SACRED SECRETS UNVEILED

Ancient Mesopotamian Magic and Mysteries

M.L. Ruscsak

Trient Press
3375 S Rainbow Blvd
#81710, SMB 13135
Las Vegas,NV 89180

Ordering Information:
Quantity sales. Special discounts are available on quantity purchases by corporations, associations, and others. For details, contact the publisher at the address above.
Orders by U.S. trade bookstores and wholesalers. Please contact Trient Press: Tel: (775) 996-3844; or visit www.trientpress.com.

Printed in the United States of America

Publisher's Cataloging-in-Publication data
Ruscsak, M.L.
A title of a book : Sacred Secrets Unveiled: Ancient Mesopotamian Magic and Mysteries

ISBN
Hard Cover   979-8-88990-106-8
Paper Back   979-8-88990-107-5
Ebook   979-8-88990-108-2

Ancient Mesopotamian Magic and Mysteries

Disclaimer:

The contents of this book, "Sacred Secrets Unveiled: Ancient Mesopotamian Magic and Mysteries," are intended for informational purposes only. The rituals, spells, and incantations presented within these pages are based on historical texts and archaeological findings related to Ancient Mesopotamian mythology. However, their efficacy and practical application in the modern world are subject to individual interpretation and belief.

It is important to note that engaging in any form of spiritual or magical practice carries inherent risks. The rituals and practices described in this book should be approached with caution and respect. Readers are advised to exercise their own discernment and take full responsibility for their choices and actions.

Furthermore, the author and publisher of this book make no claims regarding the accuracy, effectiveness, or outcome of the rituals, spells, or incantations provided. Every individual's experience with magic and spirituality may vary, and results cannot be guaranteed.

If you choose to explore the rituals and practices described in this book, it is recommended that you do so in a safe and controlled environment. Always prioritize your personal well-being and mental health. Seek guidance from experienced practitioners or spiritual advisors if needed, and consider the cultural and historical context from which these practices originated.

Lastly, this book is not meant to endorse or promote any specific religious or spiritual beliefs. It aims to provide insight into Ancient Mesopotamian mythology and its magical traditions, offering an opportunity for cultural exploration and historical understanding.

By reading and engaging with "Sacred Secrets Unveiled: Ancient Mesopotamian Magic and Mysteries," you acknowledge and accept that any choices or actions you take based on the information provided are done so at your own risk and discretion.

Remember, the true power lies within you, and it is your own responsibility to navigate your spiritual journey with wisdom and integrity.

Introduction:

Welcome to the enchanting realm of Ancient Mesopotamian mythology, where the boundaries between the mortal and divine intertwine, and the power of magic weaves its intricate web. In this tome, we delve into the depths of a civilization that flourished in the fertile lands between the Tigris and Euphrates rivers, uncovering a treasure trove of spells, incantations, and rituals that shaped the spiritual and mystical legacy of this ancient civilization.

Within the pages of this book, you will embark on a journey to explore the captivating world of Mesopotamian magic. Drawing from ancient texts, cuneiform tablets, and archaeological discoveries, we present a collection of 200 spells, incantations, and rituals that were once held sacred by the priests, priestesses, and mystics of Mesopotamia. These sacred secrets, passed down through generations, offer glimpses into the beliefs, values, and aspirations of this remarkable civilization.

As you immerse yourself in these ancient practices, you will encounter a rich tapestry of gods and goddesses, each wielding unique powers and presiding over different aspects of life. From the mighty Enki, the god of wisdom and creation, to the fierce Ishtar, the goddess of love and war, the divine pantheon of Mesopotamia awaits your discovery. Through the rituals and incantations presented in this book, you will learn how the Mesopotamians sought the favor of their deities, invoked their protection, and sought answers to life's profound mysteries.

The spells and incantations recorded herein encompass a wide range of purposes, from love and fertility rituals to healing and protection invocations. Witness the summoning of Nuska, the god of fire, for prosperity and success, or the call upon Gula, the goddess of healing, for relief from ailments. Explore the rites performed to honor the seasons and ensure abundant harvests, or the ceremonies designed to purify the body and soul.

But this book is more than a mere compendium of ancient rituals. It is an invitation to immerse yourself in the spiritual world of Mesopotamia, to engage with the profound beliefs and practices that shaped the lives of its inhabitants. As you navigate through these pages, you will gain a deeper understanding of the interconnectedness between mortals and deities, the delicate balance between light and darkness, and the enduring quest for wisdom, protection, and divine favor.

May this book serve as a key to unlock the mystical traditions and spiritual legacies of Ancient Mesopotamia. Let its spells, incantations, and rituals transport you back in time, where the ancient gods and goddesses beckon, ready to impart their ancient wisdom and bestow their blessings upon those who seek the magic that lies within.

Prepare to be captivated by the secrets of Ancient Mesopotamian mythology. The journey begins now.

Enuma Elish - The Babylonian creation epic

In the primordial depths of chaos, before the heavens and earth took form, there existed only darkness and silence. From this void emerged the great Babylonian creation epic, Enuma Elish, a testament to the creative forces that shaped the universe and the divine struggle for cosmic order.

Enuma Elish, meaning "When on High," is a poetic narrative that unfolds the captivating tale of the birth of the cosmos and the rise of the gods. Composed in ancient Mesopotamia, this epic was inscribed on cuneiform tablets and preserved as one of the oldest recorded creation myths known to humanity.

At the heart of Enuma Elish lies the grand clash between two primeval forces: Tiamat, the chaotic and primordial goddess of the saltwater depths, and Marduk, the young and powerful god of storms and civilization. As chaos threatened to engulf the universe, Marduk embarked on a perilous journey, leading to a titanic battle that would determine the fate of all existence.

The epic unfolds in seven tablets, each revealing a different aspect of the divine struggle. In vivid detail, Enuma Elish portrays Marduk's ascent to supreme power, as he defeats Tiamat and her monstrous allies with his arsenal of divine weapons. With Tiamat slain, Marduk proceeds to shape the cosmos from her fragmented body, forming the heavens and the earth, and establishing order and harmony in the universe.

Enuma Elish not only serves as a cosmological account but also carries political and religious significance. It establishes Marduk as the primary deity of Babylon and reinforces the power of Babylonian kingship. The epic emphasizes the concept of divine sovereignty and the role of the gods in maintaining the natural and social order of the world.

Through its vivid imagery and poetic verses, Enuma Elish invites us to contemplate the fundamental questions of existence, the eternal struggle between chaos and order, and the triumph of divine authority. It is a testament to the ancient Mesopotamian civilization's profound connection with the divine and their unending pursuit of understanding the mysteries of the universe.

As we delve into the mesmerizing verses of Enuma Elish, we are transported to a time long past, where gods and goddesses shaped the destinies of mortals and the celestial realms. May this epic awaken our curiosity, inspire our contemplation, and remind us of the timeless human quest for meaning and the enduring power of myth and storytelling.

Ašipu - Mesopotamian exorcist-priest

In the ancient civilization of Mesopotamia, where the boundaries between the physical and spiritual realms were believed to be intertwined, a special class of individuals emerged to navigate the invisible forces that influenced human lives. Known as the Ašipu, these exorcist-priests held a vital role in society, bridging the gap between the mortal realm and the supernatural.

The Ašipu were highly trained and knowledgeable individuals who possessed an intricate understanding of the spiritual world. Drawing from centuries of accumulated wisdom, rituals, and incantations, these priests specialized in the art of exorcism, healing, and spiritual purification. They were entrusted with the task of combating malevolent forces, protecting individuals from curses, and restoring balance to the afflicted souls.

The Ašipu's sacred duties were rooted in the belief that illness, misfortune, and psychological distress were often caused by malicious spirits or supernatural disturbances. They were called upon to diagnose the ailment's spiritual origin and employ their extensive repertoire of rituals and incantations to combat and expel these forces.

The rituals performed by the Ašipu were diverse and varied, tailored to the specific needs and circumstances of each individual. They involved elaborate ceremonies, invocations of deities, the burning of sacred herbs and incense, and the recitation of powerful incantations. These practices aimed to pacify the angered spirits, break curses, and restore harmony to both the afflicted person and the community at large.

In addition to their exorcistic roles, the Ašipu also served as counselors, offering spiritual guidance, interpreting dreams, and providing solutions to personal and societal dilemmas. They were often regarded as intermediaries between humans and the gods, capable of communicating with divine forces on behalf of the people.

The knowledge and practices of the Ašipu were passed down through generations, with secrecy and reverence, ensuring the continuity of their ancient traditions. Their skills were honed through rigorous training and study of sacred texts and were held in high regard within Mesopotamian society.

The role of the Ašipu extended beyond individual healing and spiritual protection. They played a crucial role in maintaining the overall well-being of the community, offering their services during times of crisis, such as epidemics or natural disasters. Their presence provided solace, hope, and a sense of order in times of chaos.

The Ašipu were the guardians of spiritual harmony, defenders against unseen malevolence, and custodians of the ancient wisdom that guided the Mesopotamian civilization. Through their tireless efforts, they sought to restore equilibrium and ensure the well-being of both the physical and metaphysical realms.

As we explore the history of Mesopotamia, let us remember and honor the contributions of the Ašipu, these exorcist-priests who stood at the intersection of the mortal and divine. Their enduring legacy serves as a testament to humanity's eternal fascination with the spiritual realm and the tireless pursuit of balance and serenity in the face of unseen challenges.

Barûtu - Ritual of purification

In the footsteps of our ancient Mesopotamian ancestors, we unveil the timeless ritual of Barûtu, a sacred act of purification that transcends the boundaries of time and space. Rooted in the depths of our mythological heritage, Barûtu holds the power to cleanse the spirit, restore harmony, and ignite a connection with the divine that echoes across millennia.

In the footsteps of our ancient Mesopotamian ancestors, we unveil the timeless ritual of Barûtu, a sacred act of purification that transcends the boundaries of time and space. Rooted in the depths of our mythological heritage, Barûtu holds the power to cleanse the spirit, restore harmony, and ignite a connection with the divine that echoes across millennia.

Step 1: Preparation and Sanctification
In a tranquil space, prepare a sacred altar adorned with symbols representing the elements of earth, water, fire, and air. Invoke the presence of the gods, honoring their divine authority and seeking their blessings. Light incense, such as myrrh or cedar, to purify the atmosphere and create an ambiance conducive to spiritual transformation.

Step 2: Cleansing the Body
Immerse yourself in a basin filled with consecrated water. Symbolically wash away impurities, physical and metaphysical alike. Envision the gentle touch of the sacred waters as they flow over your skin, purging negativity and preparing your being for the forthcoming journey of purification.

Step 3: Invocation of the Gods
Invoke the presence of the deities associated with purification, such as Ninhursag, the goddess of healing and renewal, and Nusku, the god of fire. Recite the ancient incantation:

"Ninhursag, mother of all life,
With your healing touch, banish strife.
Nusku, fiery guardian of purity,
Ignite my spirit with divine security."

Feel their energy enveloping you, empowering your intentions.

Step 4: Release and Letting Go
Hold a small piece of parchment or paper. Write down any negative thoughts, emotions, or burdens that weigh upon your soul. Reflect on these elements that hinder your spiritual growth. With focused intent, set the parchment aflame, chanting the words:

"As this paper turns to ash,
I release these burdens with a fiery flash.
Free from their hold, I now rise,
Embracing purity as the smoke flies."

Watch as the fire consumes the written words, transforming them into smoke that ascends to the heavens, releasing their hold on your being.

Step 5: Incantation of Purification
Chant the sacred incantation passed down through the ages:

"Barûtu, cleansing light divine,
In this sacred moment, let purity shine.
Wash away darkness, both deep and wide,
Restore my spirit with your sacred tide."

Allow the resonating sound to reverberate through your being, infusing you with purity and light. Feel the vibrations permeating every cell, dispelling darkness and inviting divine radiance.

Step 6: Anointing with Sacred Oil
Prepare a vial of sacred oil, such as olive oil infused with herbs or essences symbolizing purification. Dip your fingertips into the oil and gently anoint your forehead, heart, and palms. With each touch, visualize the oil forming a protective shield, warding off negative energies and sealing your connection to the divine.

Step 7: Gratitude and Closing
Express gratitude to the gods, acknowledging their guidance and the transformative power of the ritual. Offer prayers of appreciation and honor, expressing reverence for the ancient traditions that have brought you closer to the sacred. Slowly bring the ritual to a close, extinguishing the incense and offering final words of gratitude.

As you perform the ritual of Barûtu, remember that you walk the same path as our ancient Mesopotamian forebears. Embrace the spiritual legacies they left behind, and let the rhythm of their rivalries and mythologies guide you. May this ritual of purification awaken the light within, elevate your connection to the divine, and allow the echoes of the past to resound in the present moment.

Pazuzu Incantation - To ward off evil spirits

In the ancient land of Mesopotamia, where the forces of darkness and chaos roamed, the divine entity Pazuzu emerged as a formidable protector against malevolent spirits. With the power to banish evil and safeguard humanity, we invoke the Pazuzu Incantation, a potent invocation to ward off the presence of wicked forces and restore harmony to our lives.

As we embark on this sacred endeavor, let us gather our strength and channel the ancient words that resonate with the might of Pazuzu:

"Kima šērētu Pazuzu!
Ālātu lā tuššibta
u epšētu lā atnaddiša.
Ālātu našmētu ul išnaddiša
u kīma šērētu Pazuzu
nappīšu lā atnaddiša.
Anāku apil Pazuzu,
u Pazuzu šašī šašī
u Pazuzu pazāza šašī
u Pazuzu galla šašī
u Pazuzu mašmašī šašī."

Translated, the incantation proclaims:

"Like the form of Pazuzu,
May no evil enter
And no wickedness approach.
May no evil wind blow
For, like the form of Pazuzu,
All evil shall retreat.
I call upon Pazuzu,
The fierce Pazuzu,
The roaring Pazuzu,
The powerful Pazuzu,
The mighty Pazuzu."

As you recite these words, visualize the protective presence of Pazuzu encircling you, forming an impenetrable shield against the malevolent forces that seek to disrupt your harmony. Feel the power of Pazuzu surging through your being, banishing negativity and creating a sanctuary of divine protection.

In times of vulnerability and uncertainty, let this Pazuzu Incantation serve as a reminder of the ancient wisdom and spiritual legacy that transcends time. May Pazuzu's fierce guardianship shield you from the darkness and illuminate your path with the light of divine protection.

Note: While invoking the Pazuzu Incantation, it is crucial to approach it with respect, reverence, and a sincere intent to ward off negativity. Understanding the cultural context and historical significance of Pazuzu is essential for engaging with this ritual.

Lamashtu Ritual - Protection against the demoness Lamashtu

In the ancient realm of Mesopotamia, where the veil between the mortal and spiritual realms was thin, the menacing presence of Lamashtu, the demoness of disease and harm, cast a dark shadow over the lives of many. To counter her malicious intent and shield oneself from her malevolence, we unveil the Lamashtu Ritual, a potent invocation and ritual of protection that has been passed down through the ages.

Step 1: Sacred Preparation
In a secluded and consecrated space, create an altar adorned with symbols of divine protection, such as the symbol of the sun or the image of the warrior god Nergal. Light candles to invoke the divine presence and suffuse the surroundings with positive energy. Take a moment to center yourself and focus on your intention to shield against the influence of Lamashtu.

Step 2: Purification Bath
Prepare a basin filled with purifying water infused with herbs known for their protective properties, such as rue or sage. Immerse yourself in the basin, allowing the cleansing waters to envelop you. Visualize the water washing away any negative energy or influence associated with Lamashtu, leaving you spiritually cleansed and fortified.

Step 3: Invocation of Protective Deities
Invoke the presence and protection of deities known for their power against Lamashtu. Envision the fierce and benevolent forms of deities such as Pazuzu, Nergal, or Lamassu. Recite the following invocation:

"Mighty guardians of ancient might,
Pazuzu, Nergal, Lamassu bright,
Shield me now from Lamashtu's sway,
With your power, keep her at bay.
Wrap me in your wings of strength,
Defend me from her harmful length."

Feel their protective presence enveloping you, forming a shield against the influence of Lamashtu.

Step 4: Talisman of Protection
Create or obtain a talisman associated with protection against Lamashtu, such as an amulet or symbol. Hold the talisman in your hands and infuse it with your intent and the protective energy of the ritual. Envision the talisman radiating a vibrant light, symbolizing the divine protection it holds. Wear or carry the talisman as a constant reminder of your shield against Lamashtu's malevolence.

Step 5: Daily Affirmations
Throughout your daily life, reinforce your protection against Lamashtu through affirmations and prayers. Repeat empowering phrases such as:

"I am shielded from Lamashtu's harm,
Protected by divine light and charm.
Her influence shall not prevail,
I stand strong behind my protective veil."

These affirmations serve to strengthen your connection to the protective energies invoked during the ritual and affirm your safeguard against Lamashtu.

Step 6: Regular Maintenance
Periodically revisit the Lamashtu Ritual to renew and reinforce your protection. Perform the ritual again during times of heightened vulnerability, illness, or when feeling a sense of Lamashtu's presence. Through this ongoing commitment, you maintain a strong barrier against her influence.

As you engage in the Lamashtu Ritual, remember that you stand in the lineage of those who sought protection against the demoness. Embrace the power of ancient Mesopotamian spiritual legacies, and let the rhythm of their rituals guide you. May this ritual shield you from Lamashtu's harm and restore tranquility and well-being to your life.

Namburbi - Ritual to purify a temple

In the heart of ancient Mesopotamia, where the connection between mortals and the gods thrived, the Namburbi ritual emerged as a sacred practice to cleanse and purify the temples. Infused with mystical significance, Namburbi served as a vital ceremony to renew the sanctity of the sacred spaces and restore the divine presence that resided within.

Step 1: Invocation of the Gods
Gather within the temple, a haven where mortals meet the divine. Offer prayers and invocations to the patron deity of the temple, beseeching their presence and blessings. Call upon the gods and goddesses associated with purity and sanctification, such as Enki or Ninhursag. Humbly request their assistance in the forthcoming ritual to purify the temple and restore its spiritual vitality.

Step 2: Preparation and Symbolic Cleansing
Cleanse the physical space of the temple meticulously. Sweep away any dust or debris that may have accumulated, leaving no trace of impurity behind. Symbolically purify the temple by sprinkling consecrated water throughout its sacred chambers, using a sprig of sacred herbs or a vessel dedicated to this purpose. As the water touches the surfaces, envision it washing away any spiritual impurities and revitalizing the space.

Step 3: Incense Offering
Ignite fragrant incense, such as frankincense or myrrh, and allow its aromatic smoke to permeate the air. As the fragrant plumes rise, visualize them purifying the atmosphere and creating a spiritual ambiance conducive to divine presence. With reverence, offer the incense to the gods, inviting their ethereal essence to infuse the temple.

Step 4: Chanting of Sacred Hymns
Recite ancient sacred hymns and invocations that honor the gods and express gratitude for their benevolence. The rhythmic chants and melodic verses amplify the spiritual energy within the temple, filling it with vibrations that resonate with the divine. Let the words of the hymns reverberate through the chambers, invoking the gods' attention and inviting their divine presence to grace the purified space.

O mighty gods, we gather in this sacred space,
With hearts aflame, seeking your divine grace.
From realms unseen, we call upon your might,
To purify this temple, bathed in your sacred light.

Hear our chants, O gods of ancient lore,
In reverence, we sing, our spirits soar.
With every word, let the vibrations rise,
Purify this temple, beneath the azure skies.

Great deities, protectors of this holy shrine,
We offer devotion, our souls intertwine.
Through sacred hymns, we honor your name,
May your blessings descend, a celestial flame.

From the depths of time, your wisdom flows,
Ancient mysteries, only the faithful knows.
In this hallowed place, let your presence dwell,
Sanctify this temple, within your sacred spell.

Grant us your favor, O gods so divine,
In this blessed temple, let your essence shine.
As we chant your praise, let the vibrations soar,
Purify this sacred space, forevermore.

Step 5: Offering of Sacred Offerings
Present offerings of food, drink, and other items symbolizing abundance and
devotion to the gods. Place these offerings upon the temple altar as a gesture of
gratitude and reverence. Visualize the essence of these offerings nourishing the
spiritual realm, fostering a reciprocal relationship between mortals and the divine.

Step 6: Final Benediction and Closing
Conclude the Namburbi ritual with a final benediction, expressing gratitude to the
gods for their presence and blessings. Offer prayers for continued protection and
guidance within the purified temple. Extend your appreciation to the spiritual
legacies and traditions that have paved the way for this ritual to endure throughout
time. Conclude the ceremony with a shared moment of reflection and silence,
honoring the sanctified space.

As you perform the Namburbi ritual, immerse yourself in the ancient wisdom and
sacred practices of Mesopotamia. Feel the spiritual legacies and rivalries that
permeated the land, connecting mortals to the divine. Through this ritual, may the
temple be purified, its sanctity restored, and the presence of the gods rekindled,
bringing blessings and divine inspiration to all who enter its hallowed halls.

Enûma Anu Enlil - Series of incantations for exorcism

Within the realm of ancient Mesopotamia, where the forces of the spiritual and physical intertwine, the Enûma Anu Enlil incantation series emerged as a powerful tool in the battle against malevolent entities and spiritual afflictions. Passed down through generations, these sacred words hold the key to dispelling darkness and restoring harmony to those plagued by unholy influences.

Step 1: Invocation of Anu and Enlil
Begin by invoking the presence of Anu, the supreme god of the heavens, and Enlil, the god of breath and wind. With humility and reverence, address the divine entities, acknowledging their might and beseeching their aid in the forthcoming exorcism. Visualize their divine essence permeating the space, fortifying your connection to the celestial realms.

Step 2: Preparation and Sacred Space
Create a sacred and fortified space where the exorcism shall take place. Surround the area with symbols of divine protection and purity, such as the image of a circle or a pentagram. Light candles or incense to purify the atmosphere and enhance the spiritual energy within the space. As you prepare, clear your mind and focus your intent on banishing the dark forces that afflict the individual or space.

Step 3: Recitation of Incantations
Utter the series of incantations from the Enûma Anu Enlil with clarity and intent, while visualizing the power of the words resonating through the afflicted individual or space. Allow the vibrations of the incantations to pierce through the darkness, breaking the hold of malevolent entities. The specific incantations may vary depending on the nature of the affliction and the expertise of the exorcist.

Incantation:
By the power of Anu, king of the gods,
And Enlil, lord of the storm and wind,
I invoke the ancient forces, the divine command.

From the depths of the underworld, I call,
Banish the evil spirits, release them all.
By the authority of heaven and earth combined,
I cast out the darkness, leave no trace behind.

I summon the great gods, their names resound,

With fiery words, the demons confound.
By Shamash, the radiant sun, I decree,
Evil spirits, depart, set the possessed free.

In the name of Ea, wise god of the deep,
I break your hold, let the afflicted one sleep.
By Marduk, the champion, supreme in might,
I restore balance, dispel the blight.

By the divine word, I command and bind,
The forces of darkness, no longer blind.
Through the incantations, ancient and pure,
Exorcise the demons, make them endure.

O mighty gods, lend your power to this rite,
Drive away darkness, restore the light.
Enûma Anu Enlil, the sacred words unfold,
Purify the afflicted, let their souls be consoled.

Step 4: Symbolic Gestures and Actions
Accompany the incantations with symbolic gestures and actions that reinforce the
intent of the exorcism. These may include waving a sacred object, such as a branch
of cedar or a bundle of herbs, over the afflicted individual or space. The purpose of
these actions is to disrupt and dispel negative energies while invoking the divine
forces of Anu and Enlil.

Step 5: Dismissal of Malevolent Entities
Directly address the malevolent entities that reside within the afflicted individual or
space, commanding them to depart and relinquish their hold. With authority and
conviction, declare:

"By the might of Anu and Enlil,
I command you, spirits of darkness,
Release your grip and depart this realm.
Return to the shadows from whence you came."

Visualize the malevolent entities dispersing into the abyss, leaving behind a purified
and restored individual or space.

Step 6: Closing and Protection
Conclude the exorcism ritual by offering prayers of protection and gratitude to Anu
and Enlil. Express appreciation for their assistance and divine intervention in

banishing the darkness. Envision a shield of divine light enveloping the individual or space, safeguarding against future spiritual afflictions. Extend your blessings and well-wishes, sealing the exorcism with divine grace.

As you engage in the Enûma Anu Enlil incantation series, remember the ancient wisdom and spiritual legacies that have stood the test of time. Embrace the power of these sacred words and let their vibrations reverberate through the realms, dispelling darkness and restoring balance. May the exorcism bring solace, healing, and divine protection to all those affected.

Kettledrum Divination - Divination through the use of drums

In the realm of ancient Mesopotamia, where the mystical and the mundane intertwined, the practice of Kettledrum Divination emerged as a profound method of seeking insight into the threads of destiny. Through the rhythmic reverberations of drums, the diviner communed with the unseen realms, allowing the vibrations to reveal hidden truths and guide mortals on their paths.

Step 1: Sacred Preparation

Create a consecrated space where the divination will take place. Set up an altar adorned with symbols of divination, such as sacred stones, feathers, or incense. Light candles to illuminate the space and invite spiritual energies to converge. Center your mind and heart, grounding yourself in the present moment.

Step 2: Selection and Tuning of the Drums

Choose two kettledrums that resonate with you on an intuitive level. These drums should possess a unique and complementary sound. Tune each drum to a specific pitch, representing different aspects or domains of inquiry. The lower-pitched drum may symbolize earthly matters, while the higher-pitched drum may represent spiritual or ethereal realms.

Step 3: Invocation of Guidance

Invoke the presence and guidance of the divine or the spirits associated with divination. Offer prayers and invocations, calling upon the wisdom of the ancient Mesopotamian deities, such as Nabu, the god of writing and divination, or Ishtar, the goddess of love and prophecy. Seek their assistance in deciphering the messages that will emerge from the drums' resonance.

Step 4: Focus and Intention

Set your intention for the divination session. Clearly articulate the question or aspect of life that you seek guidance on. Concentrate on this intention, allowing it to permeate your thoughts and infuse your connection with the drums. The drums will act as the conduit between the spiritual realms and your conscious awareness.

Step 5: Drumming and Interpretation

With the drumsticks in hand, begin to play the kettledrums, allowing your intuition and the rhythms to guide your movements. Close your eyes and let the beats flow freely, connecting with the ancient echoes that reverberate through time. As the drumming continues, focus on your intention and listen to the messages that emerge through the patterns and nuances of the sound.

Pay attention to changes in tempo, intensity, and the interplay between the two drums. Each rhythm carries a distinct message or insight, unveiling aspects of the question at hand. Trust your intuition and interpret the rhythmic patterns, allowing them to shape the narrative and guide your understanding.

Step 6: Reflection and Integration
Once the drumming concludes, take a moment of silence to reflect on the insights received. Journal your experiences, impressions, and interpretations. Look for patterns, symbolism, or recurring themes that emerged through the rhythmic vibrations. Contemplate the guidance provided and how it aligns with your current circumstances.

Remember that divination is a tool for guidance and self-reflection. It offers insights and perspectives that can help you make informed choices, but ultimately, you hold the power to shape your own destiny.

As you engage in Kettledrum Divination, honor the ancient art and the spiritual legacies it carries. Embrace the rhythm of the drums, allowing their vibrations to transcend time and space, revealing the whispers of destiny. May this divination practice bring clarity, wisdom, and alignment with the cosmic currents that guide us all.

Maqlû - Ritual for removing a curse

In the ancient realm of Mesopotamia, where the echoes of mysticism and sorcery reverberated, the Maqlû ritual emerged as a powerful means of removing curses and breaking free from the malevolent grip of dark forces. Passed down through the annals of time, this sacred rite serves as a beacon of hope, offering a pathway to liberation and restoration.

Step 1: Preparation and Sacred Space
Prepare a sacred space where the Maqlû ritual will unfold. Clear the area of any disturbances or negative energies, ensuring a serene and focused environment. Light candles or incense to purify the space and invite divine energies to join the proceedings. Take a moment to center yourself, grounding your intentions and affirming your commitment to breaking the curse.

Step 2: Invocation of Protective Deities
Invoke the presence and protection of deities known for their power against curses and dark forces. Address them with reverence and sincerity, calling upon their assistance in the forthcoming ritual. Envision their radiant presence enveloping the space, forming a shield against the curse and fortifying your resolve.

Step 3: Symbolic Cleansing
Prepare a basin of pure water infused with cleansing herbs, such as rue or hyssop. Dip a clean cloth or sponge into the water and gently bathe the afflicted individual, symbolically purifying them from the taint of the curse. Visualize the water washing away the curse's malevolent influence, leaving behind a cleansed and liberated spirit.

Step 4: Incantations and Chants
Recite the sacred incantations and chants designed to unbind the curse's hold. These words, passed down through generations, carry the power to dismantle the curse's grip on the individual. Utter them with conviction and clarity, letting the vibrations of the ancient syllables resonate within and around you, piercing through the curse's veil.

Step 5: Ritual Actions
Perform symbolic actions that represent the breaking of the curse's chains. This may include the act of untying knots, breaking clay tablets, or even burning a representation of the curse itself. As you carry out these actions, visualize the curse disintegrating, its power dissipating into the ether, and the individual becoming unburdened and liberated.

Step 6: Offering and Gratitude

Offer prayers and expressions of gratitude to the protective deities and spiritual forces that have aided in breaking the curse. Show appreciation for their assistance and the divine intervention that has restored freedom and well-being. Extend blessings to the spiritual legacies and the wisdom of the ancients who forged the path of liberation.

Step 7: Daily Affirmations and Vigilance

Encourage the individual to engage in daily affirmations and practices that reinforce their newfound liberation. These may include reciting positive affirmations, visualizations of protection, or carrying a talisman symbolizing freedom from the curse. Emphasize the importance of remaining vigilant, cultivating positive energies, and guarding against future curses.

The Maqlû ritual holds the key to breaking the chains of malevolence and reclaiming one's destiny. Embrace the ancient wisdom and spiritual legacies woven into this sacred rite, allowing its power to restore balance, heal wounds, and ignite the flame of liberation. May this ritual serve as a beacon of hope, guiding the afflicted towards a life free from the curse's darkness.

Šurpu - Ritual for removing malevolent spirits

In the ancient realm of Mesopotamia, where the boundaries between the seen and unseen were intertwined, the Šurpu ritual emerged as a powerful means of dispelling malevolent spirits and restoring harmony to the afflicted. Rooted in ancient wisdom and spiritual practices, this sacred rite serves as a beacon of light, offering a pathway to liberation and protection from the forces of darkness.

Step 1: Preparation and Sacred Space
Prepare a sacred space where the Šurpu ritual will unfold. Cleanse the area of any spiritual impurities, ensuring a serene and focused environment. Light candles or burn incense to purify the space and invite divine energies to join the proceedings. Take a moment to ground yourself, centering your intentions and establishing a connection with the higher realms.

Step 2: Invocation of Protective Deities
Invoke the presence and aid of deities known for their power against malevolent spirits. Call upon them with reverence and humility, seeking their assistance in the forthcoming ritual. Envision their divine presence surrounding the space, forming a shield of protection against the forces of darkness. Trust in their guidance and benevolence throughout the ritual.

Step 3: Sacred Smoke and Purification
Ignite fragrant herbs or resins, such as sage or myrrh, and let the sacred smoke fill the space. As the smoke rises, visualize it purifying the atmosphere, dispelling negativity, and creating a sanctuary of light. Move throughout the afflicted area, fanning the smoke with a feather or your hand, focusing on corners, doorways, and areas of spiritual disturbance.

Step 4: Incantations and Prayers
Recite the ancient incantations and prayers specifically designed to banish malevolent spirits. Speak the words with conviction and authority, commanding the spirits to depart and relinquish their hold. Let the vibrations of the incantations reverberate through the space, penetrating the spirit realm and dissolving the malevolence. Trust in the power of the words and the divine forces working through you.

Incantation:
In the name of the gods, I stand strong,
With fire and smoke, I banish what's wrong.
I call upon the forces of light and might,
To cast out darkness, restore what's right.

By the power of the divine flame I hold,
I purify this space, dispel the cold.
Evil spirits, hear my voice and flee,
Leave this realm, let peace be free.

From the depths of chaos, you emerged,
But now your time here has been purged.
By Shamash, the radiant sun, I command,
Return to the shadows, meet your end.

I summon the divine, the protectors supreme,
Enki, Enlil, and all in between.
With their guidance, I banish your presence,
Restore harmony, bring divine essence.

Prayer:
O gods of light, hear my plea,
Protect this place, set the spirits free.
With your grace, remove what's impure,
Shield us from harm, make us secure.

I invoke your names, ancient and revered,
Grant us strength, let your power be near.
As I perform this ritual, I seek your aid,
To banish malevolent spirits, unafraid.

May your divine essence fill this space,
Cleansing it wholly, with your embrace.
Guide my words and actions with your might,
As we restore peace, dispelling the night.

Step 5: Symbolic Actions and Offerings
Perform symbolic actions that represent the expulsion of malevolent spirits. This
may include scattering protective herbs or salt throughout the space, symbolizing the
creation of a barrier against the dark forces. Offerings of food, drink, or other items
may also be presented as a gesture of gratitude to the protective deities and spiritual
forces assisting in the ritual.

Step 6: Sealing and Protection
Conclude the Šurpu ritual by invoking a powerful seal of protection upon the space
and its inhabitants. Visualize a radiant shield of divine light enveloping the area,

warding off any lingering malevolent energies. Express gratitude to the deities and spiritual forces, thanking them for their assistance and protection. Affirm that the space is now cleansed, purified, and guarded against further intrusion.

Step 7: Vigilance and Spiritual Maintenance
Emphasize the importance of vigilance and spiritual maintenance after the Šurpu ritual. Encourage individuals to maintain positive energies within the space, engage in regular spiritual practices, and remain aware of any signs of spiritual disturbance. Remind them to call upon the protective deities whenever needed, reinforcing the bond of divine protection.

The Šurpu ritual stands as a testament to the ancient knowledge and spiritual legacies that endure across time. Embrace the power of this sacred rite, allowing its transformative energy to banish shadows and restore harmony. May this ritual serve as a sanctuary of light, shielding individuals and spaces from malevolent spirits, and fostering a sacred haven of peace and well-being.

Amulets of Ishtar - Protection amulets associated with the goddess Ishtar

In the mystical realm of Mesopotamia, the goddess Ishtar shone brightly as the embodiment of love, beauty, and fierce protection. To safeguard against malevolent forces and invite the blessings of Ishtar, the ancient Mesopotamians crafted powerful amulets imbued with her divine essence. These Amulets of Ishtar, passed down through generations, serve as potent talismans, offering protection, empowerment, and a sacred connection to the goddess herself.

Ishtar's Star: This amulet takes the form of a star, reflecting Ishtar's celestial radiance. It symbolizes divine guidance and serves as a beacon of protection, illuminating the path and warding off negativity. Carry or wear this amulet to invoke the goddess's benevolent presence and to align with her loving energy.
Chant: "Ishtar, radiant star of the heavens, guide and protect me."

Lion's Strength: Crafted in the image of a lion, this amulet channels Ishtar's fierce and courageous spirit. It embodies her protective nature, instilling strength, confidence, and fearlessness in the wearer. Keep this amulet close to your heart or place it in your home to invoke Ishtar's guardianship and fortitude.
Chant: "Ishtar, lioness of valor, grant me strength and protection."

Love's Embrace: Shaped as a heart, this amulet represents Ishtar's embodiment of love and passion. It invites the goddess's divine love into the wearer's life, fostering harmonious relationships and attracting positivity. Wear this amulet or place it near symbols of love to invite Ishtar's blessings into matters of the heart.
Chant: "Ishtar, goddess of love's embrace, fill my heart with divine affection."

Serpent's Wisdom: This amulet takes the form of a serpent, symbolizing Ishtar's connection to ancient wisdom and intuition. It enhances psychic abilities, heightens intuition, and offers protection against negative energies. Keep this amulet close during meditation or divination practices to deepen your connection with the spiritual realms.
Chant: "Ishtar, serpent of wisdom, awaken my intuition and guard my spirit."

Crescent Moon: Crafted in the shape of a crescent moon, this amulet represents Ishtar's association with the lunar cycles and the ebb and flow of life. It bestows blessings of renewal, intuition, and emotional balance. Wear or place this amulet under your pillow during sleep to invite Ishtar's healing and harmonizing energies.
Chant: "Ishtar, moonlight's grace, bless me with renewal and emotional harmony."

When working with the Amulets of Ishtar, remember to infuse them with your intentions, prayers, and the energy of your connection to the goddess. Treat them with reverence and gratitude, recognizing the divine protection they offer. Invoke Ishtar's name and visualize her vibrant presence enveloping you as you carry or wear these amulets. May the Amulets of Ishtar serve as powerful symbols of divine protection and love, shielding you from harm and illuminating your path with the goddess's radiant blessings.

Lamastu Incantation - Protection against the demoness Lamastu

In the ancient lands of Mesopotamia, where shadows danced with the whispers of darkness, the demoness Lamastu loomed as a bringer of nightmares and chaos. To ward off her malevolent influence and safeguard against her haunting presence, the wise ancients crafted a potent incantation, a powerful shield against her wicked intentions. By invoking the divine forces and channeling their protective energies, one can repel Lamastu and find respite from her fearsome grasp.

Chant:

"Lamastu, fiend of the night,
By the power of the heavens' light,
I summon the guardians of divine,
To shield me from your cursed design.

In the name of Ea, wise and just,
I banish you with sacred trust.
By Anu's decree, I declare,
Your malevolence I will not bear.

By Ishtar's might, love's radiant grace,
I deflect your evil embrace.
With Shamash's flame, I ignite,
A shield of protection, pure and bright.

Let Lamastu's power wane and fade,
As I invoke the ancient aid.
I stand firm, resilient and strong,
Protected from the terrors, by this song.

By Ninhursag's nurturing embrace,
I find solace and healing grace.
By Enki's wisdom, I am guided,
From Lamastu's grip, I am divided.

Goddesses and gods, I call upon thee,
To banish Lamastu, set me free.
With your divine power, I prevail,

And repel her darkness without fail."

Recite this incantation with unwavering conviction, allowing the words to flow from your lips and permeate the surrounding space. Envision a radiant shield forming around you, emanating the protective energies of the deities invoked. Feel the strength and reassurance of their divine presence, shielding you from Lamastu's influence.

In times of vulnerability or when nightmares plague your slumber, repeat this incantation before sleep or whenever you feel the presence of Lamastu's looming shadow. Trust in the ancient power and the wisdom of the Mesopotamian spiritual legacies to shield you from her malevolence. May the Lamastu Incantation be your sanctuary of protection, granting you peaceful nights and a shield against the demoness's haunting touch.

Bit Rimki - Ritual for reversing evil magic

In the ancient depths of Mesopotamia, where the mysteries of magic were both revered and feared, the Bit Rimki ritual emerged as a powerful means of reversing the effects of malevolent enchantments and breaking free from their grip. Rooted in ancient wisdom and spiritual practices, this sacred rite serves as a guiding light, offering a pathway to unravel the tangled web of dark magic and restore balance to the afflicted.

Step 1: Preparation and Sacred Space
Create a sacred space where the Bit Rimki ritual will unfold. Cleanse the area of any negative energies, ensuring a serene and focused environment. Light candles or burn incense to purify the space and invoke the presence of benevolent spirits. Take a moment to center yourself, grounding your intentions and connecting with the divine forces that will aid you in this reversal.

Step 2: Invocation of Protective Deities
Invoke the presence and assistance of deities known for their power against malevolent magic. Address them with reverence and sincerity, seeking their guidance in the forthcoming ritual. Envision their divine radiance filling the space, forming a shield against the dark enchantments. Trust in their wisdom and protection as you proceed.

Step 3: Symbolic Cleansing
Prepare a basin of pure water infused with cleansing herbs, such as rosemary or sage. Dip your hands into the water and visualize it purifying your energy and intentions. Gently sprinkle the water around the afflicted person or object, symbolically washing away the effects of the dark magic. Envision the water carrying away the negative energies, leaving behind a cleansed and revitalized state.

Step 4: Incantations and Chants
Recite the sacred incantations and chants specifically designed to reverse the effects of dark magic. Speak the words with authority and clarity, commanding the malevolent energies to unravel and dissipate. Allow the power of your voice and intention to penetrate the weave of the dark enchantment, dismantling its influence and reversing its effects.

Incantation:
By the power of the gods and ancient lore,
I invoke the forces to restore,
What was twisted and cast with ill intent,

Let evil magic be swiftly unbent.

From the depths of darkness, I now call,
Undo the curses, break their thrall.
With sacred words, I command the spell,
Reverse its effects, make all be well.

Chants:

In reverse, I unwind the spell,
Turning back the twisted veil.
As I chant, its power is erased,
Evil magic, be displaced.

By fire's light, I cleanse and mend,
Undo the harm that was intended.
With each chant, I break the ties,
Reversing evil, making it unwise.

As the winds blow, the curse unwinds,
Leaving no trace of its binds.
With each word I speak, I reclaim,
The power to reverse, to heal, and tame.

Shadows fade, light takes control,
Evil magic, you have no hold.
With these chants, I restore the right,
Reversing darkness, bringing forth the light.

Step 5: Ritual Actions
Perform ritual actions that symbolize the unraveling of the dark magic's threads. This
may include the unwinding of cords or knots, the burning of symbolic
representations, or the breaking of bonds. As you carry out these actions, visualize
the dark magic weakening and disintegrating, its hold over the afflicted person or
object crumbling away.

Step 6: Offering and Gratitude
Offer prayers and expressions of gratitude to the protective deities and spiritual
forces that have aided in the reversal. Show appreciation for their assistance and the
divine intervention that has restored balance and lifted the veil of malevolence.
Extend blessings to the ancient wisdom and spiritual legacies that have guided the
ritual.

Step 7: Vigilance and Protection
Emphasize the importance of remaining vigilant and protected against future encounters with dark magic. Encourage the afflicted person or object to engage in practices that promote spiritual strength and shield against negative energies. This may include wearing protective amulets, practicing daily affirmations, or seeking the aid of knowledgeable practitioners.

The Bit Rimki ritual stands as a testament to the ancient knowledge and spiritual legacies that endure through time. Embrace the power of this sacred rite, allowing its transformative energy to unravel the threads of evil magic and restore balance and harmony. May this ritual serve as a sanctuary of light, guiding the afflicted towards liberation and protection from the forces of darkness.

Apotropaic Rituals - Rituals to ward off evil

In the enchanting realm of ancient Mesopotamia, where the forces of light and darkness engaged in eternal struggle, apotropaic rituals emerged as powerful means to repel and ward off evil influences. Rooted in deep spiritual wisdom and passed down through generations, these sacred rites stand as shields of protection against malevolent forces. By invoking divine powers, employing symbolic actions, and harnessing the strength of ancestral rituals, one can create a haven guarded against the encroachment of evil.

Step 1: Sanctify the Sacred Space
Prepare a sacred space where the apotropaic ritual will unfold. Cleanse the area thoroughly, removing any negative energies or impurities. Light candles or burn incense to purify the space and create an atmosphere conducive to spiritual work. Establish an altar adorned with symbols of protection, such as talismans, sacred objects, or images of deities associated with warding off evil.

Step 2: Invocation of Protective Deities
Invoke the presence and assistance of deities renowned for their protective qualities. Call upon their names with reverence and humility, seeking their divine intervention. Envision their radiant energy filling the space, forming a shield of light that repels all malevolent forces. Trust in their power and guidance as you proceed with the ritual.

Step 3: Symbolic Actions
Engage in symbolic actions that represent the warding off of evil. This may include gestures such as drawing protective sigils or symbols in the air, scattering salt or protective herbs around the space, or hanging amulets and charms known for their protective properties. Visualize these actions as fortifying barriers against negativity, sealing off the space from evil influences.

Step 4: Chants and Incantations
Recite ancient chants and incantations specifically designed to repel evil. Utter the words with conviction and clarity, commanding malevolent forces to retreat. Allow the power of sound and intention to reverberate through the space, resonating with divine energies and manifesting as a shield against evil's encroachment.

Incantation:
By the power of the gods and ancient lore,
I invoke the forces to restore,
What was twisted and cast with ill intent,
Let evil magic be swiftly unbent.

From the depths of darkness, I now call,
Undo the curses, break their thrall.
With sacred words, I command the spell,
Reverse its effects, make all be well.

Chants:

In reverse, I unwind the spell,
Turning back the twisted veil.
As I chant, its power is erased,
Evil magic, be displaced.

By fire's light, I cleanse and mend,
Undo the harm that was intended.
With each chant, I break the ties,
Reversing evil, making it unwise.

As the winds blow, the curse unwinds,
Leaving no trace of its binds.
With each word I speak, I reclaim,
The power to reverse, to heal, and tame.

Shadows fade, light takes control,
Evil magic, you have no hold.
With these chants, I restore the right,
Reversing darkness, bringing forth the light.

Step 5: Sacred Offerings
Make offerings to the protective deities, expressing gratitude for their intervention
and invoking their continued guidance and safeguarding. Offerings can include food,
drink, or other items of significance. Through this act of reverence, establish a
reciprocal relationship with the divine forces, deepening the bond of protection.

Step 6: Ritual Closing and Sealing
Conclude the apotropaic ritual by sealing the protective energies within the space.
Visualize a radiant sphere of light enveloping the area, acting as an impenetrable
shield against evil forces. Express gratitude to the deities and ancestral spirits,
thanking them for their presence and protection. Affirm that the space is now
consecrated and secure from malevolence.

Step 7: Vigilance and Continual Maintenance

Emphasize the importance of remaining vigilant and engaging in regular spiritual practices to maintain the shield of protection. Encourage individuals to be mindful of their surroundings, to cleanse their personal energies, and to renew the ritual's effects when needed. Remind them to trust in the power of ancestral wisdom and the divine forces that stand as guardians against evil.

Apotropaic rituals are timeless guardians, preserving the sacred balance between light and darkness. Embrace their power and wisdom, allowing them to fortify your spiritual sanctuary and shield you from the encroachments of evil. May these rituals stand as beacons of protection, weaving a shield that repels malevolence and upholds the sanctity of your being and space.

Adad Incantation - Invocation of the storm god Adad

In the ancient realm of Mesopotamia, where the heavens met the earth in a symphony of power, the storm god Adad reigned supreme. With thunder as his voice and lightning as his weapon, he embodied the forces of nature in all their awe-inspiring might. To harness the protective and transformative energies of Adad, the ancient sages crafted an incantation, a sacred invocation that calls forth the storm god's presence and blessings.

Chant:

"Adad, mighty storm god, I summon thee,
With thunderous might and lightning's decree.
Bearer of rain and purveyor of life,
Unleash your power, dispelling all strife.

In tempest and fury, your strength resides,
Commanding the winds, the earth it divides.
With every rumble and crackle of fire,
I invoke your essence, divine and dire.

O Adad, lord of the storm-tossed skies,
Bestow your protection, grant us the wise.
Shield us from harm, with your thunderous roar,
Unveil your presence, forevermore.

From your celestial abode, descend,
With crashing thunder, our spirits you mend.
Bring forth your blessings, abundant and grand,
As I chant this incantation, by your command.

By your sacred name, I call upon thee,
Adad, storm god, I offer my plea.
Grant us your favor, in times of despair,
With your protective cloak, our lives you ensnare.

Through gales and torrents, we find our way,
Under your watchful gaze, we safely stray.
O Adad, storm god, forever we praise,

In your divine presence, our spirits ablaze."

Recite this incantation with a reverent voice, allowing the words to resonate with the power and majesty of the storm god. Visualize Adad's storm clouds gathering above, feel the electric energy in the air, and sense the presence of the divine as you chant his name.

Invoke this incantation in times of turmoil or when seeking protection and guidance. Open your heart and mind to the immense power and wisdom of Adad, trusting in his ability to shield and transform. May the Adad Incantation serve as a conduit to the storm god's mighty presence, bringing forth his blessings and safeguarding you from the storms of life.

Eridu Genesis - Mythological narrative of the creation of the world

In the annals of Mesopotamian mythology, where the veil of time is woven with ancient wisdom, the Eridu Genesis stands as a sacred testament to the origins of the world. Within its timeless verses, the cosmic dance of creation unfolds, revealing the birth of the universe, the emergence of divine beings, and the intricate tapestry that weaves together the fabric of existence.

In the beginning, there was only the primordial abyss, a vast expanse of chaotic waters, and within this formless void, the gods stirred. From the depths of the watery abyss, the first city of Eridu emerged, its foundation laid by divine hands. This hallowed city became the birthplace of civilization, a beacon of enlightenment and knowledge.

Within the Eridu Genesis, the tale of the gods' endeavors unfolds, with each divine act paving the way for the next. They shaped the earth, crafted the rivers, and established the laws that govern the natural world. From the sacred clay, mankind was molded, imbued with the breath of life, destined to tend the earth and honor the gods.

Yet, as the world flourished, so too did the ambitions of mankind. The divine council, concerned by the growing hubris of mortals, resolved to teach humanity a lesson. They unleashed a catastrophic flood upon the earth, a deluge that washed away all but a select few who sought refuge in an ark. Through this cataclysmic event, the gods cleansed the world, paving the way for a new era.

In the aftermath of the flood, the gods, touched by remorse and compassion, bestowed upon humanity the gifts of civilization. They shared the knowledge of agriculture, architecture, and law, igniting the flame of progress that would guide humanity through the ages.

The Eridu Genesis is a tapestry of cosmic creation, a testament to the intricate interplay between gods and mortals. It offers a glimpse into the profound understanding of the ancient Mesopotamians regarding the origins of existence, the rise and fall of civilizations, and the enduring relationship between humanity and the divine.

Through the retelling of the Eridu Genesis, we honor the ancient wisdom and spiritual legacy that has shaped our understanding of the world. It invites us to contemplate our place within the grand tapestry of creation, to reflect upon the eternal dance between chaos and order, and to seek harmony with the divine forces that guide and shape our lives.

Let the Eridu Genesis be a source of inspiration, a reminder of our shared heritage, and a testament to the enduring power of myth and legend. May it continue to unravel the mysteries of creation and illuminate the path towards wisdom and enlightenment.

Erra and Ishum - Ritual to appease the gods of chaos and violence

In the ancient realm of Mesopotamia, where the gods of chaos and violence held sway, the rituals dedicated to Erra and Ishum emerged as a means to appease these formidable deities and restore balance to the world. Rooted in ancient wisdom and spiritual practices, this sacred invocation stands as a plea for mercy and a call for harmony amidst the tumultuous forces that threaten to engulf existence.

Step 1: Preparation and Sacred Space
Create a sacred space where the ritual will unfold. Cleanse the area, purging it of any negative energies. Light candles or burn incense to invoke the presence of the divine. Arrange symbols of Erra and Ishum, such as statues or images, as focal points of the ritual. Take a moment to center yourself, grounding your intentions and opening your heart to the gods.

Step 2: Invocation of Erra and Ishum
Invoke the presence of Erra and Ishum with reverence and respect. Address them by their sacred names, offering heartfelt prayers that express your understanding of their power and your desire for peace. Visualize their majestic forms standing before you, their wrath quelled, their guidance sought. Humbly request their mercy and benevolence during the ritual.

Step 3: Symbolic Offerings
Present offerings to Erra and Ishum as tokens of appeasement. These can include food, drink, or symbolic items representing peace and harmony. Place them before the sacred symbols, infusing them with your intentions of reconciliation and the restoration of order. Acknowledge the gods' authority and express your willingness to heed their divine wisdom.

Step 4: Chants and Invocations
Recite chants and invocations specifically crafted to invoke the mercy of Erra and Ishum. Speak the words with sincerity and conviction, expressing remorse for the chaos and violence that plagues the world. Plead for their intervention and guidance in restoring peace, beseeching them to temper their wrath and grant solace to all who suffer.

Step 5: Acts of Contrition
Engage in acts of contrition to demonstrate your genuine desire for reconciliation. This can include acts of charity, forgiveness, or self-reflection. Reflect upon the role

each individual plays in perpetuating or combating chaos and violence. Pledge to be an agent of peace and harmony, both within yourself and in your interactions with others.

Step 6: Ritual Actions for Harmony

Perform ritual actions that symbolize the restoration of harmony and balance. This can involve the symbolic extinguishing of flames or the pouring of water, representing the quenching of violence and the soothing of chaos. As you carry out these actions, envision a tranquil world emerging from the ashes of conflict, guided by the wisdom of Erra and Ishum.

Step 7: Prayer for Peace

Offer a prayer for peace, extending it to all beings affected by chaos and violence. Envision a world free from strife, where compassion and understanding reign. Express gratitude to Erra and Ishum for their presence and benevolence, trusting in their ability to calm the forces of chaos and guide humanity towards a harmonious existence.

The ritual to appease Erra and Ishum stands as a testament to the ancient understanding of the delicate balance between chaos and order. Embrace its power and wisdom, allowing it to inspire compassion, reconciliation, and a commitment to fostering peace in the world. May this invocation serve as a beacon of hope, bridging the divide between humanity and the gods, and ushering in an era of tranquility amidst the tumultuous forces of existence.

Tablet of Destinies Incantation - To gain control over destiny

In the mystical realm of ancient Mesopotamia, where the fabric of destiny was woven, the Tablet of Destinies held immense power. This sacred incantation, handed down through generations, unlocks the potential to gain control over one's own fate, to shape the tapestry of life according to one's desires. With reverence and focused intention, embark upon this journey to seize the threads of destiny.

Chant:

"By the Tablet of Destinies, I do proclaim,
I call upon the powers that shape my name.
From the cosmic tapestry, I seek control,
To weave my path, to shape my soul.

Oh, gods and goddesses, hear my plea,
Bestow upon me the power to decree.
Grant me the wisdom to understand,
The secrets of fate, at my command.

With this incantation, I claim my right,
To bend the threads of destiny with my might.
No longer a passive vessel, I shall be,
Master of my fate, boundless and free.

Tablet of Destinies, I invoke your name,
Unleash the powers, set my spirit aflame.
With unwavering intent, I take my stand,
To shape my future, guided by my hand.

Grant me the vision to see the unseen,
The strength to overcome, the will to glean,
The paths that lead to my desired goal,
And the wisdom to adapt, to achieve my soul.

By the ancient knowledge, I am imbued,
With the power to shape my fate, renewed.
I command the forces of destiny's flow,
To align with my will, my purpose to show.

By the Tablet of Destinies, I decree,
I am the weaver of my destiny.
Boundless potential lies within my grasp,
As I navigate life's labyrinthine clasp.

May this incantation empower me,
To shape my fate, to set my spirit free.
With reverence and gratitude, I claim my role,
To seize the threads of destiny, to make them whole."

Recite this incantation with unwavering belief in your ability to shape your own destiny. Visualize the Tablet of Destinies before you, radiating its ancient power, as you connect with the cosmic forces that govern the paths of life. Allow the words to reverberate within your being, infusing you with the strength, wisdom, and determination to steer your fate.

Remember, as you navigate the journey of life, to always exercise your newfound power with responsibility and compassion. May the Tablet of Destinies Incantation guide you towards a future filled with purpose, fulfillment, and the realization of your true potential.

Ištar Invocation - Invocation of the goddess Ishtar

In the mystical realm of ancient Mesopotamia, the goddess Ishtar shone as a beacon of love, beauty, and power. To invoke her presence, to bask in her divine radiance, and to seek her guidance, the ancient sages crafted this sacred invocation. With reverence and devotion, embark upon this journey to awaken the essence of the goddess within.

Chant:

"Goddess Ishtar, radiant and bright,
Mistress of love, bringer of light.
With heart and soul, I call your name,
Awaken your presence, ignite the flame.

Ishtar, queen of the heavens above,
Embodiment of beauty, embodiment of love.
Grant me your blessings, divine and true,
Fill my life with joy, as I honor you.

In your sacred temple, I kneel and pray,
I seek your wisdom, guidance today.
Unveil the secrets of passion and desire,
Ignite the flames that forever inspire.

Ishtar, Lady of the Morning and Night,
Bearer of magic, holder of delight.
Envelop me in your loving embrace,
As I walk this earthly realm with grace.

Goddess of fertility, of birth and rebirth,
Bestow your blessings upon the earth.
May love and compassion be our guiding light,
In your divine presence, all is made right.

Ishtar, I invoke your name with reverence,
With gratitude, I honor your benevolence.
Guide me on a path of love and power,
In every moment, in every hour.

Grant me strength, grant me grace,
In your eternal love, I find my place.
With devotion and awe, I seek your embrace,
Ishtar, goddess, fill me with your grace."

Recite this invocation with a heart filled with reverence and love for the goddess
Ishtar. Visualize her radiant presence before you, shimmering with divine energy.
Allow her essence to envelop you, filling you with a sense of empowerment and a
deep connection to the sacred feminine.

As you journey through life, carry the spirit of Ishtar within you, embracing love,
beauty, and the joy of existence. Let her wisdom guide your actions, and let her light
illuminate your path. May the Ishtar Invocation be a gateway to the divine,
connecting you to the eternal power and grace of the goddess.

Lullaby Incantation - To soothe a child's restless spirit

In the realm of ancient Mesopotamia, where magic and music intertwined, the Lullaby Incantation emerged as a tender enchantment to calm a child's restless spirit. Rooted in the soothing melodies of the ancients, this sacred incantation carries the power to create a serene sanctuary, to hush the worries and fears, and to embrace the child in a tranquil embrace.

Chant:

"Hush now, little one, close your eyes,
Under moonlit skies, where starlight lies.
Rest your weary soul, let dreams take flight,
In the cradle of peace, where all is right.

The world may dance with shadows deep,
But in this sacred moment, restful sleep.
Whispering breezes carry away the strife,
As we venture to the realm of dreams, so rife.

Lullaby, lullaby, let the melodies flow,
Serenading your heart, soothing the ebb and flow.
May gentle slumber find its tender hold,
As love and warmth enfold, like a story yet untold.

In the arms of dreams, you shall safely roam,
Guided by a celestial lullaby's sweet tone.
Serenading spirits, embracing tender grace,
A cradle of tranquility, a soothing embrace.

Rest now, little one, release your weary sigh,
As the moon's gentle gaze brushes the sky.
May angels watch over you, keep you near,
Guarding your dreams, banishing all fear.

Lullaby, lullaby, let your worries take flight,
In this enchanting realm, bathed in soft moonlight.
Peace be your lullaby, tranquility your guide,
As your spirit finds solace in dreams' sweet tide.

Hush now, little one, surrender to the night,
With this sacred incantation, all is set right.
In the cradle of love, drift off to dreamland,
Where the enchantment of slumber shall forever stand."

Recite this incantation with a tender and melodic voice, imbuing each word with love and compassion. Allow the soothing rhythms and gentle melodies to flow through your being, creating an atmosphere of serenity and tranquility. Cradle the child in your arms or envision their peaceful form as you chant, surrounding them with a sense of safety and peace.

May the Lullaby Incantation weave its gentle spell, bringing solace and comfort to the restless spirit of the child. May it create a sacred space of tranquility, where dreams can blossom and fears can be gently lulled to rest. Let the melodies guide the child into a realm of peaceful slumber, where their spirit may find respite and renewal.

Nuska Incantation - Invocation of the god of writing and literacy

In the realm of ancient Mesopotamia, where knowledge and wisdom flourished, the god Nuska reigned as the divine scribe, guardian of writing and literacy. To invoke his presence and seek his blessings, the sages crafted this sacred incantation. With reverence and a thirst for knowledge, embark upon this journey to connect with the god of writing and unlock the gates of wisdom.

Chant:

"Nuska, divine scribe, holder of the quill,
With reverence and awe, I seek your skill.
Bearer of wisdom, guardian of the word,
Guide me on a path where knowledge is heard.

Inscribed upon tablets of clay and stone,
The secrets of the ancients are known.
With your sacred ink, let wisdom flow,
Reveal the mysteries, help me to grow.

Nuska, I call upon your name with might,
Illuminate my path with wisdom's light.
Grant me the gift of eloquence and grace,
To express my thoughts, to leave my trace.

God of writing, master of the scroll,
Unveil the depths of knowledge untold.
Empower my pen, inspire my thought,
With words, let the universe be caught.

Grant me the keys to the realms of the mind,
Where wisdom and understanding intertwine.
Guide my hand, let words dance and sing,
As I embark on the journey of learning.

Nuska, I offer my devotion and respect,
For the gifts you bestow, I forever reflect.
May my words inspire, may they convey,
The wisdom of ages, the truths that stay.

As I write, let my thoughts find their voice,
With clarity and purpose, I shall rejoice.
Empower me, Nuska, to express and create,
To share knowledge, to elevate.

Divine scribe, I honor your sacred art,
Inscribe upon my heart, your wisdom's chart.
Nuska, god of writing, I seek your embrace,
With pen in hand, I embrace your grace."

Recite this incantation with a heart filled with reverence and a thirst for knowledge. Visualize the god Nuska before you, holding the quill of divine inspiration, as you connect with his essence. Allow his wisdom to flow through you, guiding your hand and illuminating your path of learning and self-expression.

As you journey through the realm of knowledge, may the Nuska Incantation be a powerful invocation, connecting you to the divine wellspring of wisdom. May it inspire your writing, elevate your thoughts, and unlock the gates of understanding. May Nuska, the god of writing and literacy, be your guide on the sacred journey of words.

Utukku Lemnutu Ritual - Banishment of malevolent spirits

In the ancient realm of Mesopotamia, where malevolent spirits lurked in the shadows, the Utukku Lemnutu Ritual emerged as a powerful means to confront and banish these dark entities. Rooted in the ancient wisdom of the sages, this sacred ritual invokes divine protection and empowers the practitioner to cast out the malevolent forces that seek to sow chaos and harm. With unwavering determination and spiritual fortitude, embark upon this journey to banish the shadows and restore balance.

Chant:

"Gates of protection, I call upon thee,
Unveil the powers that safeguard and decree.
Utukku Lemnutu, spirits of despair,
By the light of truth, I declare your snare.

In the sacred space, I stand prepared,
With divine guidance, no darkness is spared.
By the ancient incantations, I invoke,
To banish the shadows, their hold revoke.

In the name of the gods, I raise my voice,
To banish the malevolent, to make a choice.
Utukku Lemnutu, your reign is undone,
I call upon the power of the sun.

With sacred fire, I cleanse this place,
Purify the spirit, restore divine grace.
By the elements of earth, air, fire, and sea,
I claim the power to set the spirit free.

Shadows of darkness, I confront thee,
In the light of truth, you shall not be.
With the words of power, I cast you out,
Banished forever, there is no doubt.

Utukku Lemnutu, your presence fades,
In this sacred ritual, your grip abates.

By the strength of the gods, by their divine might,
I restore balance, banishing your blight.

By the authority bestowed upon me,
I banish the darkness, set the spirit free.
Utukku Lemnutu, your time is done,
Return to the shadows, forever shun.

As this ritual concludes, I seal the way,
Utukku Lemnutu, no longer may you sway.
By the powers of light, love, and truth,
I banish the darkness, I reclaim my youth.

May this ritual's potency endure,
Protecting me, ensuring my spirit is pure.
Utukku Lemnutu, forever be gone,
In the light's embrace, my spirit is strong."

Recite this incantation with a resolute voice, channeling the power of divine protection and casting out the malevolent spirits. Visualize a shield of divine light surrounding you, repelling the shadows and restoring a sense of peace and balance. Allow the words to resonate within you, igniting your spirit with courage and resolve.

Remember, in performing the Utukku Lemnutu Ritual, you wield the power to banish darkness and restore harmony. Approach this ritual with utmost respect, harnessing the ancient wisdom and divine energies to confront the malevolent forces that threaten your well-being. May this sacred ritual bring you solace, peace, and protection, as you banish the shadows and reclaim your spiritual sovereignty.

Sacred Marriage Rite - Ritual reenactment of the union between the gods

In the realm of ancient Mesopotamia, where the gods and goddesses held sway, the Sacred Marriage Rite stood as a profound ritual, reenacting the sacred union between deities. It was believed that through this ritual, the forces of creation, fertility, and abundance would be invoked, blessing the land and its people. Embark upon this journey as the divine energies intertwine, as you become a vessel for the union of the gods.

Chant:

"By the sacred bond of heaven and earth,
I invoke the union of divine birth.
In this rite, I stand as witness and vessel,
To embody the gods, their power I wrestle.

As Inanna and Dumuzid, in perfect harmony,
I become the conduit of their sacred unity.
The goddess of love, beauty, and desire,
The god of fertility, passion, and fire.

Inanna, radiant queen of the heavens above,
Dumuzid, the shepherd, embodiment of love.
I honor your union, your divine embrace,
I merge with your essence, your celestial grace.

In this sacred marriage, I stand betwixt,
Uniting the sacred feminine and masculine mix.
By their energies intertwined, I am blessed,
With their divine union, I am truly caressed.

I embody Inanna's allure, her captivating gaze,
Dumuzid's strength, the fire that forever stays.
As their energies entwine within my core,
I channel their power, forevermore.

May the sacred marriage bestow its grace,
Blessing the land, ensuring a fertile space.
May abundance and prosperity forever bloom,

As I invoke the gods, their union consumes.

In this rite, I merge with the divine,
As Inanna and Dumuzid, together we shine.
Through love and harmony, the world shall thrive,
As their union in me comes alive.

I embrace the divine union, my spirit aflame,
Inanna and Dumuzid, I call upon your name.
Bless this sacred marriage, bless this rite,
As I become the vessel, the conduit of your light."

Recite this chant with reverence and devotion, allowing the energies of Inanna and Dumuzid to flow through you. Visualize their divine essences merging within you, radiating a brilliant light that envelopes your being. Feel the power of their union coursing through your veins, infusing you with love, fertility, and creative energy.

As you embody the Sacred Marriage Rite, may the blessings of divine unity be bestowed upon you and all creation. May the land flourish, relationships thrive, and abundance manifest. Through the union of the gods within you, may you become a beacon of love and harmony, spreading their blessings to all those touched by your presence.

Incantation of Enki - Invocation of the god of wisdom

In the ancient realm of Mesopotamia, where knowledge and wisdom were revered, the Incantation of Enki emerged as a sacred invocation, beckoning the god of wisdom to impart his divine insights. Rooted in the depths of cosmic understanding, this incantation channels the essence of Enki, unveiling the treasures of wisdom and guiding seekers on the path of enlightenment.

Chant:

"Enki, god of boundless wisdom and might,
Bearer of knowledge, radiant with light.
With reverence, I call upon your name,
Guide me through the currents of eternal flame.

From the depths of the primordial sea,
You emerged, Enki, in all your majesty.
The mysteries of the cosmos you unfold,
Your wisdom and insights, precious gold.

Enki, great lord, your wisdom I seek,
Illuminate my mind, let understanding peak.
Grant me the keys to the hidden gate,
Unlock the doors to wisdom's divine state.

With the sacred words, I beckon your grace,
Unveil the truths, the mysteries embrace.
Enki, in your presence, I find solace and peace,
Fill my being with knowledge that shall never cease.

Flow through my veins, like a sacred river,
Awaken my mind, my soul to deliver.
Grant me discernment, the power to see,
The secrets of existence, boundless and free.

Enki, I surrender to your divine flow,
Your wisdom and guidance, in me bestow.
Through the currents of cosmic insight,
Lead me on the path of wisdom's light.

Open the gates of understanding wide,
Let divine wisdom be my eternal guide.
Enki, god of wisdom, I bow before you,
In your embrace, enlightenment anew.

By the power of your sacred name,
I am forever changed, never the same.
Enki, I am grateful for your divine presence,
Bathing me in wisdom's luminescence.

As this incantation concludes, I carry your essence,
Enki, god of wisdom, my eternal reference.
May your insights forever guide my way,
In wisdom's embrace, I forever stay."

Recite this incantation with a humble heart and a thirst for knowledge. Allow the words to resonate within you, opening the channels of divine wisdom and understanding. Visualize the radiant presence of Enki before you, his aura illuminating your being, infusing you with profound insights and cosmic understanding.

May the Incantation of Enki be a gateway to the vast realms of wisdom. May it ignite the flame of enlightenment within you, guiding you on a path of profound understanding and cosmic connection. With Enki's blessings, may your journey be filled with the treasures of wisdom, forever expanding your consciousness and enriching your existence.

Descent of Ishtar - Mythological narrative of Ishtar's journey to the underworld

In the ancient annals of Mesopotamian mythology, the Descent of Ishtar weaves a captivating tale of the goddess's journey to the underworld. Embark upon this mythological narrative as we delve into the depths of the netherworld, where Ishtar, the radiant goddess of love and war, ventures to confront the shadowy realms and unveil the mysteries of life and death.

In the realm of ancient Mesopotamia, Ishtar, adorned with her divine regalia, stands at the precipice of the underworld. Her heart brims with determination and courage, for she seeks to challenge the dominion of Ereshkigal, the queen of the dead. With unwavering resolve, Ishtar descends into the abyss, shedding her divine radiance as she traverses the seven gates.

At each gate, Ishtar must relinquish a piece of her regalia, her symbols of power and authority. She bares herself, humbled and vulnerable, as she passes through each threshold, shedding her divine aura and descending further into the realm of shadows. With each step, the air grows heavy, the darkness more palpable, and the presence of death ever more profound.

Ereshkigal, the queen of the underworld, presides over the realm of the dead with an iron grip. As Ishtar approaches her throne, the veil between the worlds thins, and a confrontation between the goddesses ensues. Ereshkigal, consumed by anguish and grief, confronts Ishtar, demanding a ransom for her release.

Undeterred, Ishtar stands resolute, refusing to yield. She channels her divine strength, calling upon her faithful followers to intercede on her behalf. Enraged by Ishtar's defiance, Ereshkigal commands the Great Bull of Heaven to be unleashed, a formidable force of destruction. But Ishtar, with unwavering determination, faces the beast with courage, subduing it and proving her worth.

Impressed by Ishtar's indomitable spirit, Ereshkigal offers a compromise. Ishtar may leave the underworld, but only if she finds a suitable replacement, someone willing to take her place. Ishtar ascends from the depths, her journey etched in the annals of mythology, forever a testament to her strength and the unyielding spirit of the divine.

The Descent of Ishtar is a testament to the cyclical nature of life, the delicate balance between light and darkness, life and death. Ishtar's journey reflects the human quest for understanding, the pursuit of knowledge, and the willingness to confront the deepest recesses of existence. Through her descent, Ishtar confronts the mysteries of the underworld, emerging with newfound wisdom and a deeper appreciation for the intricacies of the mortal realm.

May the Descent of Ishtar inspire us to confront our own shadows, to journey into the depths of our souls, and to emerge with a greater understanding of the interconnectedness of life and the enduring power of the divine.

Abnu Ritual - Ritual to remove evil from a person or object

In the ancient tradition of Mesopotamia, where the forces of light and darkness clashed, the Abnu Ritual emerged as a potent means to cleanse and purify individuals and objects tainted by evil. Rooted in the ancient wisdom of the sages, this sacred ritual invokes divine intervention and empowers the practitioner to remove the lingering presence of malevolence. With resolute determination, embark upon this transformative journey to banish the shadows and restore purity.

Chant:

"Gates of purity, open wide,
Unveil the path where darkness can't reside.
Abnu, sacred ritual, I invoke thee,
To cleanse the taint and set free.

With reverence, I stand prepared,
To confront the evil that has ensnared.
By the sacred words, I call upon divine might,
To banish the darkness, restore the light.

In this sacred space, I create a shield,
A fortress of purity, a sanctuary revealed.
By the power of the gods, I stand strong,
With their guidance, I right the wrong.

Evil's grip, I now defy,
With sacred fire, I purify.
By the elements of earth, air, fire, and sea,
I banish the darkness, I set free.

In the name of the gods, I command,
Evil's influence, no longer withstand.
Abnu, sacred ritual, your power I embrace,
To remove the taint, restore divine grace.

By the authority bestowed upon me,
I cleanse the spirit, set it free.
Evil's presence, I now dissolve,

With divine intervention, I absolve.

In this ritual's sacred flame,
Evil's hold, I now proclaim,
Banished forever, never to return,
Purity restored, its lessons learned.

As this ritual concludes, I seal the way,
Evil's taint, forever away.
By the power of the gods, by their divine might,
I banish the darkness, I restore the light.

May the Abnu Ritual be a beacon of hope,
A transformative journey to help us cope.
May its power cleanse and purify,
Removing evil's presence, bidding it goodbye.

Approach this ritual with utmost respect,
Harnessing the ancient wisdom and divine effect.
With unwavering determination, let it unfold,
Banishing the evil, restoring the untold.

May the Abnu Ritual bring solace and peace,
As it removes the darkness, brings evil's release.
May purity reign, and light forever shine,
As the taint of evil dissolves in time."

Recite this incantation with a steadfast voice, channeling the power of divine purification and banishing the malevolent presence. Visualize a brilliant light surrounding the person or object, penetrating through the layers of darkness and cleansing them to their core. Feel the purifying energy flowing through you, sweeping away the remnants of evil and restoring purity.

Remember, in performing the Abnu Ritual, you wield the power to banish darkness and restore purity. Approach this ritual with utmost respect, harnessing the ancient wisdom and divine energies to confront and remove the taint of evil. May this sacred ritual bring you solace, peace, and the restoration of divine grace as you banish the shadows and restore purity to those touched by its transformative power.

Prayer to Marduk - Prayer to the god Marduk for protection

In the ancient lands of Mesopotamia, where gods and goddesses reigned supreme, Marduk, the mighty warrior deity, stood as a beacon of strength and protection. Through this prayer, we beseech Marduk's divine presence, invoking his guardianship and seeking his powerful protection. With reverence in our hearts, we call upon Marduk, the mighty god, to shield us from harm and guide us through life's challenges.

Chant:

"Marduk, warrior of heavens high,
With reverence, to you, I raise my cry.
Master of battles, protector divine,
I seek your shelter, may your light shine.

Marduk, with your radiant shield,
Protect me from all that may yield.
Wrap me in your armor of might,
Defend me from darkness, day and night.

Mighty Marduk, with your watchful eye,
Guard me as days and nights pass by.
Guide my steps, keep evil at bay,
Lead me on the righteous way.

In your presence, I find solace and peace,
As your strength around me will never cease.
Marduk, grant me courage and fortitude,
To face life's challenges, with faith renewed.

With your divine power, I am blessed,
By your grace, I am forever impressed.
Banish the shadows, dispel my fears,
Shield me from harm, wipe away my tears.

Marduk, I stand in awe of your might,
In your embrace, I find respite.
Protect me from all that threatens my being,

With your strength, I am forever seeing.

May your divine presence be my guiding light,
In times of trouble, hold me tight.
Marduk, warrior of heavens above,
I entrust my safety to your love.

As this prayer reaches its end,
I know in your protection, I transcend.
Marduk, I am grateful for your care,
For your mighty shield, always aware."

Recite this prayer with a humble heart, calling upon Marduk's divine presence to shield you from harm and guide you through life's trials. Visualize Marduk's radiant light enveloping you, forming a protective shield that repels negativity and safeguards your path. Feel his presence beside you, instilling you with courage and fortitude to face the challenges that lie ahead.

Remember, as you offer this prayer to Marduk, you acknowledge his divine authority and seek his guardianship. Place your trust in his strength and protection, knowing that he stands as a formidable shield against adversity. May Marduk's watchful eye guide and protect you, leading you to a life filled with strength, courage, and divine favor.

Gula Incantation - Invocation of the goddess of healing

In the realm of ancient Mesopotamia, where ailments plagued both body and soul, Gula, the compassionate goddess of healing, emerged as a beacon of hope and restoration. Through this sacred incantation, we invoke Gula's divine presence, beseeching her to bring forth her healing powers and restore balance to our weary spirits. With reverence and faith, we call upon Gula, the great healer, to grace us with her compassionate touch and guide us towards wellness.

Chant:

"Gula, compassionate goddess of healing,
With reverence, your power revealing.
Great healer, with your gentle embrace,
Bring forth your blessings, bring forth your grace.

In the sacred realm where sickness resides,
Your presence, Gula, gently presides.
With your divine touch, ailments you dissolve,
Restoring vitality, evolving problems solve.

Gula, with your wisdom, profound and deep,
Guide us through afflictions, help us keep.
Grant us the strength to face each pain,
To rise above suffering, to heal and regain.

In your sacred name, I call upon thee,
Gula, goddess, hear my plea.
Blessed healer, with compassion so grand,
Extend your loving touch, extend your hand.

Bring healing to bodies, weary and worn,
Calming their pain, restoring them reborn.
Cleanse their spirits, dispel their despair,
Gula, goddess, answer this prayer.

By your divine power, illness is undone,
In your embrace, restoration is won.
Mend the broken, soothe the afflicted,

With your grace, bodies and souls uplifted.

Gula, goddess, we humbly implore,
Guide us to wellness, forevermore.
Bring forth your healing, like a gentle rain,
Washing away ailments, releasing all pain.

As this incantation reaches its end,
May your blessings upon us descend.
Gula, goddess, we offer our gratitude,
For your healing touch, our lives renewed."

Recite this incantation with heartfelt sincerity, invoking Gula's divine presence and trusting in her ability to heal. Visualize her compassionate light enveloping you, soothing and restoring your body and spirit. Feel her gentle touch, bringing relief to ailments and infusing you with renewed vitality.

Remember, as you offer this incantation to Gula, you acknowledge her as the compassionate goddess of healing. Embrace her divine wisdom and trust in her ability to restore balance and wellness. May Gula's healing powers be bestowed upon you, bringing forth a profound transformation, and guiding you towards a life of wholeness and well-being.

Ereshkigal Invocation - Invocation of the queen of the underworld

In the realms of ancient Mesopotamia, where shadows loom and the secrets of the afterlife lie veiled, Ereshkigal, the formidable queen of the underworld, reigns supreme. Through this sacred invocation, we call upon Ereshkigal, the enigmatic and powerful deity, to grant us access to the depths of her domain and bestow upon us her profound wisdom. With reverence and humility, we beseech Ereshkigal to guide us through the mysteries of life, death, and the transformative journey of the soul.

Chant:

"Ereshkigal, queen of the underworld deep,
In the realm of shadows, your vigil you keep.
Mistress of mysteries, guardian of the deceased,
We invoke your presence, may our souls be released.

With solemn hearts, we approach your throne,
Seeking your wisdom, the knowledge unknown.
Ereshkigal, in your presence we stand,
Guide us through the realm of the netherland.

In the depths of darkness, your power resides,
Unveil the secrets that in shadows hide.
Ereshkigal, we beseech your grace,
Illuminate the path to the sacred space.

Queen of the underworld, we honor your might,
In the realm of shadows, where darkness takes flight.
With reverence, we tread the path you decree,
Navigating the realms where spirits are free.

Ereshkigal, unveil the mysteries profound,
As we journey through the realms underground.
Open the gates that separate the spheres,
And grant us passage through the veils of fears.

In the name of the ancients, we call your name,
Ereshkigal, may your wisdom inflame.
Guide us through the depths of transformation,

In your embrace, we find liberation.

Grant us the courage to face our mortality,
To confront the shadows with audacity.
Ereshkigal, teach us the lessons unknown,
As we traverse the realms, our spirits are grown.

In your presence, we find solace and peace,
As our souls journey through realms that cease.
Ereshkigal, queen of the netherworld's domain,
Envelop us in your transformative reign.

As this invocation reaches its end,
May your wisdom upon us descend.
Ereshkigal, we honor your name,
And in your realm, we find eternal flame."

Recite this invocation with reverence and sincerity, immersing yourself in the presence of Ereshkigal, the queen of the underworld. Visualize her enigmatic aura surrounding you, guiding you through the depths of her domain. Feel her profound wisdom resonating within, illuminating the mysteries that lie beyond the realm of the living.

Remember, as you offer this invocation to Ereshkigal, you acknowledge her as the guardian of the underworld and the keeper of ancient wisdom. Embrace her teachings and guidance as you navigate the realms of transformation and spiritual growth. May Ereshkigal's presence be a source of enlightenment, providing you with the strength to face the shadows and emerge transformed on your soul's journey.

Etemmu Ritual - Ritual for dealing with restless spirits of the dead

In the ancient lands of Mesopotamia, where the boundaries between the living and the dead intertwined, the etemmu, restless spirits of the departed, roamed the earthly realm. Through this sacred ritual, we seek to appease these troubled souls and guide them towards their rightful place in the afterlife. With reverence and compassion, we embark on the etemmu ritual, offering solace and liberation to these wandering spirits.

Chant:

"Restless spirits, lost in the in-between,
Bound to the earthly realm, your presence keen.
Etemmu, troubled souls of the departed,
We gather here with hearts open-hearted.

With reverence, we call upon your name,
Etemmu, hear our plea, release your claim.
In the realm of the living, you linger on,
But in the embrace of the afterlife, you belong.

Through this sacred ritual, we offer respite,
A pathway to liberation, guiding your flight.
Etemmu, hear our call, heed our plea,
Embrace the freedom that waits for thee.

With cleansing fire, we purify the space,
Burning away the ties that bind your chase.
Release the earthly attachments that confine,
Embrace the ethereal, the sublime.

Etemmu, troubled souls, let go of despair,
For in the afterlife, peace is your share.
Open your hearts to the divine embrace,
Leave behind the earthly troubles you face.

With sacred chants and invocations high,
We guide you towards the celestial sky.
Etemmu, follow the guiding light,

Embrace the realm of eternal night.

In the name of the ancestors, we gather here,
To release your spirits, to make it clear.
Cross the threshold to the realm unseen,
Where serenity and tranquility convene.

Etemmu, depart from this earthly plane,
Release the burdens that cause you pain.
Be free, be at peace, in the realm anew,
Embrace the eternal, bidding this realm adieu.

As this ritual reaches its final phase,
May your spirits find eternal grace.
Etemmu, may you find your rightful abode,
Rest in the afterlife's tranquil ode."

Perform this ritual with reverence and a compassionate heart, calling upon the
etemmu, restless spirits, to release their earthly ties and find solace in the afterlife.
Create a sacred space, adorned with incense, candles, and symbols of the divine.
Recite the chants and invocations, inviting the spirits to embrace the freedom that
awaits them beyond the earthly realm.

Visualize the spirits finding peace and liberation as you guide them towards the
celestial realm. Feel the energy shifting, as their restless souls are released from the
confines of the earthly realm, ascending to their rightful place in the afterlife. Offer
gratitude to the spirits for their presence and trust that they have found eternal peace.

Remember, as you perform the etemmu ritual, you do so with respect and empathy
for these troubled souls. May your intentions be pure and your actions guided by
compassion. May the etemmu find serenity and tranquility, no longer burdened by
their earthly struggles, as they journey into the realm of eternal rest.

Nergal Incantation - Invocation of the god Nergal

In the ancient realms of Mesopotamia, where power and dominion held great sway, Nergal, the formidable god of war and the underworld, emerged as a force to be reckoned with. Through this sacred incantation, we invoke the strength and presence of Nergal, beseeching him to bestow his mighty protection and grant us the courage to face our battles. With reverence and determination, we call upon Nergal, the fierce god of conquest, to awaken his divine essence within us.

Chant:

"Nergal, god of battle, hear our call,
Mighty warrior, standing tall.
With your presence, courage ignites,
Grant us strength in our perilous fights.

God of war, with fiery might,
In your name, we claim our right.
Nergal, bringer of victory's flame,
In your honor, we kindle the same.

By your side, we march with pride,
Through the fields where battles reside.
Nergal, guide our hand and our aim,
Unleash your power, our foes to tame.

In the depths of Hades, your kingdom prevails,
Where darkness and conquest leave their trails.
Nergal, god of the underworld's might,
Bestow upon us your formidable sight.

Grant us the courage to face our fears,
As we traverse the battlefield's tears.
With your wrath, our enemies we subdue,
Nergal, god of war, we honor you.

Awaken within us your warrior's fire,
Fierce determination, never to tire.
Nergal, lend us your commanding gaze,

Lead us through battles, to victory's blaze.

In your name, we invoke your power,
In our veins, the warrior's hour.
Nergal, god of war, accept our plea,
Envelop us in your might, fierce and free.

As this incantation reaches its end,
May your essence upon us descend.
Nergal, god of battle, we adore,
Our hearts and souls forevermore."

Recite this incantation with unwavering conviction, invoking the presence of Nergal, the god of war and the underworld. Visualize his fierce aura enveloping you, empowering you with the strength and determination to face any challenge. Feel his indomitable spirit coursing through your veins, igniting the warrior within.

Remember, as you offer this incantation to Nergal, you acknowledge him as the god of war and conquest. Embrace his power, but also respect the responsibilities that come with it. May Nergal grant you the courage to face your battles, whether they be physical or metaphorical, and may his divine presence guide you to victory in all your endeavors.

Namtar Incantation - Invocation of the god of fate and death

In the ancient realms of Mesopotamia, where the threads of life and death are intricately woven, Namtar, the god of fate and death, holds sway over the destiny of all beings. Through this sacred incantation, we call upon Namtar, the arbiter of mortal existence, to bestow his wisdom and guidance upon us. With reverence and acceptance, we invoke Namtar, the harbinger of fate, to help us navigate the mysteries of life and find solace in the inevitability of death.

Chant:

"Namtar, god of fate, we seek your embrace,
Guide us through life's intricate maze.
In your presence, we humbly stand,
Grant us insight, destiny's hand.

Master of mortality, your judgment prevails,
We surrender to you, as every life entails.
Namtar, we embrace your wisdom profound,
In your realm of fate, our destinies are bound.

Through the veil of uncertainty, you shed light,
Revealing the path that leads to eternal night.
Namtar, we accept the cycles of life,
Embracing the ebb and flow, embracing the strife.

As we traverse the tapestry of existence,
We surrender to your divine persistence.
Namtar, help us understand and learn,
To embrace each moment, in its turn.

In the face of mortality, grant us grace,
As we journey towards the unknown space.
Namtar, god of death, we offer our trust,
In your embrace, we find solace and adjust.

Guide us through the thresholds of life's transitions,
In each passing moment, in all its renditions.
Namtar, god of fate, we honor your reign,

Accept our reverence, let our voices sustain.

As this incantation reaches its conclusion,
May your presence fill us with resolution.
Namtar, god of fate, we are humbly in awe,
Embrace us, guide us, as our lives withdraw."

Recite this incantation with solemnity and acceptance, inviting the presence of Namtar, the god of fate and death, into your space. Visualize his profound wisdom enveloping you, granting you the ability to navigate the intricacies of life's journey. Feel a sense of surrender and peace as you acknowledge the inevitability of death and the cycles of existence.

Remember, as you offer this incantation to Namtar, you acknowledge his role as the arbiter of fate. Embrace his wisdom and guidance, finding solace in the understanding that life is transient and every moment is precious. May Namtar's presence help you appreciate the ebb and flow of life, and may his divine wisdom guide you to embrace the mysteries that lie ahead.

Divination by Oil - Divination using oil and light

In the ancient lands of Mesopotamia, where the interplay of light and darkness weaves the tapestry of destiny, the art of divination by oil has been practiced for centuries. Through this sacred method, we seek to illuminate the path of fate, gazing into the depths of oil and light to discern the hidden truths that lie beyond. With reverence and focused intent, we embark on the journey of divination, using oil and light as our guides.

Step 1: Preparation
Create a sacred space where you can perform the divination ritual undisturbed. Clear your mind and set your intentions for seeking guidance and insight into the mysteries of life. Choose a small, shallow dish or bowl to hold the oil, and place a floating wick or a small candle within it. Ensure that the oil is of high quality and pure, as it represents the medium through which messages will be revealed.

Step 2: Invocation
Light the wick or candle, allowing the flame to flicker and dance in the darkness. As the glow of the flame grows, speak an invocation to the gods or spirits you wish to call upon for guidance. Offer your respect and request their presence and wisdom throughout the divination process. You may choose to invoke deities associated with divination, such as Nabu, the god of writing and knowledge, or Ishtar, the goddess of love and wisdom.

Step 3: Focus and Concentration
Sit before the oil and flame, gazing upon the surface of the liquid. Relax your mind and enter a state of focused concentration. Let your breathing become steady and calm as you attune yourself to the subtle energies surrounding you. Allow your awareness to merge with the dancing reflections upon the oil's surface.

Step 4: Pose Your Questions
With clarity and intention, formulate the questions or concerns you wish to seek answers for. Phrase your questions in a concise and specific manner, avoiding ambiguity. Hold the questions in your mind, letting them reverberate within you as you maintain your gaze upon the oil. Visualize the questions sinking into the depths of the liquid, seeking the hidden truths.

Step 5: Interpretation
As you continue to gaze at the oil, observe any patterns, images, or symbols that may appear upon its surface. Pay attention to the way the light interacts with the liquid, casting shadows and reflections that hold significance. Allow your intuition to guide you in interpreting these signs and symbols, trusting the messages that unfold before you.

Step 6: Closing and Gratitude
Once you have received the messages and insights from the oil, express your gratitude to the deities or spirits you invoked for their guidance. Extinguish the flame, symbolizing the end of the divination session. Reflect on the messages received and contemplate how they may inform your actions and decisions moving forward.

Remember, divination by oil is a sacred practice that requires focus, patience, and an open mind. Interpretations may vary, and it is essential to trust your intuition and personal connection to the divine. With practice and experience, the art of divination by oil can provide profound insights, shedding light upon the path of fate and offering guidance in the journey of life.

Incantation of Nabu - Invocation of the god of writing and divination

In the realm of ancient Mesopotamia, where the power of the written word holds sway, Nabu, the god of writing and divination, emerges as the guardian of sacred knowledge. Through this sacred incantation, we seek the presence and wisdom of Nabu, beseeching him to share his divine insight and illuminate our path with his celestial light. With utmost reverence, we call upon Nabu, the master of the written word, to bestow upon us his profound wisdom.

Chant:

"Nabu, divine scribe, we invoke your might,
Bearer of knowledge, guide us in your light.
With sacred quill and tablet in hand,
Your wisdom flows like a river grand.

God of writing, your essence we seek,
Through your divine words, our spirits speak.
Unveil the secrets of the ancient tome,
Illuminate our minds, our hearts to roam.

Nabu, revealer of hidden truths,
We beseech you, bless our quest for clues.
Grant us the power to interpret signs,
To decipher symbols in cryptic lines.

Inscribe upon our souls the ancient lore,
With your divine guidance, we explore.
Nabu, grant us the gift of prophecy,
To glimpse the future, to comprehend the decree.

Open our minds to the celestial realm,
Where knowledge and wisdom forever overwhelm.
Nabu, your presence fills our sacred space,
Empower us with your divine grace.

By the might of your sacred pen,
We invoke your presence again and again.
Nabu, god of writing, we offer our plea,

Grant us the wisdom to truly see.

As this incantation reaches its end,
May your wisdom upon us descend.
Nabu, god of writing, we honor your name,
Inscribe upon us your eternal flame."

Recite this incantation with reverence and clarity, invoking the presence of Nabu, the god of writing and divination. Envision his divine aura surrounding you, enlightening your mind and connecting you to the cosmic flow of knowledge. Feel the profound influence of Nabu as you embrace the power of the written word and the art of divination.

Remember, as you offer this incantation to Nabu, you acknowledge his role as the guardian of wisdom and the facilitator of divine communication. Embrace his guidance with humility and respect, recognizing the sacred responsibility that comes with seeking knowledge and understanding. May Nabu's presence empower you to channel divine insights, unveil hidden truths, and honor the transformative power of the written word.

Prayer to Ninurta - Prayer to the god Ninurta for protection in battle

In the realm of ancient Mesopotamia, where conflicts and challenges abound, Ninurta, the god of war and protection, stands as a beacon of strength and courage. Through this solemn prayer, we beseech Ninurta, the mighty warrior, to grant us his divine protection in the midst of battle. With utmost reverence and unwavering faith, we call upon Ninurta, the vanquisher of enemies, to shield us with his formidable might.

Prayer:

"Ninurta, god of war, we turn to you,
In this hour of battle, our plea we renew.
Mighty warrior, with your spear and mace,
Protect us in this perilous embrace.

Giver of victories, master of the fight,
Unleash your power, like a tempest's might.
Ninurta, we seek your shield and blade,
In your presence, no enemy shall evade.

Grant us strength, O divine protector,
Guide our hands in this fierce sector.
Like an eagle soaring through the skies,
Let our spirits ascend, unyielding and wise.

In the face of adversity, we stand tall,
With your divine intervention, we shall not fall.
Ninurta, grant us your invincible might,
To triumph in battle, to defend what's right.

Wrap us in your impenetrable armor,
Shield us from harm, both near and far.
As we march into the heat of strife,
Be our guiding star, our guardian of life.

O Ninurta, we offer this prayer to thee,
With hearts resolute, courageous and free.
Grant us victory, protect us in war's dance,

Our devotion to you, we forever enhance."

Recite this prayer with reverence and conviction, directing your words to Ninurta, the god of war and protection. Meditate upon his divine presence, visualizing his formidable figure standing beside you, guarding and empowering you in the midst of battle.

Remember, as you offer this prayer to Ninurta, you acknowledge his role as the defender and champion of warriors. Approach him with humility and respect, embracing his guidance with a pure heart. May Ninurta's divine protection envelop you, empowering you to face adversity with unwavering strength and emerge victorious on the battlefield.

Adapa's Prayer - Prayer for divine wisdom

In the ancient realm of Mesopotamia, where the pursuit of wisdom and divine knowledge was held in high regard, Adapa, the sage and seeker of truth, uttered a sacred prayer to the gods. Through this prayer, we humbly seek divine wisdom and understanding, following in the footsteps of Adapa, the embodiment of intellectual enlightenment. With reverence and a thirst for knowledge, we raise our voices in prayer, seeking the grace and guidance of the gods.

Prayer:

"O great gods, hear my plea,
In this sacred prayer, I bend my knee.
Adapa, the seeker of wisdom, am I,
Yearning for knowledge that reaches the sky.

Grant me, gods, your divine insight,
Unveil the mysteries hidden from sight.
With open heart and mind, I implore,
Fill my being with wisdom's sacred lore.

Enki, god of wisdom and deep waters,
Share with me your boundless treasures.
Let the streams of knowledge flow,
So my understanding may eternally grow.

Nabu, master of writing and divine speech,
Grant me the power of your teachings to reach.
Inscribe upon my heart the sacred words,
So I may comprehend the secrets of the gods.

Anu, supreme ruler of the heavens high,
Illuminate my path, as the sun in the sky.
Bless me with celestial wisdom and might,
To navigate the realms of knowledge's light.

Marduk, champion of justice and truth,
Guide my steps on the path of wisdom's route.
Grant me the discernment to distinguish,
Between falsehood and knowledge I wish.

With reverence, I offer this plea,
To the gods who hold wisdom's key.
May their divine presence grace my soul,
And grant me understanding, making me whole.

As I walk the path of enlightenment's grace,
May wisdom's blessings light my face.
Let my mind be a vessel, pure and true,
Filled with divine wisdom, ever anew.

I am but a humble seeker, gods divine,
Yearning for knowledge that's truly mine.
Bless me, gods, with wisdom's embrace,
That I may navigate life's intricate space."

Recite this prayer with sincerity and humility, directing your words to the gods of wisdom and knowledge. Meditate upon their divine presence, envisioning their radiant light illuminating your path and infusing your being with profound understanding.

Remember, as you offer this prayer, you follow in the footsteps of Adapa, the ancient seeker of divine wisdom. Approach the gods with reverence and a genuine thirst for knowledge, acknowledging their role as bestowers of enlightenment. May their wisdom and guidance grace your life, opening the doors to profound insights and deep spiritual understanding.

Akitu Festival - New Year festival and ritual

In the ancient realm of Mesopotamia, where the cycles of nature and the celestial spheres governed the lives of its people, the Akitu Festival emerged as a grand celebration of the new year and a sacred ritual of renewal. Through this festival, we honor the eternal cosmic order and the divine cycle of creation and rebirth. With reverence and jubilation, we partake in the Akitu Festival, embracing its profound significance and the spiritual legacy it carries.

During the Akitu Festival, the divine drama unfolds, symbolizing the victory of order over chaos, and the renewal of cosmic harmony. With elaborate processions, chants, and rituals, the people engage in acts of devotion and thanksgiving, seeking blessings and divine favor for the year to come.

As the festival commences, the city is adorned with vibrant decorations, symbolizing abundance and fertility. The streets resound with the rhythmic beats of drums and the joyous melodies of hymns, echoing the harmonious rhythms of the cosmos. The people, dressed in splendid attire, gather in anticipation, as the divine drama of the gods' triumph over chaos is reenacted.

The central moment of the Akitu Festival arrives with the arrival of the sacred barge, carrying the statue of the presiding deity. Amidst the fervent cheers of the crowd, the god is paraded through the city, bestowing blessings upon the land and its people. Offerings of food, drink, and incense are presented to the gods, expressing gratitude and seeking their benevolence.

The ritual culminates in a solemn ceremony, where the old year is ceremonially concluded, and the new year is joyously inaugurated. Prayers are offered, invocations are chanted, and the divine oracles are consulted to seek guidance for the year ahead. The people, filled with hope and renewed vigor, make vows and resolutions, promising to embrace the opportunities and challenges of the coming year with determination and virtue.

As the Akitu Festival draws to a close, the people carry with them the blessings and the spiritual legacy of this sacred celebration. They embark on a new chapter, guided by the harmonious rhythms of the celestial spheres and the knowledge that the eternal cycle of creation and rebirth continues unabated.

In the present day, we honor the legacy of the Akitu Festival by rekindling its spirit in our hearts. Through rituals, gatherings, and acts of gratitude, we celebrate the arrival of the new year, embracing the opportunity for personal and spiritual renewal. Just as our ancient ancestors sought divine blessings and guidance, we too partake in the Akitu Festival, affirming our connection to the cosmic order and our place within the grand tapestry of existence.

May the Akitu Festival inspire us to embrace the cycles of life, to honor the divine within and around us, and to embark on each new year with hope, resilience, and a deep reverence for the eternal renewal of the cosmos.

Prayer to Enlil - Prayer to the god Enlil for guidance and protection

Enlil, mighty god of the heavens and earth,
We bow before your majestic presence, in humble reverence and awe.
As the lord of wisdom and divine authority,
We seek your guidance and protection in this sacred prayer.

Enlil, you hold the threads of destiny in your hands,
We beseech you to guide us along the path of righteousness.
With your keen insight and unwavering justice,
Illuminate our way and shield us from harm's reach.

Great Enlil, protector of the cosmic order,
In your divine wisdom, we place our trust.
Guard us against the tides of chaos and discord,
Wrap us in the mantle of your powerful might.

O Enlil, lord of the earth and the winds that blow,
With your breath, sweep away the obstacles in our path.
Grant us clarity of thought and discernment of heart,
That we may navigate life's challenges with wisdom and art.

In your divine presence, we find solace and strength,
A shelter from the storms that beset our lives.
Like a beacon of light in the darkest night,
Lead us to safety and illuminate our way with your celestial might.

Enlil, we offer this prayer with hearts sincere,
Seeking your divine favor, protection, and care.
May your watchful eye be upon us every day,
Guiding us on our journey, lest we stray.

With gratitude and devotion, we raise our voices high,
Enlil, hear our prayer, as it soars through the sky.
Guide us, protect us, with your divine hand,
As we traverse this mortal realm, a sacred land.

In your name, Enlil, we place our hopes and dreams,
May your benevolence flow like a life-giving stream.

We walk in harmony with your divine will,
Forever grateful for your guidance and protection, still.

As we offer this prayer to Enlil, the god of wisdom and divine authority, let our words echo through the celestial realms. Meditate upon his presence, visualizing his radiant energy surrounding us, providing guidance and protection. Approach Enlil with reverence and humility, acknowledging his role as the guardian of the cosmic order. May his wisdom illuminate our path and his protection shield us from harm, as we journey through the tapestry of life.

Giparu Ritual - Ritual for the consecration of a temple

In the ancient realm of Mesopotamia, where the divine and mortal realms intersected, the Giparu Ritual emerged as a sacred ceremony of profound significance. Through this ritual, a temple was consecrated, transforming it into a sacred space where the divine and human realms converged. With utmost reverence and devotion, we embark on the Giparu Ritual, embracing its ancient wisdom and spiritual legacy.

As the appointed time of the ritual approaches, the temple stands adorned in splendor and sanctity. The air carries a sense of anticipation, as priests and priestesses prepare themselves for the sacred task ahead. The temple, a bridge between the human and divine, is about to be consecrated, making it a dwelling place for the gods.

The Giparu Ritual commences with purification, a cleansing of the temple's physical and spiritual essence. Through the burning of incense, the sprinkling of sacred waters, and the recitation of invocations, the space is rid of any impurities, allowing the divine presence to descend and bless the sacred precinct.

Next, the statues of the patron deities are brought forth, and with great reverence, they are placed within the inner sanctum of the temple. Offerings of food, drink, and precious artifacts are presented, symbolizing the devotion and gratitude of the worshipers. Chants and hymns resound, filling the air with melodic waves of adoration and awe.

The high priest or priestess, a conduit between the realms, stands at the threshold of the temple, invoking the blessings of the gods. With arms raised in supplication, they channel divine energy, calling upon the gods to infuse the temple with their sacred presence. Prayers are offered, expressing the hopes and aspirations of the community, and seeking the divine favor for prosperity, protection, and spiritual guidance.

In a climactic moment, the sacred fire, a symbol of divine illumination and purification, is lit. Its flames dance with vigor and radiance, carrying the blessings and presence of the gods throughout the temple. The fire serves as a beacon, signifying the eternal flame of devotion and the perpetual connection between the human and divine realms.

As the Giparu Ritual concludes, the temple stands consecrated, transformed into a sacred abode where the gods reside. Its walls vibrate with spiritual energy, inviting worshipers to enter and commune with the divine. The consecrated temple becomes a beacon of light, a sanctuary of solace, and a vessel of divine wisdom.

In the present day, we honor the legacy of the Giparu Ritual by infusing our own sacred spaces with reverence and devotion. Through rituals of purification, invocation, and offerings, we create sanctuaries where the divine presence may be felt. In consecrating our temples, be they physical or symbolic, we establish connections with the eternal realms and invite the blessings of the gods into our lives.

May the Giparu Ritual inspire us to recognize the sanctity within and around us, to nurture our connection with the divine, and to create spaces where the sacred may flourish. As we embark on this sacred journey, let us remember the ancient wisdom of consecration and embrace the eternal bond between humanity and the divine.

Prayer to Inanna - Prayer to the goddess Inanna for fertility and love

Inanna, radiant goddess of the heavens and earth,
We come before you with hearts brimming with devotion and reverence.
As the embodiment of beauty, passion, and fertility,
We humbly seek your blessings and guidance in this sacred prayer.

Inanna, mistress of desire and divine sensuality,
We beseech you to grace our lives with your abundant love.
In your presence, relationships flourish and hearts unite,
Illuminate our paths with the flame of passion, burning bright.

Goddess Inanna, you are the nurturer of life's sacred seed,
Bless us with fertility, both in body and in spirit.
Grant us the bountiful blessings of fruitful abundance,
That we may experience the joy of creation, in love's dance.

We entreat you, Inanna, to open the gates of our hearts,
To embrace love's sweet enchantment and tender caress.
Guide us in the art of nurturing relationships,
That they may blossom and flourish, bringing joy and happiness.

Radiant Inanna, queen of divine sovereignty,
We seek your wisdom in matters of the heart.
Lead us on the path of love and harmony,
Shield us from heartache and grant us love's serenity.

Inanna, as we offer this prayer, our souls resonate,
With the eternal longing for love and fertility, innate.
May your divine presence grace our lives each day,
Empowering us to love, to create, and to find our way.

With gratitude and devotion, we raise our voices high,
Inanna, hear our prayer, as it soars through the sky.
Bless us with your sacred touch, divine and pure,
That love and fertility may forever endure.

In your name, Inanna, we offer this plea,
May your blessings shower upon us, so mote it be.

With love and gratitude, we honor your divine power,
Radiant goddess, guide us in love's sacred hour.

As we offer this prayer to Inanna, the goddess of fertility and love, let our words echo through the celestial realms. Meditate upon her presence, visualizing her radiant energy surrounding us, bestowing her blessings upon our lives. Approach Inanna with love, gratitude, and openness, acknowledging her as the source of divine fertility and passion. May her grace and guidance ignite the flames of love within us and bless us with abundant fertility in all aspects of our lives.

Nergal and Ereshkigal Incantation - Invocation of the gods Nergal and Ereshkigal

In the depths of the ancient underworld,
Where shadows dance and secrets unfurl,
We call upon Nergal and Ereshkigal,
Mighty deities of the netherworld's hall.

Nergal, fierce god of war and plague,
With your fiery might, battles you wage.
Ereshkigal, queen of the underworld's domain,
Guide us through darkness, release us from pain.

Together, Nergal and Ereshkigal, we invoke,
Through this sacred incantation, our spirits evoke.
Grant us strength and courage, O divine pair,
As we navigate life's challenges with utmost care.

Nergal, with your wrathful power and might,
Banish our fears, bring victory to our fight.
Empower us with the fire of your divine rage,
To overcome obstacles, turn the page.

Ereshkigal, ruler of the realm below,
In your presence, shadows ebb and flow.
Guide us through the depths of our own soul,
Teach us wisdom, make us whole.

As we utter your names, Nergal and Ereshkigal,
The boundaries between realms start to fall.
In this sacred moment, we embrace the dark,
Honoring the depths, where secrets embark.

Grant us insight into the mysteries profound,
As we traverse the realms where you are found.
Illuminate our path, reveal hidden truths,
From your ancient wisdom, we seek our roots.

Nergal and Ereshkigal, we offer this plea,
As we enter the realm of the underworld's decree.

Guide us, protect us, as we tread this sacred ground,
In your divine presence, may our spirits be bound.

With reverence and humility, our voices unite,
Nergal and Ereshkigal, hear our call tonight.
Bring forth your blessings, embrace us with your might,
As we honor your ancient legacy, shining bright.

In your names, Nergal and Ereshkigal, we pray,
May your presence guide us on our sacred way.
As we invoke your power, let our spirits align,
Nergal and Ereshkigal, your devotees we will forever be thine.

In this invocation of Nergal and Ereshkigal, we honor the gods of the underworld and seek their guidance and protection. Meditate upon their names, visualizing their presence, and connect with their ancient power. Approach them with respect and reverence, acknowledging their roles as guardians of the netherworld. May their strength and wisdom empower us as we navigate the depths of our own journey, embracing the mysteries and lessons that await.

Incantation of Šamaš - Invocation of the sun god Šamaš

Šamaš, radiant and resplendent god of the sun,
Whose golden rays illuminate the world we live in,
We call upon your divine presence and power,
To guide us on our path and bless us in every hour.

Mighty Šamaš, source of light and life,
With each rising dawn, you dispel the night's strife.
As you ascend the heavens in celestial grandeur,
We beseech you, hear our invocation, pure.

From the eastern horizon, you emerge anew,
A beacon of warmth, shining bright and true.
With your radiant gaze, you bless the land,
Filling our hearts with courage and a helping hand.

Šamaš, god of justice and righteousness,
We seek your wisdom to discern truth's finesse.
Illuminate our minds with your divine clarity,
That we may walk the path of integrity.

Through your fiery chariot, you traverse the skies,
Witnessing the world with all-seeing eyes.
Grant us the clarity to see beyond the veil,
To discern the right path when our spirits fail.

Šamaš, god of healing and restoration,
Infuse our bodies and souls with revitalization.
With your nurturing warmth, heal our wounds,
And bathe us in your divine energy, like a soothing tune.

We offer our gratitude for each day you bestow,
For the blessings you bring and the wisdom you show.
Šamaš, as we call upon your sacred name,
Fill our lives with abundance, free from blame.

In this sacred moment, we invoke your might,
Šamaš, sun god, shining with pure light.

Guide us on our journey, inspire us to be,
Radiant beacons of love and harmony.

As we utter your name, Šamaš, feel our devotion,
May our spirits align with your divine motion.
Bless us with your radiant energy, eternal and true,
Šamaš, sun god, we honor and worship you.

In this invocation of Šamaš, the sun god, we embrace the power and warmth of the celestial deity. Meditate upon his name, visualizing the sun's brilliance and the life-giving rays that he bestows upon the world. Approach Šamaš with reverence and gratitude, acknowledging his role as the illuminator and sustainer of life. May his divine presence shine upon us, guiding our paths and infusing our lives with his radiant energy and blessings.

Ekur Ritual - Ritual for the blessing of a royal palace

In the grandeur of the royal palace, adorned with splendor,
We gather to perform the sacred Ekur ritual with fervor.
May the gods bestow their blessings upon this regal abode,
As we invoke their presence and seek their divine code.

O majestic palace, symbol of power and authority,
We embark on this ritual with utmost solemnity.
May your walls stand strong, steeped in sanctity,
As we beseech the gods for their eternal loyalty.

We call upon the divine assembly, with voices raised,
To witness this sacred rite, in awe and praise.
Mighty Anu, ruler of the heavens and earth,
Bless this palace with your divine worth.

Enlil, lord of the winds and supreme in command,
Let your protective embrace across these walls expand.
Ninhursag, mother goddess of the fertile lands,
Grant abundant blessings and harmony that withstands.

Inanna, radiant queen of beauty and desire,
Infuse this palace with passion and divine fire.
Shamash, god of justice and radiant light,
Illuminate every corner, banishing darkness from sight.

Let the sacred smoke of incense rise, fragrant and pure,
Cleansing the palace, ensuring blessings endure.
May the sacred waters of purification flow,
Washing away impurities, letting positive energies grow.

The priest, adorned in sacred vestments, chants the hymn,
Invoking the gods, their presence drawing near, not dim.
The ritual vessels, filled with offerings and reverence,
Symbolize the unity of gods and earthly presence.

With each step, the palace is blessed and consecrated,
By the divine energies, its destiny dictated.

May prosperity and harmony forever reside,
Within these walls, where royalty does preside.

In this Ekur ritual, we honor the royal palace,
Seeking the gods' favor and blessings, never callous.
May the spirits of divinity grace this regal space,
Infusing it with their sacred essence and grace.

As the ritual concludes, we offer gratitude and praise,
To the gods who have witnessed this sacred display.
May the Ekur ritual's blessings endure and unfold,
Within this royal palace, radiant and bold.

Prayer to Nanna - Prayer to the moon god Nanna for divine favor

Oh, Nanna, divine ruler of the night sky,
Guiding light that graces our world from up high,
With each crescent and full moon that you display,
We humbly approach you, our hearts in fervent sway.

Mighty Nanna, radiant moon god so fair,
Your gentle glow bathes the earth with a celestial flair,
Your luminous presence brings solace and calm,
As we seek your divine favor, with uplifted palm.

In the stillness of the night, we raise our voice,
Offering prayers to you, O god of choice.
Grant us your blessings, Nanna, from above,
Illuminate our path with your celestial love.

With each lunar cycle, you guide the tides,
As we navigate life's challenges and divides,
We beseech you, Nanna, to lend us your aid,
And shower us with the blessings we have prayed.

Like the ever-changing moon, we too transform,
In your cosmic radiance, we find strength to perform,
Grant us wisdom to make choices that are right,
And fill our hearts with divine insight.

Nanna, ancient deity of the heavenly sphere,
Your grace and wisdom we humbly revere,
With devotion, we offer this heartfelt plea,
Grant us your favor, that we may succeed and be free.

In this sacred moment, we bow our heads,
Seeking your guidance on life's intricate threads,
May your divine light shine upon our path,
Protecting us from harm, shielding us from wrath.

Oh, Nanna, hear our prayer, offered with respect,
Embrace us with your celestial intellect,

As we honor you, moon god, with devotion profound,
May your divine favor in our lives resound.

Ereshkigal and Nergal Ritual - Ritual to appease the gods Ereshkigal and Nergal

In the depths of the underworld, where shadows reside,
We embark on a sacred rite, with reverence as our guide.
To Ereshkigal and Nergal, we offer our devotion,
Seeking their mercy and favor, with heartfelt emotion.

Ereshkigal, mighty queen of the netherworld,
Whose dominion holds the spirits unfurled,
We approach your realm with utmost respect,
To honor your power and show our prospect.

Nergal, fierce and formidable god of war,
Whose presence brings destruction near and far,
We acknowledge your might and invoke your name,
As we seek your blessings and quell any flame.

In this ritual, we acknowledge the balance they hold,
For life and death, their power so bold.
Ereshkigal, compassionate in your domain,
Guide us through darkness, easing our pain.

Nergal, fierce warrior, guardian of the gate,
Lend us your strength, our fears to abate.
Together, you reign in the realm below,
In this ritual, we honor both high and low.

We offer libations, symbols of life's flow,
As a gesture of reverence, our devotion on show.
With each pour, we honor your sacred might,
May our offering bring solace, shining bright.

In sacred space, adorned with symbols of death,
We invoke their presence, with each prayer's breath.
Words of supplication rise from our lips,
Seeking their mercy, as the ritual eclipse.

With candles flickering, casting shadows on the wall,
We chant incantations, a beckoning call.

May Ereshkigal's sorrow find solace in our plea,
And Nergal's wrath be tempered, setting our spirits free.

In this union of underworld and mortal plane,
We seek harmony, our intentions made plain.
May Ereshkigal and Nergal find favor in our plight,
As we navigate life's journey, both day and night.

As the ritual concludes, we express our gratitude,
For the gods' presence, their divine fortitude.
May Ereshkigal and Nergal, in their sacred grace,
Grant us protection and blessings in every place.

Prayer to Ashur - Prayer to the god Ashur for protection

Oh, Ashur, mighty ruler of the heavens,
Whose presence brings strength to our mortal endeavors,
With awe and reverence, we turn to you,
Seeking your divine protection, strong and true.

Ashur, god of gods, supreme in your might,
Your watchful gaze guides us day and night,
Grant us your shield, unwavering and firm,
As we face life's challenges, let your blessings confirm.

In times of peril, we seek your aid,
Your divine protection, our fears allayed,
Wrap us in your mantle, secure and serene,
Shield us from harm, O majestic deity unseen.

With every step we take, let your wisdom guide,
Through shadows and trials, our fears subside,
May your presence surround us like a sacred fire,
Uplifting our spirits, filling us with divine desire.

Ashur, lord of the cosmic realm,
Let your power protect, overwhelm,
Stand as our guardian, tower of strength,
Defend us from harm, throughout life's length.

In your sacred name, we offer this plea,
For your divine favor, we humbly decree,
Watch over us, Ashur, with vigilant care,
Shield us from danger, answering our prayer.

Oh, Ashur, we beseech you, hear our call,
As we entrust our lives to your celestial thrall,
Guide us, protect us, with your mighty hand,
And lead us to safety, across life's shifting sand.

In times of darkness, we find solace in your light,
Your presence dispels the shadows of the night,

With gratitude and reverence, our spirits ascend,
As we honor you, Ashur, our eternal friend.

Note: It is important to note that specific prayers and practices may vary within Mesopotamian mythology and historical context.

Eridu Lament - Ritual lamentation for the destruction of the city of Eridu

Oh, Eridu, once majestic city of old,
Whose glory and splendor now lie untold,
We gather in sorrow, our hearts heavy with grief,
To lament the loss, seeking solace and relief.

In the shadow of ruins, where greatness once stood,
We mourn the destruction, the loss of all that was good.
Eridu, cradle of civilization, revered and renowned,
Your fall leaves us with a sense of profound.

With tear-stained cheeks and voices of lament,
We mourn the loss of your grandeur, now spent.
The great ziggurat, towering high above,
Now reduced to rubble, devoid of your love.

We remember your temples, once bustling with life,
Now silenced and empty, amid the wreckage and strife.
Your sacred waters, once a source of nourishment and grace,
Now tainted and forgotten, a reflection of our displaced.

Oh, Eridu, your demise echoes through time,
A testament to the fleeting nature of all sublime.
We honor your memory, with each mournful cry,
And vow to keep your legacy alive, though you lie.

With lamentation, we channel our grief,
The tears we shed bring some relief.
In sorrow's embrace, we find unity,
Binding our hearts in shared community.

Through solemn songs and mournful dirges,
We commemorate your fall, as history urges.
May your spirit find solace in our mourning,
As we remember your past, forever adorning.

Eridu, your lament echoes through the ages,
A poignant reminder of mortality's stages.

In our sorrow, we hold your memory dear,
And honor your legacy with reverence sincere.

Incantation of Ninhursag - Invocation of the goddess Ninhursag

Oh, Ninhursag, mother of all creation,
Goddess of fertility, nurturing foundation,
With reverence and awe, we call upon your name,
To seek your wisdom and blessings we acclaim.

Ninhursag, primordial goddess of the earth,
Whose fertile embrace gives life its worth,
From your sacred womb, all beings were born,
With your divine touch, the world was adorned.

Mistress of the mountains, lush and green,
Your bountiful fields, a sight to be seen,
In your presence, nature thrives and flourishes,
Grant us your blessings, O goddess who nourishes.

With each chant and incantation we utter,
We invoke your essence, O benevolent mother,
Let your creative force flow through our veins,
Awakening our spirits, releasing life's chains.

Oh, Ninhursag, your healing touch we implore,
Restore our bodies, minds, and spirits to the core,
Infuse us with vitality, strength, and grace,
As we walk the path of life, at your divine pace.

Guide us with your wisdom, O goddess profound,
Teach us the secrets of the fertile ground,
Help us sow the seeds of harmony and love,
As we honor you, Ninhursag, in realms above.

In this sacred space, we offer our devotion,
To the goddess of life, with heartfelt emotion,
May your blessings rain upon us, like gentle showers,
Nurturing our souls, blooming life's flowers.

Ninhursag, we beseech you, hear our plea,
Grant us your favor, for all eternity,

Embrace us with your motherly embrace,
And shower us with your abundant grace.

Prayer to Enki - Prayer to the god Enki for wisdom and blessings

Oh, Enki, divine bringer of wisdom and knowledge,
With reverence and humility, I approach your sacred edge.
Grant me your wisdom, O god of the deep waters,
Fill my mind with insight, as the river's gentle murmurs.

Enki, compassionate ruler of the cosmic domain,
Guide me through life's challenges, alleviate my strain.
Bestow upon me the gift of discernment and understanding,
That I may navigate the world with wisdom commanding.

In your sacred presence, I find solace and inspiration,
For you hold the key to profound revelation.
Unveil the mysteries that lie beyond mortal sight,
Illuminate my path with your divine and guiding light.

Oh, Enki, grant me the strength to seek truth and clarity,
In the depths of my soul, let your wisdom find solidarity.
Bless me with insight, that I may make choices wise,
And with each decision, may your guidance materialize.

Enki, lord of abundance and prosperity untold,
I beseech you to bless me with blessings manifold.
Open the floodgates of abundance and wealth,
That I may prosper and thrive, in spiritual and material health.

With gratitude and reverence, I offer this prayer,
To the god of wisdom, who deeply cares.
May your blessings descend upon me like gentle rain,
Filling my life with purpose and removing every strain.

Oh, Enki, your presence brings me peace and serenity,
I thank you for the wisdom and blessings bestowed upon me.
Guide me, protect me, in your divine embrace,
Enki, I offer my devotion, forever in your grace.

Eunuch Exorcism Ritual - Ritual to exorcise a possessed eunuch

Step 1: Preparation

Create a sacred space by cleansing and purifying the area where the ritual will take place.
Set up an altar with candles, incense, blessed herbs, and a vessel of purified water.
Gather the participants and ensure they are spiritually prepared and focused on the task at hand.

Step 2: Invocation and Protection

Begin the ritual by invoking the presence of the gods, specifically Nergal and Ishtar, through prayers and chants.
Light the candles and the incense to purify the space and invoke divine protection.
Use the purified water to consecrate the participants and create a protective barrier around them.

Step 3: Cleansing and Purification

Approach the possessed eunuch and offer words of reassurance and support.
Begin the cleansing process by gently washing the eunuch's face and hands with the purified water, using a soft cloth or sponge.
Recite incantations and chants specific to exorcism and purification, invoking the power of Nergal and Ishtar to banish the possessing entity.

Step 4: Drumming and Chanting

Start the rhythmic drumming, creating a steady beat that resonates with the spiritual realm.
Encourage the participants to join in with chanting, using the incantations and prayers specific to exorcism and spiritual liberation.
The drumming and chanting should gradually intensify, building energy to confront and dispel the malevolent forces.

In the realm where spirits intertwine with flesh,
Where darkness can consume and souls are enmeshed,
We gather with purpose, wielding sacred might,
To free a tormented eunuch from the grip of the night.

Divine Dynamics

With resolute hearts and unwavering devotion,
We invoke the powers of divine intercession,
Calling upon the gods, guardians of light,
To banish the malevolent forces, restoring what's right.

In the sanctified space where rituals unfold,
With incense and candles, the scene takes hold,
We create a shield, a barrier of divine grace,
To protect us from harm and invoke sacred space.

With purified water and blessed herbs in hand,
We cleanse the afflicted eunuch, where darkness has banned,
Chanting ancient incantations, invoking divine names,
Breaking the bonds that hold them, extinguishing infernal flames.

We call upon Nergal, god of pestilence and might,
To cast out the demon, restore the eunuch's light,
With flames of purification, let the malevolence be consumed,
And restore the eunuch's spirit, from darkness exhumed.

We beseech the aid of Ishtar, goddess of love and war,
To wrap the eunuch in her protective and healing lore,
With her divine presence, let strength and courage abound,
As we cleanse the afflicted, restoring their lost ground.

Through rhythmic drumbeats and chants that resonate,
We break the chains that bind, liberating the eunuch's fate,
In this sacred dance of exorcism, we weave,
A tapestry of healing, helping the eunuch to retrieve.

As the ritual crescendos, the possessed is released,
Their spirit unburdened, their anguish finally eased,
With gratitude and reverence, we bid farewell,
To the forces of darkness, their power dispelled.

May the exorcised eunuch now find solace and peace,
With the scars of possession, their spirit will cease,
And in the embrace of the divine, they shall thrive,
Forever protected, as their soul begins to revive.

Step 5: Release and Healing

As the energy peaks, focus the collective intent on freeing the eunuch from the possession.
Channel the divine energy through the drumming, chanting, and prayers, directing it towards the eunuch.
Visualize the dark entity being expelled from the eunuch's body, consumed by divine flames, and banished from their presence.
Step 6: Closure and Gratitude

Once the intensity subsides, gradually ease the drumming and chanting, allowing the energy to settle.
Offer prayers of gratitude to Nergal, Ishtar, and any other deities invoked during the ritual, expressing appreciation for their assistance.
Provide a moment of silence and reflection to allow the eunuch to regain composure and integrate the healing energies.

Prayer to Shamash - Prayer to the god Shamash for justice

Mighty Shamash, radiant god of justice and truth,
I stand before you, seeking your divine presence and soothing truth.
With humble words and a heart filled with righteousness,
I invoke your name, seeking your guidance and fairness.

Shamash, dispenser of wisdom and impartiality,
You hold the scales of justice with unwavering clarity.
Illuminate my path with your radiant light,
Guide me through the shadows, dispelling all blight.

I implore you, O Shamash, to hear my plea,
Grant me the strength to champion what is right and decree.
Grant me the discernment to see through deceit,
And the courage to stand firm against injustice I meet.

Like the golden sun, your presence shines bright,
I seek your wisdom and insight, like a guiding light.
Bring forth justice, O Shamash, with your righteous hand,
Let fairness prevail in every corner of the land.

In courtrooms and councils, let your influence be known,
As the ultimate arbiter, seated on your celestial throne.
Dispense justice with your divine authority,
Weave together the threads of truth and equity.

Shamash, protector of the weak and oppressed,
Empower me to fight for justice, to never rest.
Grant me the words to speak truth without fear,
And the conviction to stand up when injustice draws near.

May your radiant beams guide the righteous way,
As I strive for justice with each passing day.
With your divine presence, let justice prevail,
And may your wisdom and fairness never fail.

Shamash, I offer this prayer with devotion and trust,
In your hands, I place my hopes, knowing justice is just.

Bless me with your divine grace, and let justice be served,
In your name, O Shamash, may justice be preserved.

Ishtar's Descent Incantation - Invocation of Ishtar during her descent to the underworld

In the realm of shadows and the land of the dead,
I invoke the name of Ishtar, the Queen to be led.
With solemn reverence and a heart full of devotion,
I call upon Ishtar, seeking her mighty ocean.

Ishtar, radiant goddess of love and desire,
You descended to the underworld, fueled by fire.
With your divine presence and unyielding will,
You traversed the realms, defying death's chill.

I stand before you, O Ishtar, with awe and respect,
In this sacred moment, my voice I direct.
Through the gates of Kur, where darkness resides,
You journeyed fearlessly, with unwavering strides.

I seek your guidance, O Ishtar, in times of despair,
As you faced the trials and depths of the underworld's lair.
Grant me strength and resilience in my darkest hour,
As I navigate the challenges that life does devour.

Ishtar, as you were stripped of your divine attire,
You faced the shadows, their torment and their ire.
But your power remained unbroken, your spirit intact,
You emerged triumphant, radiant and exact.

In your descent, you witnessed the secrets of the abyss,
Gaining wisdom and understanding, amidst darkness amiss.
I beseech you, Ishtar, share your sacred knowledge with me,
Illuminate my path, that I may walk with clarity.

Let your presence be felt, O Ishtar, in realms above and below,
Empower me with your love, courage, and sacred glow.
As you rose from the underworld, restored and renewed,
May I too find strength, as your divine essence imbued.

Ishtar, I offer my devotion and utmost respect,
As I invoke your name, your power I reflect.

Guide me through challenges, both great and small,
With your divine presence, I shall conquer them all.

Prayer to Nergal - Prayer to the god Nergal for protection from evil

Mighty Nergal, fearsome god of war and protection,
I call upon your name, seeking your divine direction.
With reverence and humility, I bow before your might,
Asking for your presence, shining like a guiding light.

Nergal, warrior of the gods, fierce and brave,
I beseech you, safeguard me from evil's dark wave.
Protect me from harm, shield me from all ill,
Grant me strength and courage, as I climb life's steep hill.

With your flaming sword and unwavering gaze,
Banish evil forces that seek to cause dismay.
Stand by my side, O Nergal, with unwavering might,
Keep me safe and secure, both day and night.

In your divine presence, evil trembles and retreats,
Your power and vigilance, none can defeat.
I invoke your name, O Nergal, with trust and respect,
May your protection surround me, as I navigate life's sect.

Grant me the fortitude to face adversity with resolve,
Guide my steps, that I may evolve.
Infuse me with your fiery essence, Nergal so bold,
Protect me from wickedness, as your grip takes hold.

In your fierce embrace, evil shall falter and cower,
As you guard my spirit in every passing hour.
With your divine strength, I stand tall and resolute,
Repelling darkness, with your light absolute.

Nergal, I offer this prayer, with utmost devotion,
Seeking your protection from evil's dark commotion.
May your vigilance shield me, both near and far,
Preserve my soul, like a guiding northern star.

Etemenanki Ritual - Ritual for the sanctification of a ziggurat

Preparation: Gather the necessary ritual tools and offerings. Cleanse yourself and the area where the ritual will take place.

Invocation: Begin the ritual by invoking the divine presence of the gods associated with the ziggurat, such as Marduk, Nabu, or Shamash. Offer prayers and words of reverence to invite their divine energies.

Purification: Perform a ritual purification by sprinkling sacred water or burning purifying herbs such as myrrh or frankincense. Walk around the base of the ziggurat, spreading the purifying elements to cleanse the space.

Offerings: Prepare offerings such as food, drink, flowers, or symbolic items that represent the gods and their attributes. Place them at the designated altar or shrine within the ziggurat.

Chant and Incantation: Stand at the base of the ziggurat and chant the following incantation:
"Etemenanki, sacred and grand,
Pillar of heaven, reaching high to land.
May your foundations be blessed and strong,
Anointed by gods, where they belong."

Ascend the Ziggurat: Begin climbing the ziggurat, step by step, symbolizing the ascent to the divine realms. As you climb, maintain a reverent and focused mindset, connecting with the energies of the gods.

Blessing and Sanctification: Upon reaching the top of the ziggurat, stand before the altar or shrine. Extend your hands towards the sky, channeling your intention for the sanctification of the ziggurat. Recite prayers and invocations, asking the gods to bless and consecrate the structure.

Offerings and Gratitude: Make additional offerings at the altar, expressing gratitude to the gods for their presence and blessings. Offer words of thanks for the opportunity to partake in this sacred ritual.

Closing: Descend the ziggurat, step by step, symbolizing the return from the divine realms. Offer a final prayer of gratitude and bid farewell to the gods, acknowledging the conclusion of the ritual.

Chant:
Etemenanki, Etemenanki, soaring high,
Divine abode reaching towards the sky.
Sanctified and blessed, may you forever stand,
Anchored in earth, touched by gods' command.

Prayer to Nabu - Prayer to the god Nabu for wisdom and learning

Nabu, god of wisdom and writing divine,
I call upon your name, with reverence I incline.
Grant me your knowledge, O wise and learned one,
Illuminate my path, as the rising of the sun.

Nabu, son of Marduk, with your tablet and stylus,
You record the truths and the knowledge that is.
Guide me in my pursuit of wisdom and insight,
Bestow upon me the gift of intellectual might.

Inscribe upon my heart the wisdom of the ages,
That I may understand the world's ancient pages.
Open my mind to the mysteries and truths untold,
As I seek knowledge, let your blessings unfold.

Nabu, teacher and scribe, I beseech your aid,
In my quest for wisdom, let me not be swayed.
Grant me clarity of thought, a discerning mind,
That I may unravel the secrets I long to find.

As you stand at the gates of heaven and earth,
I seek your guidance, your wisdom, your worth.
Inspire my words and thoughts with your divine fire,
That I may aspire to greatness and never tire.

Nabu, I offer my devotion and utmost respect,
As I seek your wisdom, I humbly reflect.
Grant me the understanding and knowledge to grow,
In your presence, O Nabu, may my intellect glow.

In your name, I pray, with a humble heart,
Grant me wisdom, knowledge, and a scholarly art.
Guide me on the path of learning, ever true,
Nabu, I honor you, and my studies I pursue.

Gula's Healing Incantation - Invocation of the goddess Gula for healing

Gula, great and compassionate goddess of healing,
I invoke your name, seeking your divine revealing.
With reverence and trust, I turn to you this hour,
Asking for your mercy, your soothing healing power.

Gula, gentle and caring, with your loving touch,
Bring forth your remedies, for ailments I clutch.
By your grace and wisdom, restore my body's ease,
Banish sickness and pain, let my health find release.

With your radiant presence, heal the wounds within,
Mend the broken, soothe the weary, and cleanse the sin.
Pour forth your healing balm, O Gula so fair,
With your divine intervention, let wellness repair.

In your hands lie the herbs and medicines of old,
With your knowledge and skill, ailments are consoled.
I implore your aid, O Gula, so benevolent,
Guide the healers' hands, with your wisdom ever present.

Gula, I offer my gratitude and utmost devotion,
As I seek your healing, with unwavering emotion.
Grant me your compassion, your divine intervention,
Restore my health, O Gula, with your gentle attention.

By your healing touch, may my body be made whole,
With every ailment cured, every pain released, every toll.
Gula, I trust in your grace, in your power so vast,
Wrap me in your healing embrace, until the sickness is past.

In your name, I pray, with faith in your divine art,
Bring forth your healing energy, let it swiftly impart.
Gula, goddess of compassion and restoration,
I honor you in this invocation, seeking your healing manifestation.

Prayer to Sin - Prayer to the moon god Sin for protection during the night

Sin, mighty and radiant god of the moon,
I beseech your presence, your divine boon.
As darkness descends, and shadows cast their might,
I seek your protection throughout the long night.

Bathed in your ethereal glow, O celestial guide,
Watch over me, keep me safe, my fears subside.
With your lunar brilliance, illuminate my way,
Guard me from harm until the break of day.

Sin, dispenser of dreams, keeper of secrets untold,
In your gentle embrace, may peace unfold.
Shield me from the terrors that the night may bring,
With your divine presence, let tranquility sing.

As I venture into the realm of the nocturnal hour,
I seek your watchful gaze, your protective power.
Wrap me in your celestial light, O Sin so wise,
Guide my steps, let no harm in darkness arise.

From the heavens above, you watch with grace,
Preserve me from darkness, from dangers I face.
Keep me safe from malevolent spirits that roam,
May your divine radiance be my sacred home.

Sin, I offer my devotion, my prayers sincere,
As I implore your protection, your presence near.
In your lunar realm, let me find solace and peace,
As I rest under your watchful eye, may my fears cease.

In your name, I pray, O Moon God so bright,
Keep me guarded and sheltered throughout the night.
Grant me your blessings, your divine intervention,
Sin, I seek your protection with utmost veneration.

Anunnaki Invocation - Invocation of the Anunnaki, the gods of the underworld

In the depths of the underworld, where shadows dwell,
I call upon the Anunnaki, those who rule this realm.
Mighty deities of ancient times, hear my plea,
As I invoke your presence, bend your ear to me.

Anunnaki, masters of the netherworld so vast,
With reverence and awe, I approach you at last.
Grant me audience, O guardians of the abyss,
As I seek your wisdom, in darkness and in bliss.

From the great abzu, your realm of primordial might,
You emerged, divine beings, shining with celestial light.
Enki, Enlil, Nergal, Ereshkigal, and more,
I beseech your favor, on this sacred floor.

By the gates of Kur, the land of no return,
You hold dominion, where mortal souls discern.
Guide me through the realms of death and rebirth,
As I navigate the mysteries of the vast underworld's girth.

Anunnaki, judges of souls, weigh my heart true,
Grant me passage, let my spirit journey anew.
In your presence, I seek solace and understanding,
Reveal the secrets of the afterlife, so commanding.

In your names, I chant the ancient incantations,
Invoking the Anunnaki with utmost dedication.
Open the gates to your realm, O mighty ones,
Let me commune with the spirits, daughters and sons.

Anunnaki, I offer my reverence and devotion,
As I seek your guidance, with utmost emotion.
Grant me insight, wisdom, and protection divine,
In the realm of the Anunnaki, may my spirit align.

Prayer to Ninhursag - Prayer to the goddess Ninhursag for fertility and abundance

Ninhursag, nurturing mother of all creation,
Goddess of fertility, hear my supplication.
With reverence and gratitude, I call upon your name,
Asking for your blessings, your abundant flame.

In your sacred embrace, life finds its birth,
You, who shapes the earth, the cradle of our worth.
Mistress of the mountains, guardian of the fields,
Fruitful Ninhursag, to you my heart yields.

Goddess of vegetation, of bountiful harvest,
Pour forth your blessings, abundant and steadfast.
Grant fertility to the land, and abundance to the crops,
Let the seeds of life flourish, from the smallest tops.

Ninhursag, divine midwife, who brings forth life,
Guide the growth of all beings, relieve their strife.
From the fertile soil, let life's essence spring,
Grant us your favor, and prosperity you bring.

In your care, may the fields yield plentiful grain,
May the orchards bear fruit, ripe and sweet in the main.
Let the rivers flow, nourishing the land anew,
With your touch, may abundance always ensue.

Ninhursag, I offer my prayers, my devotion true,
As I seek your blessings, fertility imbued.
Grant me the joy of motherhood, if it be my fate,
Let your nurturing presence guide me, never abate.

With your wisdom and grace, bless our homes and kin,
Let love and abundance reign, deep from within.
In your name, I praise, O Ninhursag so divine,
Fertility and abundance, with your blessings intertwine.

Nergal and Ereshkigal Offering - Offering to the gods Nergal and Ereshkigal

In the depths of the underworld, where darkness thrives,
I come before you, Nergal and Ereshkigal, with humble lives.
Mighty gods of the netherworld, rulers of the abyss,
Accept this offering, an act of devotion and bliss.

To Nergal, fierce warrior and lord of the dead,
And to Ereshkigal, queen of the underworld, dread,
I present this tribute, a gesture of reverence profound,
May it please you, as my devotion resounds.

Nergal, your might is unmatched, your wrath severe,
With your flaming sword, you instill both hope and fear.
Accept this offering, an homage to your power,
May it please you, in this sacred hour.

Ereshkigal, ruler of the land of no return,
In your domain, spirits of the dead sojourn.
Accept this offering, a token of respect and honor,
May it please you, as my devotion you ponder.

This offering, carefully chosen and prepared,
Symbolizes my devotion, my soul bared.
I present it with utmost reverence and care,
May it find favor with you, Nergal and Ereshkigal, fair.

In this moment of communion, I seek your grace,
Guide me through the shadows, show me your face.
Accept this offering, an act of devotion sincere,
May it please you, as my words reach your ear.

Nergal and Ereshkigal, I offer my devotion true,
As I honor your might and the darkness you imbue.
May this offering strengthen our connection so deep,
As I tread the path of the underworld, in your keep.

Prayer to Enlil and Ninlil - Prayer to the gods Enlil and Ninlil for protection

Mighty Enlil, father of the gods so grand,
And Ninlil, revered goddess at your right hand,
I come before you, seeking your divine embrace,
In this prayer, I beseech your protection and grace.

Enlil, lord of the storms and ruler of the skies,
With your thunderous voice, let evil forces demise.
Ninlil, gentle goddess of the harvest and fertility,
Wrap us in your loving care, shield us with your purity.

Together, your powers combine, an unyielding force,
Protectors of the heavens, our safeguard and resource.
Grant us strength in times of trials and strife,
May your divine presence guide us through life.

Enlil, in your wisdom, bring clarity and insight,
Illuminate our paths, keep us on the righteous flight.
Ninlil, in your nurturing embrace, grant us peace,
Shield us from harm, as our worries cease.

We seek your protection from malevolent intent,
Guard our homes, our loved ones, wherever they're sent.
With your divine presence, may our fears be allayed,
Enlil and Ninlil, in your shelter, we find aid.

Enlil and Ninlil, I offer this prayer with devotion,
Seeking your benevolence and divine protection.
Keep us safe from harm, both day and night,
Surround us with your love, your celestial light.

Eridu Lamentation - Ritual lamentation for the city of Eridu

Preparation:

Find a quiet and secluded space where you can perform the ritual undisturbed.
Create an altar or sacred space to honor the spirit of Eridu. You can adorn it with symbols or representations of the ancient city, such as miniature ziggurats or images of Mesopotamian deities.
Light a candle or incense to create a solemn atmosphere.
Invocation:

Begin by standing or sitting before the altar, facing the representation of Eridu.

Take a few deep breaths to center yourself and create a connection with the energy of the ritual.

Speak an invocation to the spirit of Eridu, expressing your intention to lament and honor its memory. You can use your own words or a scripted invocation, such as:

"Oh, spirit of Eridu, ancient city of splendor,
I call upon you now with reverence and surrender.
In this sacred space, I mourn your fate,
And offer this lamentation to commemorate."

Lamentation:

Close your eyes and allow yourself to feel the sorrow and sadness for the decline of Eridu. Let the emotions rise within you.
Begin the lamentation by speaking or chanting verses that express your grief and longing for the city. You can use the words from the Eridu Lamentation poem provided earlier or compose your own heartfelt verses.
Let the words flow naturally, allowing your voice to convey the depth of your emotions. You may choose to speak softly or sing the lamentation if you feel inclined.
Reflection and Connection:

After the lamentation, take a few moments of silence to reflect on the significance of Eridu and its place in history.
Visualize the grandeur and vitality of the ancient city, and imagine the spirit of Eridu responding to your lamentation.

During this time, you can also offer personal prayers or thoughts of gratitude for the wisdom and contributions that emerged from Eridu.
Closing:

Conclude the ritual by expressing gratitude to the spirit of Eridu for allowing you to connect with its essence and honor its memory.
Blow out the candle or extinguish the incense, symbolizing the end of the ritual.
Take a moment to ground yourself, feeling your connection with the present moment and the world around you.

Uruanna Ritual - Ritual for the consecration of a city

The Uruanna Ritual is a sacred ceremony performed to consecrate a city, invoking the divine energies and seeking blessings for its inhabitants. This ritual signifies the establishment of a spiritual connection between the city and the gods, ensuring its prosperity, protection, and harmony. Below are the steps to perform the Uruanna Ritual:

Selection of a Sacred Site:

Choose a central location within the city that holds significance or aligns with the city's spiritual essence. It can be a prominent hill, a temple complex, or any place deemed sacred.
Prepare the site by clearing away any debris or unwanted materials, creating a clean and sanctified space.
Preparation and Purification:

Gather the necessary ritual items, including offerings, incense, sacred objects, and representations of deities associated with the city or the local pantheon.
Perform a personal purification ritual by cleansing your body and mind. Bathe, wear clean attire, and center yourself through meditation or deep breathing.
Opening Invocation:

Stand at the designated sacred site and face the direction that aligns with the city's significance or the rising sun.
Begin the ritual with an opening invocation, calling upon the gods and goddesses associated with the city, expressing gratitude, and seeking their presence and blessings.
Offering and Blessings:

Place offerings, such as grains, fruits, flowers, and sacred herbs, in a designated area within the sacred site.
Invoke the gods and goddesses, offering prayers and expressing the intentions of the city's consecration. Request their blessings for the city's prosperity, protection, and harmonious existence.
Light incense or candles to symbolize the presence of divine energy and to purify the surroundings.
Sacred Walk or Procession:

Perform a sacred walk or procession around the designated sacred site, carrying the representations of deities or sacred objects.

Chant prayers, invocations, or hymns specific to the city or the gods and goddesses invoked, invoking their presence and protection as you move.

Blessing the City:

Return to the central sacred site and offer additional prayers, expressing gratitude for the blessings bestowed upon the city and its inhabitants.

Sprinkle holy water or sacred oils on the ground as a symbolic act of consecration, signifying the divine presence permeating the city.

Closing Invocation:

Conclude the ritual with a closing invocation, expressing gratitude to the gods and goddesses for their presence and blessings.

Offer a final prayer, asking for the continued guidance, prosperity, and protection of the city and its people.

Prayer to Dumuzid - Prayer to the god Dumuzid for abundance and prosperity

Mighty Dumuzid, god of abundance and fertility,
I come before you with reverence and humility.
In this prayer, I seek your divine presence,
To bless me with prosperity and sustenance.

Dumuzid, beloved shepherd of the land,
Your bountiful gifts, I now understand.
You bring forth the golden harvest in the fields,
And ensure abundance that nature yields.

I pray to you, O Dumuzid, with a grateful heart,
For your blessings and abundance, I impart.
Grant me the wisdom to sow and reap,
To nurture the fruits of the earth, so deep.

Bless my endeavors, both great and small,
With success and prosperity, may I stand tall.
Guide my hands as I toil in the fertile soil,
Grant me abundance, my efforts to foil.

Dumuzid, provider of wealth and fortune,
May your blessings shower upon me soon.
Open the doors of opportunity and gain,
Let abundance flow like a gentle rain.

I pledge to honor you, O Dumuzid, in return,
To share my blessings, to give and discern.
As abundance fills my life, I will share,
With those in need, my love and care.

Dumuzid, hear my prayer, I beseech,
Grant me prosperity, in abundance, I reach.
With gratitude, I embrace your divine grace,
Bless me, O Dumuzid, in every time and space.

Prayer to Anu - Prayer to the god Anu for divine favor and protection

O mighty Anu, ruler of the heavens,
I bow before you with reverence and devotion.
In this prayer, I seek your divine favor,
To receive your blessings and protection forever.

Anu, supreme god of the celestial realm,
Your wisdom and power overwhelm.
As the lord of the divine council, you preside,
With justice and mercy by your side.

I beseech you, O Anu, with a humble heart,
Grant me your divine favor, a precious art.
Guide my steps with your celestial light,
Protect me from harm both day and night.

You hold the cosmic keys to destiny's gate,
Grant me the favor I seek, for my fate.
With your blessings, let opportunities unfold,
And may success and prosperity take hold.

In times of darkness, be my guiding star,
Shield me from misfortune, near and far.
Let your divine presence surround me,
With your protection, I feel safe and free.

Anu, the great celestial king on high,
Hear my prayer, as I look to the sky.
Grant me your favor, I humbly implore,
And I shall forever honor and adore.

Inanna's Descent Incantation - Invocation of Inanna during her descent to the underworld

O Inanna, Queen of Heaven and Earth,
I invoke your presence with sacred mirth.
As you descended to the underworld's embrace,
I call upon your power, seeking your grace.

Inanna, radiant goddess of love and war,
Through the realms of darkness, you did soar.
Grant me strength as I face life's trials,
Through your guidance, let me find my smiles.

In the depths of the underworld's domain,
You faced challenges, enduring the pain.
With your courage and wisdom as my guide,
I too shall triumph, standing tall with pride.

Inanna, wearer of the sacred Me,
Descend with me into the depths, set me free.
Grant me the courage to face my shadows,
To embrace transformation, as life's current flows.

In the realm of Ereshkigal, the queen below,
You navigated the trials, I seek to know.
Guide me through the darkness, illuminate the way,
Lead me back to the light, I humbly pray.

Inanna, I offer my devotion and trust,
As I tread the path of descent, I adjust.
Grant me the power to release what no longer serves,
To emerge reborn, with a soul that observes.

As you ascended, clothed in divine light,
Bestow upon me your blessings, shining bright.
Let your wisdom and compassion fill my being,
Inanna, goddess of transformation, I am seeing.

By your grace, O Inanna, I find my strength,
In your embrace, I go to any length.

Through the descent, I reclaim my power,
Inanna, guide me in this transformative hour.

Prayer to Enki and Ninhursag - Prayer to the gods Enki and Ninhursag for fertility

O Enki, wise and generous god of wisdom,
And Ninhursag, nurturing goddess of the earth,
I beseech your divine presence and grace,
As I offer this prayer for fertility's embrace.

Enki, master of creation and abundance,
You hold the secrets of life's inception.
With your guidance, let fertility flow,
May barrenness and sorrow find no place to grow.

Ninhursag, bountiful mother of all living things,
You bring forth life with nurturing wings.
With your fertile embrace, let new life arise,
And bless us with abundance that never dies.

Together, Enki and Ninhursag, I implore,
Pour your blessings upon the land I adore.
Favor us with fertility in body and soul,
Let the seeds of life in us take their toll.

Grant us the gift of healthy conception,
That new life may form in divine connection.
Bless us with children, a joyous heritage,
To carry forward the love and wisdom we cherish.

Enki and Ninhursag, I bow before your might,
In this prayer, seeking your divine light.
Guide us on the path of fertility's grace,
And bless us abundantly in every embrace.

May our bodies be fertile like the earth's soil,
And may our spirits flourish in joyful toil.
With your blessings, may our lives bloom and grow,
Filling our hearts with love's radiant glow.

I offer my gratitude for your benevolent care,
Enki and Ninhursag, hear my heartfelt prayer.

May fertility's blessings forever abound,
In your divine presence, may I be found.

Prayer to Nusku - Prayer to the god Nusku for protection from fire

O Nusku, divine guardian of the flame,
I come before you, calling out your name.
In this prayer, I seek your watchful eye,
To protect me from fire, drawing nigh.

Nusku, radiant deity of light and warmth,
You hold the power to shield from fire's harm.
With your divine presence, I feel secure,
Guiding me through dangers, steadfast and sure.

I beseech you, O Nusku, with reverence deep,
Protect me and my loved ones as we sleep.
Keep our homes and hearths safe and sound,
Shield us from fire's destructive bound.

You, who guard the sacred flame of life,
I call upon you to avert all strife.
With your fiery essence, create a shield,
That fire's destructive force may be repealed.

Nusku, vigilant deity of the flickering fire,
Grant us your protection, never to tire.
Keep calamity and disaster at bay,
Preserve our lives, day by day.

In moments of peril, be our guiding light,
Illuminate the path, dispelling the fright.
Through your watchful gaze, danger shall cease,
And we shall find solace, tranquility, and peace.

O Nusku, mighty god of fiery glow,
Embrace us with your protective glow.
With gratitude and reverence, we pray to thee,
May your shielding presence forever be.

Prayer to Inanna and Dumuzid - Prayer to the gods Inanna and Dumuzid for love and fertility

Mighty Inanna, radiant queen of heaven,
And noble Dumuzid, the beloved king,
I kneel before you with humble reverence,
Seeking your divine blessings this day I bring.

Inanna, goddess of passion and desire,
With your beauty and grace that never tire,
I beseech you to bestow your love's fire,
Igniting my heart's deepest yearning and aspire.

Dumuzid, tender shepherd of the land,
Whose love and fertility are vast and grand,
I implore you to bless me with your gentle hand,
So that love and abundance may forever expand.

Goddess of love, Inanna, hear my plea,
Grant me the love I seek, pure and free,
Guide my steps in matters of the heart,
That I may find a love that shall never depart.

Dumuzid, guardian of the fertile earth,
Bring forth your blessings, an abundant birth,
Let fertility and growth be felt in every girth,
Blessing my life with joy, love, and mirth.

Inanna and Dumuzid, united divine pair,
Embodying love's essence, so rare and fair,
I offer my devotion and heartfelt prayer,
Grant me love's bliss, beyond compare.

May my heart be filled with love's gentle embrace,
And may my life be blessed with fertility and grace,
Inanna and Dumuzid, I offer my gratitude and praise,
May your divine blessings guide me through life's maze.

Gilgamesh's Lament - Lamentation for the death of Gilgamesh's companion, Enkidu

O Enkidu, my cherished companion and friend,
In the depths of sorrow, my heart does rend.
With tears that flow like a ceaseless stream,
I mourn your loss, as if in a dream.

We embarked on countless adventures together,
Facing trials, both fierce and clever.
Side by side, we conquered all in our path,
But now, alone, I face the aftermath.

O Enkidu, you were my strength and shield,
In battle, our bond could never yield.
Your laughter echoed through every endeavor,
Now silenced forever, gone from me forever.

We swore to stand united, till the end of days,
But fate has torn us apart, in mysterious ways.
The weight of grief, like a heavy stone,
Crushes my spirit, leaving me alone.

In the vast wilderness, we roamed with pride,
But now, I wander, lost without my guide.
Your absence leaves a void I cannot fill,
Aching emptiness, a sorrow that's so real.

O Enkidu, my dearest companion, I lament,
Your departure has left me deeply bent.
I grieve for the moments we can never share,
Longing for your presence, feeling the despair.

In my heart, your memory shall forever reside,
A flame of friendship that will never subside.
Though you have passed beyond the mortal realm,
In my thoughts, your spirit will forever overwhelm.

O Enkidu, may the gods welcome you with grace,
Embrace you in their eternal embrace.

In the land of shadows, may you find peace,
While here on Earth, your memory shall never cease.

Enuma Anu Enlil Exorcism - Exorcism using the Enuma Anu Enlil incantation

The Enuma Anu Enlil incantation holds ancient power,
A sacred formula to banish spirits that devour.
With the words of the gods, we confront the unseen,
Expelling malevolence, bringing purity serene.

Step 1: Preparation
In a sacred space, purified and consecrated,
Gather the tools and offerings, fully dedicated.
Light incense and candles, creating a sacred atmosphere,
Invoking the presence of divine forces near.

Step 2: Invocation
Stand in the center, arms raised to the heavens high,
With conviction and reverence, call upon the sky.
Speak the words of the Enuma Anu Enlil with might,
Invoking the divine powers to banish the blight.

Step 3: Incantation
Enûma Anu Enlil,
May the heavens and earth align,
With divine authority, I repel the malign.
By the decree of Anu, the supreme lord,
By the wisdom of Enlil, the one adored.

Step 4: Visualization
Envision a radiant light surrounding your being,
Expanding outward, a protective shield, all-seeing.
See the darkness dispersing, giving way to divine grace,
As the ancient incantation fills the sacred space.

Step 5: Banishment
With firm resolve, speak the words of banishment,
Commanding the malevolent spirits to relent.
Invoke the power of the gods to cast them away,
To restore harmony and keep darkness at bay.

Step 6: Offering
Present an offering to the gods, a token of gratitude,
For their aid in the exorcism, their interlude.
Express thanks for their protection and divine might,
As you conclude the ritual, bathed in their light.

Note: The Enuma Anu Enlil incantation is a powerful ancient Mesopotamian exorcism formula. This adaptation of the ritual incorporates the use of the incantation as a means of spiritual purification. It is essential to approach such practices with respect and understanding, adapting them to your own belief system and personal connection to the divine.

Prayer to Nergal and Ereshkigal - Prayer to the gods Nergal and Ereshkigal for protection in the underworld

O Nergal, fearsome god of the underworld,
And Ereshkigal, queen of the realm so cold,
I humbly beseech you, with reverence and might,
To grant me protection in the darkest of night.

As I descend into the depths of the abyss,
Guide my steps through the shadows, I insist.
Shield me from the perils that lie in wait,
And guard me from the spirits that seal my fate.

Nergal, with your fierce and fiery essence,
Grant me strength to face the trials, relentless.
Defend me from the malevolent forces that dwell,
In the realms where darkness and chaos swell.

Ereshkigal, queen of the underworld's domain,
Extend your mercy and shield me from pain.
As I tread upon your sacred, hallowed ground,
Grant me your favor, let safety be found.

O mighty gods, rulers of the netherworld's domain,
I seek your shelter and your divine reign.
Protect me from the judgment and wrath that lie,
In the depths where souls of the departed cry.

Grant me passage through the gates of death,
Preserve my spirit with each passing breath.
Guide me through the trials of the afterlife's test,
And ensure my soul finds eternal rest.

In your divine embrace, I find solace and peace,
May your presence in the underworld never cease.
With gratitude and reverence, I offer my plea,
Nergal and Ereshkigal, hear my prayer and see.

Note: This prayer is intended to invoke the protection of the gods Nergal and Ereshkigal in the realm of the underworld. It acknowledges their power and seeks their benevolence for safe passage and protection against the perils that may be encountered in the realms beyond. Adapt and personalize this prayer according to your beliefs and connection with the divine.

Gudam Ritual - Ritual for the consecration of a royal tomb

Step 1: Preparation
Select a suitable location for the royal tomb,
A sacred space where ancestral spirits will roam.
Cleanse the area, purify it with sacred rites,
Creating a sanctified space, free from mundane sights.

Step 2: Invocation
Gather the participants, priests, and attendants all,
To witness the consecration, heeding the sacred call.
Invoke the blessings of the gods with reverence profound,
Seeking their favor as the tomb is hallowed ground.

Step 3: Purification
With sacred water and incense, purify the tomb's entrance,
Cleansing it of impurities, removing any malevolent presence.
Sprinkle the holy water, warding off evil's blight,
While incense smoke fills the air, guiding spirits to the light.

Step 4: Offerings
Present offerings of food, drink, and precious items rare,
To honor the deceased and show respect and care.
Invoke their spirits, inviting them to dwell,
In the consecrated tomb, their eternal abode to tell.

Step 5: Ritual Chants and Prayers
Utter ancient chants and prayers, invoking divine grace,
Seeking the blessings of the gods, their eternal embrace.
Call upon the deities, guardians of the afterlife's gate,
To watch over the tomb, ensuring the departed's fate.

Step 6: Sealing
Seal the entrance to the tomb with sacred symbols and signs,
Protecting it from desecration, preserving its divine design.
Mark it as a place of rest for the revered departed,
A sanctuary where their legacy is forever charted.

Step 7: Final Benediction
Offer final prayers and blessings, expressing gratitude and awe,
For the consecration completed, fulfilling ancient law.
May the spirits of the departed find eternal peace,
And may their tomb be honored, as their legacy will never cease.

Prayer to Utu - Prayer to the sun god Utu for justice and protection

Mighty Utu, radiant and resplendent,
Golden charioteer of the heavens,
I bow before you, seeking your divine presence,
And invoke your name with reverence and reverence.

Utu, lord of justice and truth,
Dispenser of divine retribution,
I beseech you to shine your righteous light,
And illuminate the path of justice, pure and bright.

As you traverse the celestial expanse,
Guiding the sun's chariot with steadfast stance,
I implore you, O Utu, to extend your protection,
And shield me from all harm and affliction.

Grant me the strength to face life's trials,
To uphold truth and vanquish falsehood's wiles,
Illuminate the darkness that veils the way,
And lead me towards justice day by day.

O Utu, arbiter of right and wrong,
Grant wisdom and discernment strong,
Let your radiance shine upon the unjust,
Exposing their deeds, and in justice, they shall adjust.

In your hands, the scales of justice rest,
Balancing the hearts of the deserving best,
Guide my steps with your divine light,
So that I may walk the path of righteousness, upright.

Protect me from those who seek to deceive,
And grant me the courage to stand and believe,
In the power of justice, fairness, and truth,
With your benevolent gaze, blessings imbue.

O Utu, sun god, I offer my heartfelt plea,
Fill my life with justice and harmony,

As you rise and set in the eternal sky,
May your presence forever be nigh.

Note: This prayer is intended to invoke the sun god Utu for justice, protection, and guidance. Adapt and personalize it according to your beliefs and connection with Utu or any other solar deity. Remember to approach prayer with sincerity and reverence, acknowledging the divine power and seeking its influence in your life.

Eridu Purification Ritual - Ritual purification for the city of Eridu

Step 1: Gathering of the Community
Gather the community of Eridu, both young and old,
United in purpose, with hearts and spirits bold.
Come together at the sacred center of the city,
To cleanse and purify, invoking divine purity.

Step 2: Ritual Preparations
Prepare a sacred fire, ablaze with sacred light,
Its flames representing the gods' benevolent might.
Arrange sacred herbs and incense, aromatic and pure,
Their fragrances invoking blessings that endure.

Step 3: Cleansing Offerings
Prepare offerings of water, grains, and sacred bread,
Symbols of sustenance and purity widely spread.
Present them to the gods with reverence and devotion,
Seeking their blessings and divine intercession.

Step 4: Chanting of Purification Hymns
Chant ancient hymns of purification and renewal,
Words resonating with the gods, ancient and eternal.
Let the powerful vibrations cleanse the city's essence,
Restoring its sacredness and divine presence.

Step 5: Ritual Purification Baths
Partake in ritual purification baths or ablutions,
Symbolically washing away impurities and illusions.
Submerge in sacred waters, cleansing body and soul,
Absorbing the divine grace that makes one whole.

Step 6: Sacred Procession through the City
Form a solemn procession, led by the priestly class,
Carrying symbols of divine power, strong as brass.
Walk through the city's streets, spreading purifying rites,
Dispelling negative energies and restoring cosmic rights.

Step 7: Final Blessings and Invocations
Conclude the ritual with final blessings and invocations,
Calling upon the gods for their divine restorations.
May the city of Eridu be cleansed, renewed, and pure,
A haven of sacredness, with blessings to endure.

Note: The Eridu Purification Ritual described here is a symbolic ceremony for cleansing and renewing the city of Eridu. Adapt the steps and practices according to your own beliefs and traditions. The intention is to invoke the gods' blessings and restore the city's sacredness, fostering a sense of spiritual well-being and community unity.

Prayer to Ninshubur - Prayer to the goddess Ninshubur for divine assistance

Glorious Ninshubur, faithful servant and friend,
With utmost reverence, to you I extend,
In times of need, I seek your guiding hand,
Grant me your divine assistance, ever so grand.

Ninshubur, messenger of the heavens above,
Bearer of tidings, embodiment of love,
I call upon your wisdom, strength, and grace,
To aid me in life's challenges I face.

Goddess of loyalty, unwavering and true,
You stand by the side of the great Inanna, too,
I beseech you now, with a heart sincere,
To listen to my plea and draw near.

Ninshubur, intercessor between realms divine,
Bridge the gap between mortal and sacred shrine,
Guide me through trials, both dark and rough,
Empower me with resilience, courage, and enough.

Grant me your wisdom, so profound and deep,
To navigate life's paths with discernment and keep,
Bless me with clarity, vision, and insight,
To make decisions that lead to what is right.

Ninshubur, guardian of secrets and whispers,
Bearer of messages, both subtle and blizzards,
I implore you, in your divine splendor,
To intercede on my behalf, my defender.

In times of hardship, grant me strength to persevere,
In times of doubt, fill my heart with faith clear,
Assist me in finding solutions and resolutions,
And lead me towards divine revelations.

Ninshubur, goddess of support and aid,
In your presence, may my worries fade,

With gratitude, I offer this prayer to you,
Believing in your blessings, pure and true.

Note: This prayer is intended to invoke the goddess Ninshubur for divine assistance. Adapt and personalize it according to your own beliefs and connection with this deity. Approach prayer with sincerity and reverence, expressing your specific needs and seeking her divine guidance and support.

Giparu Offering - Offering to the gods for the consecration of a temple

In reverence to the gods, with sacred intent,
I come forth bearing offerings, humble and bent.
To consecrate this temple, a haven divine,
With gratitude and devotion, this act shall align.

Step 1: Purification
Cleanse the sacred space, free from any taint,
With sacred water and incense, remove any constraint.
Invoke the gods' presence, their blessings implore,
Purifying the temple, now and forevermore.

Step 2: Preparation
Arrange the altar with reverence and care,
Adorned with flowers, symbols, and incense to share.
Offerings of food, drink, and precious gifts,
Laid before the gods, uplifted spirits they uplift.

Step 3: Invocation
Invoke the gods, one by one,
With words of praise, let your voice be spun.
Call upon their names with honor and respect,
Inviting their divine presence, this sacred connect.

Step 4: Offering
Present your offerings, one by one,
Food and drink, symbolic of what is done.
Show gratitude for the gods' divine grace,
As you place each offering in its rightful place.

Step 5: Prayer
Offer a heartfelt prayer, filled with devotion,
Expressing your gratitude and deep emotion.
Seek the gods' blessings for this sacred shrine,
That it may be a place of power, divine.

Step 6: Closing
Express gratitude for the gods' presence here,

And thank them for their blessings, sincere.
Close the ritual with reverence and grace,
Knowing their divine energy fills this sacred space.

May the gods accept this offering with delight,
And bless this temple with their presence, shining bright.
May it be a sanctuary where mortals find solace,
And a conduit for divine energies to interlace.

Note: This ritual is a general framework for the Giparu Offering, which is performed to consecrate a temple in the ancient Mesopotamian tradition. Adapt and personalize it according to your specific beliefs, practices, and the deities you wish to honor.

Prayer to Ashnan - Prayer to the goddess Ashnan for abundance and sustenance

Oh, Ashnan, bountiful goddess of the fields,
Whose hands nurture the seeds that the earth yields,
I beseech you now with a humble plea,
Grant me your blessings, I implore thee.

Goddess of abundance, provider of grain,
Your touch brings forth sustenance and gain,
As you tend to the crops with gentle care,
May your blessings fill the land and the air.

Ashnan, hear my prayer, my heartfelt cry,
In your divine presence, I draw nigh,
Bestow upon me your gifts of plenty,
That I may flourish in life's journey.

In times of hunger, provide me with food,
Nourish my body, uplift my mood,
Bless my table with sustenance and grace,
Fill my pantry with abundance, a plentiful space.

Goddess of the harvest, I acknowledge your might,
The golden wheat fields, a magnificent sight,
As you bless the grains with your loving touch,
May I be blessed with prosperity, oh goddess, so much.

Ashnan, embodiment of fertility and growth,
In your hands, the seeds of life you sow,
I seek your blessings for a fruitful yield,
In every endeavor, may success be revealed.

Guide me in cultivating the seeds of my dreams,
Grant me the wisdom to tend to them, it seems,
May they blossom and flourish under your care,
As I walk upon life's path, with love and share.

Oh, Ashnan, hear my prayer, my plea,
Fill my life with abundance, full and free,

With gratitude in my heart, I express my devotion,
To you, goddess of plenty, in this sacred motion.

Note: This prayer is intended to invoke the goddess Ashnan for abundance and sustenance. Adapt and personalize it according to your own beliefs and connection with this deity. Approach prayer with sincerity and reverence, expressing your specific needs and desires for abundance in your life.

Incantation of Iškur - Invocation of the storm god Iškur

In the roaring thunder and the crackling skies,
I call upon thee, Iškur, with sacred cries.
Mighty god of storms, ruler of the tempest's might,
Unleash your power, manifest your divine light.

Iškur, I invoke your name with reverence and awe,
Master of lightning, enforcer of natural law.
From your celestial abode, descend to this earthly plane,
Let your presence be known, let your energy sustain.

By your command, the rains shall pour,
Cleansing the earth, renewing its core.
With each thunderous clap, your voice resounds,
Stirring awe and fear, as the tempest surrounds.

Iškur, I call upon your lightning's fierce blaze,
To strike down obstacles, to clear my life's maze.
Grant me strength and courage, in times of strife,
To weather the storm, to embrace a transformed life.

Oh, storm god Iškur, protector and guide,
With your blessings, let me safely abide.
Drive away misfortune, dispel all harm,
Shield me from danger with your mighty arm.

As I speak your name, let the winds obey,
Sweeping away darkness, bringing a brighter day.
Grant me your favor, oh divine storm god,
In your presence, I find solace, my spirit awed.

Iškur, I offer my devotion and respect,
As your power and might I humbly reflect.
Accept this invocation, this sacred plea,
And in your grace, I forever shall be.

Prayer to Ninhursag and Enki - Prayer to the gods Ninhursag and Enki for healing and wisdom

Oh, Ninhursag, divine mother of all,
Whose gentle touch brings forth life's call,
And Enki, wise god of knowledge and might,
I come before you, seeking your healing light.

Ninhursag, goddess of the fertile earth,
You nurture and heal, granting us rebirth.
With your compassionate embrace, restore my being,
Heal my body, my spirit, my very meaning.

Enki, god of wisdom, holder of deep insight,
Bestow upon me knowledge, pure and bright.
Grant me the wisdom to understand and perceive,
The mysteries of life, the lessons to receive.

In your divine presence, I find solace and peace,
A sanctuary where my worries and ailments cease.
May your healing energies flow through my veins,
Revitalizing my body, releasing all pains.

Ninhursag and Enki, hear my humble plea,
Wrap me in your embrace, set my spirit free.
With your wisdom and healing powers combined,
May I find wholeness, restoration of body and mind.

I seek your guidance, oh benevolent gods,
To navigate life's challenges, to overcome odds.
Grant me the strength to face each day anew,
With your wisdom and healing, I shall pursue.

In your names, I offer my heartfelt devotion,
Seeking your blessings, your boundless compassion.
Ninhursag and Enki, hear my prayer,
Grant me healing and wisdom, beyond compare.

Eridu Fertility Ritual - Ritual for the fertility of the land in Eridu

Step 1: Preparation

Choose a sacred outdoor space in Eridu, preferably near a body of water or fertile land.
Gather the necessary ritual items, including offerings of grain, fruits, and flowers, as symbols of abundance and fertility.
Purify yourself by washing your hands and face with clean water.
Step 2: Invocation of the Divine

Face the direction of the rising sun, symbolizing the dawning of new life and fertility.
Raise your hands to the sky and call upon the gods and goddesses associated with fertility, such as Ninhursag, Enki, and Inanna.
Offer a prayer, expressing your sincere desire for the fertility and prosperity of the land in Eridu.
Step 3: Offerings to the Earth

Place the offerings of grain, fruits, and flowers on a clean and elevated surface, symbolizing the bountiful earth.
Express gratitude to the earth for its nourishing and life-giving qualities.
Pour a libation of water onto the ground as an offering to the earth, signifying the renewal of life and the replenishment of the land.
Step 4: Chanting and Dancing

Begin chanting rhythmic and uplifting songs, praising the fertility and abundance of the land.
Dance in a circular motion, symbolizing the cycles of nature and the interconnectedness of all living beings.
Let your movements and voice become one with the energy of the earth, invoking its life-giving force.
Step 5: Blessing of the Land

Take a handful of fertile soil and scatter it gently across the ground, symbolizing the spreading of blessings and fertility.
Offer prayers for the growth of crops, the health of livestock, and the overall prosperity of the land and its inhabitants.
Visualize the land flourishing with abundant vegetation, thriving wildlife, and a harmonious balance of nature.

Step 6: Closing and Gratitude

Conclude the ritual by expressing gratitude to the gods, goddesses, and the land itself for their participation and blessings.
Thank the earth for its generosity and promise to honor and care for it in return.
Take a moment to reflect on the power of fertility and the interconnectedness of all life.
Note: This ritual is inspired by ancient Mesopotamian practices and adapted for modern use. It aims to connect with the fertility energies of the land in Eridu, symbolizing the cycle of life, growth, and abundance.

Prayer to Tiamat - Prayer to the primordial goddess Tiamat for protection

Mighty Tiamat, Primordial Mother,
Goddess of Chaos and Creation,
I stand before you with reverence and awe.
In your ancient wisdom, I seek your protection.

Tiamat, Lady of the Deep Waters,
Guardian of the Primordial Forces,
I call upon your immense power and strength.
Surround me with your divine presence.

As chaos swirls around me, Tiamat,
I seek your shield of protection.
Wrap me in your primordial embrace,
Shield me from all harm and malevolent forces.

With your serpentine form, Tiamat,
Unleash your fury upon my enemies.
Let your scales be my armor,
Your roars strike fear into their hearts.

Oh Tiamat, Ancient Mother,
In your vast wisdom, grant me discernment.
Guide me through the treacherous waters of life,
Protect me from those who seek to do me harm.

I embrace your chaotic essence, Tiamat,
For in chaos lies great power and transformation.
May your boundless energy flow through me,
Granting me the strength to overcome all obstacles.

Tiamat, Divine Creatrix,
I offer my gratitude and devotion.
May your protective presence be with me always,
As I navigate the ever-changing tides of existence.

Hail Tiamat, Primordial Goddess of Protection,
I humbly bow before your majesty and might.

In your name, I seek shelter and guidance,
As I walk this mortal realm, forever blessed by your presence.

Note: This prayer is a heartfelt invocation to Tiamat, the primordial goddess of chaos and creation in Mesopotamian mythology. Seek Tiamat's protection and guidance with sincerity and respect, acknowledging her as a powerful and ancient deity.

Eannatum Ritual - Ritual for the sanctification of a kingdom

Step 1: Preparation
Gather the necessary ceremonial items, including a sacred incense, a ceremonial robe, and offerings of food and drink. Cleanse yourself and the ritual space to create a sacred atmosphere.

Step 2: Invocation
Stand at the entrance of the kingdom and face the four cardinal directions. Raise your hands to the sky and call upon the deities of the heavens, the earth, and the underworld. Invoke their blessings and presence to witness and sanctify the upcoming ritual.

Step 3: Offering
Approach the central shrine of the kingdom and place the offerings of food and drink. Express gratitude to the deities for their continuous support and guidance. Pray for the prosperity, stability, and well-being of the kingdom and its people.

Step 4: Incantation
Recite sacred incantations, calling upon the divine forces that protect and govern the kingdom. Invoke the names of the patron deities and the ancestors who have guarded and guided the land throughout history. Seek their blessings and ask for their continued favor and protection.

From the heavens to the earth, let the divine power descend,
Sanctify this land, its rulers, and its people, without end.
By the gods' decree, let prosperity and harmony unfold,
In this kingdom, may blessings and abundance be forever told.

O mighty deities, guardians of the land and sky,
Pour your blessings upon us, as your divine presence draws nigh.
With sacred words and ancient rites, we purify this realm,
A sanctuary of prosperity and peace, where goodness overwhelms.

By the power of the gods, this kingdom is bestowed,
With strength, wisdom, and fortune, its rulers endowed.
Let justice and righteousness prevail in every decree,
May this land flourish, united and prosperous, for eternity.

As we gather here, with reverence and solemnity,
We invoke the gods, embracing their divine authority.
Grant us their guidance, their favor, and their grace,
As we dedicate this kingdom, a sacred and hallowed place.

Step 5: Anointing
Take the sacred incense and pass it over the altar, allowing its fragrant smoke to purify and sanctify the space. With reverence, anoint yourself and other participants with a few drops of sacred oil, symbolizing the divine blessings and protection bestowed upon the kingdom.

Step 6: Benediction
Raise your hands in prayer and offer a heartfelt benediction for the kingdom. Express gratitude for the land, its resources, and the unity of its people. Pray for prosperity, peace, and harmony to prevail within the kingdom's borders.

Step 7: Closing
Offer a final prayer of gratitude to the deities for their presence and blessings. Lower your hands, bow in reverence, and thank the divine forces for their participation in the ritual. Express your commitment to upholding the sanctity and well-being of the kingdom.

Note: The Eannatum Ritual is a symbolic representation of the sanctification and consecration of a kingdom. The specific steps and incantations may vary depending on the traditions and beliefs associated with the kingdom. It is important to approach the ritual with sincerity, respect, and a deep connection to the divine forces invoked.

Prayer to Ningal - Prayer to the goddess Ningal for protection during childbirth

Goddess Ningal, radiant and wise,
I call upon you with humble cries.
In this sacred hour of childbirth's embrace,
Wrap your gentle arms around this sacred space.

Goddess of the moon, with nurturing care,
Guide and protect, let no harm come near.
As life emerges, like the moon's gentle glow,
Watch over us, keep us safe, as we ebb and flow.

Ningal, mother goddess of tender grace,
In your presence, fears find their rightful place.
With each contraction, strength and courage we seek,
May your presence empower, soothing and meek.

Guide the hands of the midwife, skilled and kind,
Grant her wisdom, blessings, and a steadfast mind.
May she be an instrument of your divine light,
A channel of comfort, easing pain with all her might.

Oh, Ningal, hear our plea, our fervent prayer,
Wrap the mother and child in your loving care.
Shield them from harm, bestow your gentle touch,
As new life emerges, we honor you so much.

In this sacred moment, we surrender and trust,
Knowing that your divine love will guide and adjust.
Ningal, goddess of protection and grace,
Bless this birth with your tender embrace.

Anu Offering - Offering to the god Anu for divine favor

Step 1: Preparation
Gather the necessary items for the offering, including a clean and sacred space, a small altar or table, a bowl or dish for the offering, and any symbols or representations of the god Anu.

Step 2: Purification
Before approaching the altar, purify yourself by washing your hands and face, and center your mind and heart in a state of reverence and respect.

Step 3: Invocation
Stand before the altar and light a candle or incense to signify the presence of the divine. Close your eyes and take a moment to connect with the energy of Anu, the god of the heavens and divine favor. Speak the following invocation or create your own heartfelt words:

"Mighty Anu, ruler of the heavens above,
I come before you with reverence and love.
You who hold the power of divine favor,
I offer this humble tribute to savor.
May your blessings shower upon my path,
Guiding me with wisdom, shielding me from wrath."

Step 4: Offering
Place the offering, which can be a small portion of food, drink, or symbolic items such as grains or flowers, into the bowl or dish on the altar. As you do so, visualize the offering as a gesture of gratitude and devotion to Anu.

Step 5: Prayer of Offering
With your hands extended over the offering, recite a prayer expressing your intentions and gratitude. You may use the following prayer or create your own:

"Mighty Anu, I offer this gift to thee,
In humble gratitude, I bend my knee.
May your divine favor shine upon my days,
Guiding me through life's intricate maze.
Accept this offering, a token of my devotion,
And bless me with your grace and protection."

Step 6: Meditation and Connection
Sit or stand before the altar and enter a meditative state. Close your eyes and focus your awareness on the presence of Anu. Feel the divine energy surrounding you, enveloping you in a comforting embrace. Spend a few moments in silent communion, expressing your hopes, dreams, and desires to Anu.

Step 7: Closing
Conclude the ritual by expressing your thanks and reverence to Anu. You may use the following words or modify them to suit your own style:

"Great Anu, I thank you for your divine presence,
For your favor and blessings, I feel your essence.
May your guidance and protection be my eternal guide,
As I walk this earthly path with you by my side.
In gratitude and reverence, I bid you farewell,
Knowing your divine favor in my life shall dwell."

Step 8: Extinguishing the Candle or Incense
Gently extinguish the candle or incense, symbolizing the end of the ritual and the departure of the divine presence. Take a moment to reflect on the experience and carry the blessings of Anu with you as you continue your journey.

Prayer to Enlil and Ninurta - Prayer to the gods Enlil and Ninurta for victory in battle

Mighty Enlil, god of the storm and lord of the winds,
And valiant Ninurta, warrior of great might,
I come before you with a fervent plea,
To seek your favor and blessings in the heat of battle's fight.

Enlil, you are the commander of the divine army,
Your voice thunders through the heavens, striking fear,
Grant me strength and courage to face my adversaries,
Guide my hand and protect me as I draw near.

Ninurta, with your mighty bow and fierce spear,
You are the protector of the land, the guardian of the people,
Bestow upon me your prowess and valor,
Lead me to victory, with each step resolute and steeple.

Grant me, O Enlil and Ninurta, your divine aid,
In the face of danger and amidst the chaos of war,
Bless my weapons, my armor, and my heart,
Let victory be mine, by your mighty power and lore.

In the name of Enlil, the lord of the heavens,
And Ninurta, the champion of the battlefield,
I offer this prayer, my plea for strength and triumph,
May your blessings upon me be forever sealed.

Hear my prayer, O Enlil and Ninurta,
In this moment of need and perilous strife,
Grant me victory, honor, and glory,
As I march forward, upheld by your divine life.

In your names, I pray, O Enlil and Ninurta,
May your divine presence be ever near,
Grant me triumph and success in battle,
And fill my heart with courage and fearlessness, clear.

I offer my devotion and loyalty to you,
Enlil and Ninurta, gods of war and might,

Divine Dynamics

Guide me on the path of victory and glory,
And protect me as I fight the noble fight.

Enlil and Ninurta, hear my plea,
Grant me victory and courage, I beseech thee.

Eshnunna Divination Ritual - Divination ritual practiced in the city of Eshnunna

The Eshnunna Divination Ritual, practiced in the ancient city of Eshnunna, is a sacred method of seeking divine guidance and insight into the future. It is performed with reverence and deep respect for the gods. Here are the steps involved in the ritual:

Preparation:

Create a sacred space, purified and free from disturbances.
Gather the necessary divination tools, such as clay models, cuneiform tablets, or other symbolic items associated with the ritual.
Light incense or candles to create an atmosphere of spiritual connection.
Invoke the presence of the gods, expressing your intention and seeking their guidance.

Invocation of the Gods:

Begin by offering prayers and invocations to the gods, specifically those associated with divination and oracles, such as Shamash, Nisaba, or Ishtar.
Call upon their divine wisdom and insight to guide the divination process.

Ritual Purity:

Purify yourself and the divination tools using water or sacred substances, symbolizing the cleansing of any impurities and ensuring a clear connection with the divine.
Casting of Lots or Interpretation of Signs:

Depending on the specific divination method used in Eshnunna, either cast lots or interpret signs and symbols to gain insight into the question or situation at hand.
The lots may be small clay objects or marked stones, each representing a specific meaning or outcome.
The signs and symbols may be observed in natural phenomena, such as the flight of birds, the position of stars, or the patterns formed by smoke.

Divine Dynamics

Interpretation and Communication:

Engage in a deep state of concentration and focus, allowing the divine messages and insights to flow through you.

Carefully interpret the meaning of the lots or signs, considering their context and any associated omens or traditional interpretations.

Communicate the divinatory message, whether through oral recitation, writing, or other means, conveying the guidance received from the gods.

Reflection and Action:

Reflect upon the divinatory message and its implications for the situation or question.

Consider any necessary actions or decisions that need to be taken based on the guidance received.

Show gratitude to the gods for their guidance and assistance.

Remember, the Eshnunna Divination Ritual should be performed with sincerity, humility, and a genuine desire to seek divine wisdom.

Prayer to Nanna and Inanna - Prayer to the gods Nanna and Inanna for fertility and love

Oh Nanna, radiant moon god,
Your gentle glow illuminates the night sky,
Your celestial presence brings calm and peace.
Bless us with your divine light,
Fill our lives with fertility and abundance,
May your soothing influence guide us on our path.

Inanna, mighty goddess of love and desire,
Your beauty captivates all who behold you,
Your passion ignites the flames of love.
We beseech you, grant us your favor,
Bestow upon us the gift of love and passion,
May our hearts be filled with joy and devotion.

Together, Nanna and Inanna, we call upon you,
Unite your powers, weave your blessings,
Illuminate our lives with the sacred union of fertility and love.
Grant us the fertility of the land, the bountiful harvest,
And bless our relationships with love that knows no bounds.

Nanna and Inanna, we offer our gratitude and praise,
May your divine influence grace our lives,
May fertility and love flow abundantly within and around us.
We honor you with our hearts and souls,
And forever cherish the blessings you bestow.

In the name of Nanna and Inanna, we pray,
Amen.

Prayer to Nabu and Marduk - Prayer to the gods Nabu and Marduk for wisdom and protection

Mighty Nabu, god of wisdom and writing,
You hold the knowledge of the ages,
Your words shape the destiny of mortals.
We seek your guidance and enlightenment,
Bless us with the gift of wisdom and understanding,
Illuminate our minds with your divine light.

Oh Marduk, glorious god of protection and justice,
You wield the power of the heavens,
Your might shields us from all harm.
We turn to you in times of need,
Wrap us in your protective embrace,
Defend us against the forces of darkness.

Nabu and Marduk, patrons of knowledge and strength,
We offer our prayers and devotion to you,
Bestow upon us your divine favor and blessings.
Grant us the wisdom to make wise choices,
And the strength to overcome any obstacles,
May your watchful eyes guide and guard us.

In your wisdom, Nabu, we find clarity,
In your protection, Marduk, we find solace,
Together, you offer us wisdom and safety.
May your divine presence be with us always,
Grant us the courage to face challenges,
And the knowledge to navigate the complexities of life.

In the name of Nabu and Marduk, we pray,
Amen.

Enki's Wisdom Incantation - Invocation of the god Enki for divine wisdom

Oh Enki, wise and compassionate god,
Fountain of knowledge and understanding,
I call upon you, the bringer of wisdom,
To grant me your divine insight and guidance.

From the depths of your sacred abode,
Where the waters of wisdom flow,
I seek your divine presence and favor,
To illuminate my path and fill my mind.

Enki, lord of all crafts and arts,
You hold the key to the mysteries of the universe,
With your divine wisdom, unlock the gates of knowledge,
And bestow upon me your profound understanding.

In your infinite wisdom, Enki, I place my trust,
Open my mind to new insights and perspectives,
Grant me clarity and discernment in my thoughts,
So that I may make wise choices and decisions.

Oh Enki, grant me the ability to discern truth,
To see beyond the surface and grasp deeper meanings,
May your wisdom flow through me like a river,
Empowering me with the knowledge I seek.

I invoke your name, Enki, with reverence and gratitude,
Thankful for the wisdom you bestow upon those who seek,
Guide me on the path of enlightenment and growth,
And let your divine wisdom be my eternal companion.

In the name of Enki, the god of wisdom, I pray,
Amen.

Prayer to Ishtar - Prayer to the goddess Ishtar for love and beauty

Prayer to Ishtar - Goddess of Love and Beauty

Oh Ishtar, radiant and enchanting goddess,
Whose beauty and grace captivate all hearts,
I come before you with reverence and love,
Seeking your divine presence from above.

Ishtar, goddess of love and desire,
You hold the power to ignite passion's fire,
With your divine essence, fill my heart and soul,
Grant me the gift of love, pure and whole.

In your divine presence, Ishtar, I find solace,
Your love's embrace brings joy and grace,
Shower me with your blessings of affection,
And guide me to experience love's perfection.

Goddess of beauty, Ishtar, I implore,
Illuminate my being, inside and out, forevermore,
Grant me the radiance that comes from within,
So that my beauty may shine and never dim.

Ishtar, I pray to you with utmost devotion,
Wrap me in your love's gentle ocean,
Bless my relationships with tenderness and care,
And let love's magic permeate the air.

May your divine influence fill every day,
With love's enchantment in every way,
I honor you, Ishtar, goddess divine,
In your loving embrace, eternally, I shall shine.

In the name of Ishtar, the goddess of love, I pray,
Amen.

Prayer to Shamash and Ishtar - Prayer to the gods Shamash and Ishtar for justice and protection

Mighty Shamash, radiant sun god,
You are the dispenser of justice and truth,
Your watchful eye sees all deeds under the sun.
We call upon your divine presence,
Illuminate our path with your righteous guidance,
May your justice prevail in every aspect of our lives.

Oh Ishtar, powerful goddess of love and war,
Your strength and beauty are unmatched,
You protect those who seek your aid.
We invoke your mighty name,
Wrap us in your protective embrace,
Shield us from harm and bring us victory.

Shamash and Ishtar, celestial guardians,
We turn to you with humble hearts and sincere prayers,
Grant us your divine protection and justice.
In times of darkness, be our guiding light,
In moments of injustice, be our voice of truth,
May your powerful presence bring balance and harmony.

Together, Shamash and Ishtar, we honor you,
We acknowledge your might and grace,
Grant us the strength to face challenges with courage,
And the wisdom to uphold justice in our actions.
Bless us with your divine favor and protection,
And may your influence be felt in our lives.

In the name of Shamash and Ishtar, we pray,
Amen.

Prayer to Nergal and Ereshkigal for the Dead - Prayer to the gods Nergal and Ereshkigal for the souls of the deceased

Oh Nergal, mighty god of the underworld,
And Ereshkigal, queen of the realm of the dead,
I humbly come before you with reverence and awe,
Seeking your divine guidance for the souls we shed.

In the depths of your domain, you hold great power,
As the guardians of the realm beyond this mortal coil,
I beseech you, Nergal and Ereshkigal,
To watch over the departed with compassion and toil.

Guide them through the darkness of the underworld's embrace,
Protect their spirits from harm and anguish they may face,
Grant them solace and peace in their eternal abode,
And let their journey be smooth along the righteous road.

Nergal, fierce warrior and ruler of the netherworld,
With your strength and might, protect them unfurled,
Ereshkigal, queen of the dead, in your wisdom and grace,
Provide them solace and comfort in this eternal space.

May their souls find rest in the land of the departed,
Surrounded by the love and care that you imparted,
Grant them peace and liberation from earthly strife,
As they embark on the journey to eternal life.

Nergal and Ereshkigal, hear my humble plea,
Embrace the souls of the departed and set them free,
In your divine presence, let them find serenity,
As they rest in the realm of eternity.

In the name of Nergal and Ereshkigal, I pray,
May the souls of the deceased find eternal peace each day,
Guide them, protect them, and shower them with grace,
As they dwell in the realm beyond, in a sacred space.
Amen

Lament for Uruk - Lamentation for the city of Uruk

Oh Uruk, once mighty and grand,
Your walls now crumble, your glory disband.
Once bustling streets filled with vibrant life,
Now echo with emptiness, sorrow, and strife.

Your temples, once adorned with sacred grace,
Lie in ruins, a somber and desolate place.
The echoes of prayers and chants now fade,
As sorrowful winds sweep through the arcade.

Gone are the days of prosperity and might,
When Uruk shone as a beacon of light.
No longer do your people dance and sing,
For their hearts are heavy with loss and longing.

Oh Uruk, city of heroes and tales,
Your fall brings forth lamentations and wails.
Your kings and queens, now but memories in time,
Leave behind a legacy of splendor and prime.

We weep for your streets, once bustling with life,
For the craftsmen and poets who brought you to life.
Your gardens, once lush with green and bloom,
Now lie in ruins, consumed by gloom.

But even in your desolation and decay,
The spirit of Uruk shall never fade away.
Your name, immortalized in history's scroll,
Shall forever be cherished in our heart and soul.

Oh Uruk, though your glory may have waned,
Your legacy and spirit can never be restrained.
We lament for you, dear city of old,
And in our memories, your stories unfold.

May your name be whispered in reverence and awe,
As we recall the grandeur of Uruk once more.

Divine Dynamics

Lament for Uruk, a tribute we pay,
To the city that shall never fade away.

Oh Uruk, city of beauty and might,
May your spirit forever shine bright,
In the annals of history, your name shall remain,
A testament to the greatness you once attained.

Lament for Uruk, we sing with heavy hearts,
For the city that was, and shall never depart.
May your memory live on, through song and verse,
Uruk, dear Uruk, may you find eternal solace.

Lament for Uruk, our voices raised high,
To honor your glory and bid you goodbye.
Though you may be gone, your spirit lives on,
In the hearts of those who loved you, long gone.

Farewell, dear Uruk, your lament we will sing,
And forever cherish the memory you bring.
May your soul find peace in the realm beyond,
As we bid you farewell with an eternal bond.

Farewell, dear Uruk, your lament we will sing,
And forever cherish the memory you bring.
May your soul find peace in the realm beyond,
As we bid you farewell with an eternal bond.

Prayer to Enlil and Ninhursag - Prayer to the gods Enlil and Ninhursag for fertility and protection

Oh Enlil, mighty god of the heavens high,
Master of the winds that sweep across the sky.
With reverence, I bow before your divine might,
Seeking your blessings and guidance day and night.

Ninhursag, gracious goddess of the fertile earth,
Nurturer of life, bestower of abundant birth.
I humbly beseech you, hear my fervent plea,
Grant us your blessings, that we may thrive and be free.

Enlil, with your strength and wisdom so grand,
Guide us on the path with your mighty hand.
Protect our lands, our homes, and our kin,
Shield us from harm, let no evil seep in.

Ninhursag, embodiment of nature's grace,
Bless our fields, our crops, and our sacred space.
Grant us bountiful harvests, abundance untold,
Fill our lives with prosperity, as your blessings unfold.

Together, Enlil and Ninhursag, we pray,
For fertility, protection, and blessings each day.
May your union bring forth a fruitful land,
Where life flourishes, guided by your loving hand.

Enlil, lord of the storm and the thunderous roar,
Protect us from calamity, forevermore.
May your watchful eye guard us from all harm,
As we seek your shelter, safe and warm.

Ninhursag, mother of all, with nurturing embrace,
Wrap us in your love, shower us with grace.
In your embrace, may we find strength and peace,
As your gentle touch brings our worries to cease.

Divine Dynamics

Oh Enlil and Ninhursag, gods of fertility and might,
We offer our prayers with hearts pure and bright.
Guide us, protect us, in your divine care,
May our lives be blessed, beyond compare.

As we honor your sacred union, we believe,
That your blessings upon us, we shall receive.
Enlil and Ninhursag, hear our prayer this day,
Grant us fertility, protection, and blessings, we pray.

In your divine presence, we find solace and peace,
As we surrender to your will, may our troubles cease.
Enlil and Ninhursag, we offer our devotion,
With gratitude and reverence, in heartfelt emotion.

Oh Enlil and Ninhursag, gods of boundless love,
We thank you for your blessings from above.
May our lives be filled with abundance and grace,
Forever protected in your divine embrace.

Enlil and Ninhursag, hear our prayer,
In your sacred names, we solemnly declare.
Grant us fertility, protection, and prosperity,
Oh mighty gods, blessed be, blessed be.

Incantation of Gugalanna - Invocation of the Bull of Heaven, Gugalanna

Gugalanna, Bull of Heaven, fierce and strong,
With thunderous hooves and a bellowing song.
I invoke your power, I call out your name,
Come forth, mighty Gugalanna, to this earthly plane.

From the heavens above, you descend with might,
With divine authority, you bring forth light.
Your presence commands respect and awe,
As the Bull of Heaven, your power we draw.

Gugalanna, guardian of the celestial realm,
With your strength, chaos and darkness you overwhelm.
Your horns, like crescent moons, pierce the sky,
Symbol of your might, elevated high.

By your side, Ishtar, the queen, stands tall,
Together, your wrath upon the wicked will fall.
I beseech you, Gugalanna, lend me your power,
To overcome obstacles and triumph in every hour.

Oh, Bull of Heaven, your fury is feared,
But your divine protection, by the righteous, is revered.
I seek your aid, in times of strife and strife,
To vanquish evil, to restore balance and life.

Gugalanna, let your roar shake the ground,
As I utter your name, let your strength resound.
Guide me through battles, fierce and wild,
Protect me, O Bull of Heaven, like a shield.

I invoke your ancient might, O Gugalanna,
As I call upon your name, I feel your aura.
Grant me courage and unwavering resolve,
To face life's challenges, with you, I evolve.

Bull of Heaven, your power is supreme,
With your presence, darkness is but a dream.

Divine Dynamics

I honor you, Gugalanna, with reverence and praise,
In your divine presence, my spirit finds solace and raise.

By the celestial order, by the heavens above,
I invoke your essence, O Gugalanna, with love.
May your strength guide me on this earthly plane,
As I invoke the Bull of Heaven, again and again.

Gugalanna, Bull of Heaven, I offer my plea,
Grant me your protection, let your essence be free.
As I speak your name, may your energy ignite,
And lead me to victory, under your celestial light.

In your divine presence, I find strength and might,
Gugalanna, Bull of Heaven, shine forth your light.
I am grateful for your presence, for your power divine,
I honor you, Gugalanna, for you are truly sublime.

As I conclude this incantation, I offer my praise,
To Gugalanna, the Bull of Heaven, I forever raise.
Guide me, protect me, with your celestial grace,
In your name, Gugalanna, I find my rightful place.

Prayer to Ninurta and Nergal - Prayer to the gods Ninurta and Nergal for victory and protection

Mighty Ninurta, warrior of valor and might,
With your divine strength, vanquish the enemies in sight.
I kneel before you, with reverence and awe,
Grant me your guidance, protect me with your awe.

Nergal, fearsome god of the underworld and strife,
With your fierce determination, bring victory to my life.
I invoke your name, I seek your divine embrace,
Shield me from harm, and grant me strength in every chase.

Ninurta, with your celestial bow and thunderous roar,
Lead me to triumph, on the battlefield, I implore.
In your hands, the power of storms and thunder,
Grant me courage, as I face challenges and plunder.

Nergal, ruler of the realm of the dead,
Shield me from evil, with your fiery dread.
Lend me your might, in times of trial and despair,
Protect me from danger, with your vigilant stare.

Ninurta, valiant god of the cosmic order,
Guide my steps, as I face trials with fervor.
Grant me victory in battles, both near and far,
Bless me with your wisdom and your guiding star.

Nergal, fierce guardian of the underworld's gate,
Watch over me, as I navigate life's uncertain fate.
Keep evil at bay, with your infernal might,
Protect me day and night, from darkness and blight.

Together, Ninurta and Nergal, I beseech your aid,
In this mortal realm, where challenges invade.
Grant me strength and courage, to overcome all strife,
And emerge victorious, in this tumultuous life.

Divine Dynamics

I offer my prayers, my devotion to your names,
Ninurta and Nergal, with reverence, my spirit claims.
Guide me, protect me, in times of need and despair,
With your divine presence, I know you'll be there.

I honor your might, your wisdom, and your power,
Ninurta and Nergal, in you, I find solace every hour.
Grant me victory, protect me from harm and woe,
With your divine favor, I shall surely grow.

As I conclude this prayer, I offer my gratitude,
To Ninurta and Nergal, for their unwavering fortitude.
May their blessings surround me, both day and night,
And lead me towards victory, in their eternal light.

Eridu Blessing Ritual - Ritual for blessing a house or dwelling in Eridu

Step 1: Preparation
Gather the necessary items for the ritual: a small bowl of pure water, a handful of sacred herbs (such as myrrh or frankincense), and a lit candle. Enter the house or dwelling that is to be blessed and ensure it is clean and ready for the ritual.

Step 2: Purification
Begin by purifying the space. Walk through each room, carrying the bowl of water, and sprinkle a few drops in each corner while reciting a purifying incantation, such as:
"With this sacred water, I cleanse this space,
Removing any impurity, leaving only grace.
May the energies be pure and bright,
Blessed by the divine, filled with light."

Step 3: Invocation of the Gods
Stand in the central area of the house or dwelling and light the candle. Close your eyes and visualize the presence of the gods. Invoke the deities of Eridu, such as Enki and Ninhursag, and call upon their blessings. Offer a few words of praise and gratitude, expressing your desire for their divine presence and protection within the space.

Step 4: Blessing Chant
Recite a blessing chant, either in your own words or using a traditional hymn, while moving through each room. Let the chant resonate in your voice, filling the space with positive vibrations. You can use the following as an example:
"May Eridu's ancient power, within these walls reside,
Bless this house, its inhabitants, with joy and love inside.
May every corner, every room, be filled with divine grace,
Protecting all who dwell within, in every time and space."

Step 5: Offering and Gratitude
After completing the blessing chant, offer a small token of gratitude to the gods. It can be a handful of the sacred herbs or a small offering of food or drink. Place it on a designated altar or in a central location within the house, expressing your thanks for the divine blessings received.

Step 6: Closing

Conclude the ritual by expressing your gratitude once again to the gods and closing the connection with a final prayer. Thank Enki, Ninhursag, and any other deities invoked for their presence and blessings. Extinguish the candle and leave the space with a sense of reverence and serenity.

Prayer to Enki and Inanna - Prayer to the gods Enki and Inanna for divine guidance and favor

Oh Enki, wise and compassionate god,
You who hold the knowledge of the universe,
I come before you seeking your guidance and favor.
In this moment of uncertainty, I ask for your wisdom to light my path,
That I may make choices aligned with divine will and for the highest good.

Glorious Inanna, radiant goddess of love and power,
You who embody strength and grace,
I humbly invoke your presence and seek your favor.
Grant me your guidance and protection,
That I may navigate life's challenges with confidence and love.

Enki, with your deep understanding of the mysteries of existence,
Help me uncover hidden truths and find solutions to my questions.
Inanna, with your fierce determination and boundless love,
Empower me to express my true self and embrace my passions.

Together, Enki and Inanna, I seek your divine intervention,
Bless my endeavors and shower me with your grace.
Guide my thoughts, words, and actions,
So that they may be in harmony with your divine plan.

Enki, Inanna, I offer my gratitude for your presence in my life,
For the gifts of wisdom, love, and protection you bestow upon me.
May I be a vessel of your divine light and an instrument of your will.

In the name of Enki and Inanna, I pray,
With love and reverence in my heart.

Prayer to Enki and Nanna - Prayer to the gods Enki and Nanna for wisdom and divine guidance

Oh Enki, wise and mighty god,
Grant me your boundless wisdom and understanding.
Guide my steps and illuminate my path,
That I may walk in alignment with divine knowledge.

Nanna, radiant moon god of wisdom,
Pour forth your celestial light upon my mind.
Illuminate my thoughts and grant me clarity,
That I may discern truth from falsehood.

Enki, source of all knowledge and creativity,
Bestow upon me your profound wisdom.
Inspire my words and actions with your divine insight,
That I may bring forth blessings and harmony.

Together, Enki and Nanna, hear my prayer,
Grant me the gift of wisdom and divine guidance.
In your presence, may I find enlightenment and purpose,
And may my life be a reflection of your divine wisdom.

I offer my gratitude and reverence to you,
Enki and Nanna, gods of wisdom and illumination.
May your blessings flow through me,
And may I walk the path of wisdom and divine truth.

Eridu Offering Ritual - Ritual offering to the gods for blessings in the city of Eridu

Step 1: Purification
Prepare yourself for the ritual by cleansing your body and mind. Bathe or wash your hands and face with pure water, allowing the impurities to be washed away. Clear your mind of distractions and enter a state of reverence and focus.

Step 2: Altar Preparation
Create a sacred space for the ritual by setting up an altar or designated area. Place a clean cloth or sacred cloth on the altar as a symbol of purity. Arrange offerings and sacred objects on the altar, such as fruits, flowers, incense, and candles.

Step 3: Invocation
Stand before the altar and invoke the presence of the gods of Eridu. Offer a heartfelt invocation, expressing your reverence and inviting their presence. Call upon the gods by their names, such as Enki, Nammu, or Inanna, and express your intentions for the ritual.

Step 4: Offerings
Present your offerings to the gods on the altar. Offer fruits, grains, or other food items as symbols of abundance and sustenance. Light incense to create a fragrant atmosphere and symbolize the rising of prayers to the divine. Light candles to represent the illumination of blessings in the city of Eridu.

Step 5: Prayer of Blessing
Offer a prayer of blessing, expressing your gratitude and asking for divine blessings upon the city of Eridu. Pray for the well-being of its inhabitants, the prosperity of its land, and the harmony of its community. Ask the gods to shower their blessings upon Eridu and its people.

Divine gods of Eridu, hear my prayer,
As I stand before you in humble reverence and care.
Bless this sacred city with your divine grace,
Fill its streets with abundance, love, and embrace.

Enki, the wise and mighty lord,
Pour forth your wisdom, blessings, and reward.
Guide the people of Eridu with your deep insight,

Divine Dynamics

Illuminate their paths and lead them to the light.

Nammu, ancient mother goddess so grand,
Protect this city with your nurturing hand.
Guard its waters, fertile fields, and shores,
Let prosperity flow like rivers forevermore.

Inanna, radiant queen of heaven and earth,
Bestow upon Eridu your love and rebirth.
Infuse its people with passion and desire,
Ignite their hearts with a burning inner fire.

Let harmony dwell within each home and street,
May conflicts and strife find swift defeat.
Bless the crops, the gardens, and the land,
Grant Eridu abundance, fruits in every hand.

Oh, gods of Eridu, with gratitude we pray,
For your blessings upon this city every day.
May its people thrive in joy and unity,
Under your watchful eyes, in eternal serenity.

Accept this offering, our humble tribute,
As we seek your favor and divine attribute.
Blessings upon Eridu, its people, and its soil,
May your presence and grace forever coil.

In the name of the gods of Eridu, we say,
So be it, let it be, this prayer we convey.
May the blessings flow and never subside,
In Eridu's embrace, may goodness reside.

Hear our prayer, O gods of Eridu divine,
And bless this city, till the end of time.

Step 6: Communion
Take a moment to connect with the divine presence and feel their energy and blessings. Open your heart and mind to receive any messages or guidance that may be offered to you. Feel the divine presence surrounding you and infusing the space with their blessings.

Step 7: Closing

Conclude the ritual with words of gratitude and reverence. Thank the gods for their presence and blessings. Express your commitment to honor them and their sacred city, Eridu, in your thoughts, words, and actions. Close the ritual by extinguishing the candles and offering a final expression of gratitude.

May the gods of Eridu accept your offerings and bestow their blessings upon the city and its people.

Prayer to Ninlil - Prayer to the goddess Ninlil for protection and fertility

Oh Ninlil, mighty goddess of protection and fertility,
I bow before your divine presence and seek your blessings.
You who bring forth abundance and ensure the growth of life,
I humbly invoke your name and offer my heartfelt prayers.

Ninlil, radiant and compassionate goddess,
Wrap your loving arms around me and shield me from harm.
Guard my path from evil forces and guide me towards goodness.
May your divine protection surround me like a strong fortress.

Goddess of fertility, Ninlil, I beseech you for your favor,
Bless my womb with fertility and grant me the gift of life.
In your infinite wisdom, help me bring forth healthy and happy children,
That they may thrive under your loving gaze and grow in strength.

Ninlil, mother of all, hear my plea,
Fill my life with abundance, prosperity, and joy.
As I walk the path of life, be my guiding light,
Lead me towards success, fulfillment, and spiritual growth.

I offer my gratitude for your divine presence, Ninlil,
For your unwavering protection and boundless blessings.
May I be worthy of your favor and live in accordance with your teachings.

In the name of Ninlil, I pray,
With reverence and gratitude in my heart.

Incantation of Nuska - Invocation of the god Nuska for protection and prosperity

Nuska, guardian and provider of divine blessings,
I invoke your presence, your power, your essence.
With humble words and utmost respect,
I seek your protection and prosperity to collect.

From the heavens above, you descend,
A radiant deity, a loyal friend.
With unwavering loyalty, you guard and guide,
Shielding us from harm, walking by our side.

Oh Nuska, mighty god of wealth and gain,
Bestow upon us your bountiful reign.
Protect our homes, our businesses, and lands,
Fill our lives with abundance, held in your hands.

By the power of your divine might,
Banish darkness and bring forth the light.
Strengthen our endeavors, our every stride,
With your wisdom and blessings, be our guide.

Grant us prosperity, in every endeavor,
May our fortunes flourish and never sever.
Open the doors of success wide and free,
Let your blessings flow abundantly.

Oh Nuska, guardian of fortune and might,
In your presence, we find solace and delight.
Wrap us in your protective embrace,
And shower us with abundance, grace by grace.

I offer my reverence, my heart's plea,
For your blessings to shower upon me.
With gratitude and devotion, I implore,
Nuska, hear my prayer, forevermore.

In your name, I chant this invocation,
With faith and trust in your divine manifestation.

Divine Dynamics

Protect us, bless us, and light our way,
Nuska, hear our plea, today and every day.

Amen.

Prayer to Dumuzid and Inanna - Prayer to the gods Dumuzid and Inanna for love and fertility

Dumuzid, radiant shepherd of the flock,
Inanna, radiant goddess, bearer of luck,
I beseech your divine presence here,
To grant me love and fertility, sincere.

Dumuzid, embodiment of youthful desire,
Inanna, embodiment of passionate fire,
Join your powers, intertwine your grace,
Bless my life with love's warm embrace.

Inanna, queen of heaven and earth,
Dumuzid, the one of noble birth,
Unite your energies, merge as one,
Infuse my heart, let love be spun.

Grant me a love that's deep and true,
A partnership blessed, steadfast and new.
May our hearts beat in perfect harmony,
Bound together in eternal unity.

Dumuzid, bring forth fertility's gift,
Inanna, bestow upon me love's uplift.
Fill my life with joy and bliss,
With the tender touch of your divine kiss.

In the sacred union of body and soul,
May love's sacred flame forever console.
Bless our union with fertility's delight,
Grant us the gift of children, shining bright.

Oh Dumuzid and Inanna, I implore,
Pour your blessings upon me, I adore.
Guide my steps on love's sacred path,
And let me experience love's sweet aftermath.

Divine Dynamics

In your names, I offer this prayer,
With love and devotion, I solemnly swear.
Dumuzid and Inanna, hear my plea,
Bring love and fertility, blessed be.

Amen.

Gula's Healing Ritual - Ritual for invoking the healing powers of the goddess Gula

To invoke the healing powers of the goddess Gula,
Follow this ritual, both sacred and profound.
Prepare a sacred space, pure and serene,
Where the presence of Gula can be keen.

Light a sacred flame, a beacon of divine light,
Inviting Gula's essence to shine so bright.
Let the gentle glow illuminate the room,
As we call upon Gula, dispelling gloom.

Create an altar adorned with symbols of healing,
A vessel of offerings, love, and deep feeling.
Place herbs and flowers known for their cure,
With reverence and intention, pure and sure.

Anoint yourself with oils, fragrant and pure,
As you prepare to invoke Gula's allure.
Dab them on your temples, your heart, and your hands,
Feeling her healing touch, like golden sands.

Close your eyes and enter a meditative state,
Inwardly, connect with Gula, the healer great.
Feel her presence surrounding you, warm and serene,
Embracing you with her love, vibrant and keen.

Recite these words, heartfelt and sincere,
Calling upon Gula, the goddess so dear:
"Oh, Gula, compassionate healer divine,
With your gentle touch, let healing enshrine.
Release your power, your wisdom and grace,
Heal our bodies, minds, and spirits' embrace."

Visualize Gula's energy flowing through,
Infusing your being with health and renewal.
See her healing light, vibrant and bright,
Restoring balance, dispelling all blight.

Divine Dynamics

Extend your hands, palms open and wide,
Feeling the energy of Gula, a healing tide.
Let it flow through your fingertips and palms,
Healing those in need, like sacred psalms.

Take a moment to express your gratitude,
For Gula's presence and blessings imbued.
Thank her for her healing touch and care,
For being with you in this sacred prayer.

As you conclude the ritual, slowly open your eyes,
Feeling Gula's healing power, a wondrous surprise.
Carry her essence with you throughout your day,
Embracing her healing energy in every way.

In Gula's name, this ritual is done,
May her healing power shine like the sun.
Blessed be the goddess Gula, divine and true,
Thank you for your healing, in all that we do.

Amen.

Prayer to Ninhursag and Enlil - Prayer to the gods Ninhursag and Enlil for abundance and protection

Oh Ninhursag and Enlil, mighty gods of abundance and protection,
We come before you with hearts full of devotion.
Grant us your blessings, shower us with your grace,
As we seek abundance and safety in this sacred space.

Ninhursag, mother of all, nurturing and wise,
With your fertile lands, let prosperity arise.
Bless us with bountiful harvests, crops that grow,
And abundance that flows like rivers that gently flow.

Enlil, protector and guardian of the realms,
Shield us from harm, as the storm overwhelms.
Wrap us in your loving embrace, strong and true,
Keep us safe and secure, in all that we do.

Together, we call upon your divine might,
To bring us abundance, both day and night.
Protect us from adversity, shield us from strife,
And guide us on the path to a prosperous life.

Ninhursag, Enlil, hear our heartfelt plea,
Grant us your blessings, so mote it be.
With gratitude in our hearts, we offer our praise,
To you, divine gods, in this sacred space.

May our fields be fruitful, our homes secure,
With your presence, our lives will endure.
We thank you for your guidance and protection,
And seek your blessings, in every direction.

Oh Ninhursag and Enlil, hear our prayer,
With your divine presence, we're forever aware.
Abundance and protection, we humbly request,
And in your blessings, we are truly blessed.
Amen

Incantation of Ninkasi - Invocation of the goddess Ninkasi for brewing beer

Ninkasi, goddess of brewing, hear our call,
With barley and water, we stand tall.
By your divine grace, we seek your aid,
In the sacred art of beer that we have made.

From the golden fields, the grain we take,
With care and reverence, the foundation we make.
We grind and crush, the kernels so fine,
Preparing the mash, a precious sign.

Into the vessels, the water we pour,
Mixing with grain, a symphony to adore.
Sacred alchemy, the transformation begins,
Ninkasi, guide us, as the fermentation spins.

Your divine touch, we implore you to share,
Infuse our brew with your magic, so rare.
With every bubble, with every yeast's dance,
We honor you, Ninkasi, in this brewing trance.

From the vessel, the aroma rises high,
A symphony of flavors, pleasing to the sky.
In every sip, we taste your grace,
Ninkasi, goddess, bless this sacred space.

As the beer is poured, a tribute to your name,
We raise our glasses, in honor and acclaim.
To Ninkasi, the brewer's muse so fair,
We offer our gratitude and heartfelt prayer.

Oh Ninkasi, goddess of beer divine,
In our hearts and cups, your blessings we find.
Guide us in the craft, with your wisdom and flair,
As we celebrate the gift of beer we share.

Ninkasi, we honor you in this rite,
In every sip, your presence shines bright.

Bless our brew, with your touch so divine,
May it bring joy and merriment, glass after glass, every time.

So, with gratitude and reverence, we say,
Ninkasi, goddess, on this blessed day,
Accept our offering, our humble brew,
And in return, we honor and praise you.

Hail Ninkasi, goddess of beer,
In your presence, our hearts cheer.
Bless this brew, we raise our voice,
With your guidance, our craft we rejoice.

Amen.

Prayer to Adad - Prayer to the storm god Adad for rain and fertility

Adad, mighty storm god, we beseech thee,
Bearer of thunder and bringer of rain so free.
From the heavens, unleash thy bountiful showers,
Quench the parched earth, revive its powers.

With roaring thunder and lightning's bright gleam,
Bring forth the life-giving waters in a glorious stream.
Let the droplets fall upon the fields and the land,
Nourishing the soil, creating abundance so grand.

O Adad, master of the tempest's might,
We pray to thee, bring rain in the darkest night.
Fill the rivers, the lakes, and the fertile ground,
Let growth and prosperity be forever found.

In your divine presence, we find solace and peace,
Grant us fertility, blessings that never cease.
May crops flourish, livestock thrive with glee,
Under your watchful eye, a fruitful destiny.

Adad, we honor thee, ruler of the storm,
With reverence, our prayers take form.
Pour down thy rain, O gracious deity,
Bless us with abundance, rain-soaked and free.

As the droplets fall, let life blossom anew,
Bringing forth prosperity, a world vibrant and true.
We offer our gratitude, Adad, for thy sacred gift,
Rain and fertility, in our hearts, forever lift.

Hail Adad, bringer of rain and fruitful grace,
In your name, our voices rise and embrace.
With reverence, we seek thy benevolent reign,
O storm god, bless us with thy life-giving rain.

Amen.

Ereshkigal's Descent Ritual - Ritual reenactment of Ereshkigal's descent to the underworld

The reenactment of Ereshkigal's descent to the underworld is a sacred ritual,
A journey through the realms of darkness, where the goddess holds her rule.
With reverence and awe, we recreate her descent, paying homage to her might,
Unveiling the mysteries of the underworld, where darkness and death unite.

Step 1: Preparation
Gather in a sacred space, adorned with symbols of the underworld's domain,
Create an altar, with offerings of incense, candles, and sacred grains.
Enter with a heart open and pure, ready to embrace the underworld's embrace,
Let the veil between the realms thin, as we embark on this sacred chase.

Gather in a sacred space:

Choose a quiet and secluded area where you can perform the ritual undisturbed.
Decorate the space with symbols and imagery that represent the underworld's domain. This can include images or statues of Ereshkigal, symbols of death and rebirth, or representations of the underworld creatures.
Create an ambiance that evokes the atmosphere of the underworld, using dim lighting, dark colors, and soothing, mysterious music.
Create an altar:

Set up an altar as the focal point of your ritual space.
Place a cloth or fabric in dark colors such as black or deep purple on the altar to symbolize the realm of the underworld.
Arrange items on the altar that are associated with Ereshkigal, such as her symbols or representations.
Include offerings of incense, candles, and sacred grains as a sign of reverence and invitation to the divine presence.
Enter with a heart open and pure:

Before entering the sacred space, take a moment to center yourself and clear your mind.
Purify yourself through a ritual bath, smudging with sacred herbs, or any personal cleansing practice you prefer.

Approach the ritual space with a sense of humility, respect, and openness to the energies of the underworld.

Let go of any distractions or mundane thoughts, allowing yourself to fully immerse in the experience.

Let the veil between the realms thin:

As you step into the sacred space, visualize a thinning of the veil between the physical world and the realm of the underworld.

Invoke the presence of Ereshkigal and the energies of the underworld, inviting them to join you in the ritual.

Engage in grounding and centering practices, connecting with the earth's energies and the depths of your own being.

Embrace the anticipation and the transformative power that comes with stepping into the realm of the underworld.

By creating a sacred space adorned with symbols, setting up an altar with offerings, approaching with an open heart, and thinning the veil between realms, you create an environment conducive to connecting with Ereshkigal and the energies of the underworld. These details enhance the ritual experience and deepen your connection with the divine forces you seek to honor and invoke.

Step 2: Invocation
Invocation:

Take a moment to center yourself and establish a connection with the energy of the sacred space.

Stand before the altar or in a position where you feel grounded and connected to the earth.

Close your eyes and take a few deep breaths to calm your mind and focus your intention.

Begin the invocation by addressing Ereshkigal directly, using words that resonate with you and reflect your reverence for her.

Chant and Call upon Ereshkigal:

Start by chanting the name of Ereshkigal, repeating it with intention and clarity. You can chant softly or aloud, allowing the sound to reverberate within you and in the ritual space.

Feel the vibrations of the chant resonating in your body, creating a connection between you and the energy of Ereshkigal.

Following the chant, proceed with the invocation, expressing your respect and admiration for Ereshkigal as the mighty queen of the realms below.

State your purpose clearly and humbly, acknowledging the depths and shadows of the underworld and seeking Ereshkigal's guidance and empowerment.
Proclaim the Invocation:

Conclude the invocation with a proclamation of your intent to invoke Ereshkigal's presence and to receive her wisdom and courage as you embark on the journey by her side.
Speak the proclamation with conviction and sincerity, projecting your voice to fill the sacred space.
Visualize Ereshkigal's presence enveloping you and the ritual space, her power and energy flowing through you as you declare your intention.
Remember that the words provided here are a starting point, and you can modify and personalize them to resonate with your own beliefs and connection with Ereshkigal. The key is to approach the invocation with reverence, respect, and a sincere desire to connect with the queen of the underworld.

Step 3: Descent
Create a symbolic descent, moving towards a designated underworld space,
A representation of the depths where Ereshkigal's rule takes place.
As you descend, let go of earthly attachments and embrace the unknown,
Allow the darkness to envelop you, as the underworld's essence is shown.

Step 4: Ritual Actions
Reenact the trials and tribulations faced by Ereshkigal in the underworld's domain,
Symbolically representing her journey, her sacrifices, and her pain.
Engage in acts of purification, releasing what no longer serves your soul,
Let go of burdens and attachments, allowing transformation to take its toll.

Step 5: Communion
Connect with the spirits of the underworld, with reverence and care,
Seek wisdom from departed souls, as they guide you through this sacred affair.
Offer prayers, libations, and offerings to honor the spirits of the deceased,
Creating a bridge between realms, where the living and the dead find peace.

Step 6: Ascent
After communing with the underworld, it is time to ascend once more,
Emerging from the depths, with newfound wisdom and an enlightened core.
Express gratitude to Ereshkigal for her guidance and the lessons learned,
Carrying the essence of the underworld within, forever transformed.

Divine Dynamics

Step 7: Closing
Conclude the ritual with gratitude and reverence in your heart,
Thank Ereshkigal for her presence and the wisdom she imparts.
Extinguish the candles, clear the space, and offer final words of praise,
Honoring Ereshkigal's descent, and the sacredness of the underworld's ways.

May this ritual reenactment of Ereshkigal's descent bring enlightenment and
transformation, honoring the depths of the underworld and the mysteries it holds.

Prayer to Ishtar and Shamash - Prayer to the gods Ishtar and Shamash for justice and protection

Divine Ishtar, radiant goddess of love and passion,
And Shamash, brilliant sun god of justice and protection,
I humbly kneel before your sacred presence, seeking your divine guidance.

Ishtar, mighty queen of heaven and earth,
You who wield the power of love and desire,
I beseech you to shine your light upon us,
Illuminate our paths with your benevolent grace.
Grant us the wisdom to navigate the intricacies of justice,
And the strength to stand for what is right and true.

Shamash, radiant sun of the heavens,
You who govern the laws and uphold righteousness,
I implore you to bestow your protective mantle upon us,
Shield us from harm and injustice that may befall.
Grant us the courage to face adversity with unwavering resolve,
And the discernment to discern truth from falsehood.

Together, O Ishtar and Shamash,
Your divine partnership brings balance and harmony.
May your combined power safeguard our lives and endeavors,
May justice prevail and righteousness triumph.
We place our trust in your guidance and protection,
And offer our gratitude for your eternal watch over us.

In your names, Ishtar and Shamash, we pray,
With hearts open and humble, our voices lifted high,
May justice be served, and our lives be blessed,
Now and forevermore. Amen.

Anunnaki Offering - Offering to the Anunnaki, the ancient Mesopotamian gods

Gathered here, in reverence and devotion,
We offer our humble tribute to the Anunnaki,
The ancient gods of Mesopotamia, mighty and divine.

With hands outstretched and hearts filled with awe,
We present these offerings as tokens of our gratitude,
To honor your eternal presence and benevolence.

We offer you the finest fruits of the earth,
The sweet nectar of the vine, a libation of delight,
Symbolizing the abundance and richness you bestow.

We present before you fragrant incense,
Whose swirling smoke carries our prayers,
Ascending to the heavens, reaching your divine ears.

With each flickering flame upon the altar,
We kindle the light of devotion and reverence,
Invoking your presence and guidance in our lives.

We offer you grains, symbolizing sustenance,
The bread that nourishes our bodies and souls,
A reminder of the eternal cycle of life and abundance.

And with each heartfelt word of gratitude and praise,
We honor your names, O Anunnaki,
Acknowledging your wisdom, power, and dominion.

Accept our offerings, O mighty Anunnaki,
Let your divine blessings rain upon us,
Guiding us on the path of enlightenment and harmony.

May our devotion and offerings find favor with you,
And may your divine presence forever dwell among us.
In the name of the Anunnaki, we offer our humble gifts,
With reverence and gratitude, our spirits uplifted. Amen.

Prayer to Enki and Ninhursag - Prayer to the gods Enki and Ninhursag for fertility and abundance

O Enki, wise and benevolent god of the waters,
And Ninhursag, nurturing and fertile goddess of the earth,
We come before you with hearts filled with reverence and hope.

Enki, from the depths of your divine wisdom,
You bring forth the life-giving waters that flow,
Nourishing the earth and all living beings.
Grant us your blessings of fertility and abundance,
That our fields may yield bountiful harvests,
And our homes may be filled with prosperity and joy.

Ninhursag, mother of all living creatures,
You shape the earth and cultivate its fertility,
Bringing forth the abundance of nature's gifts.
We beseech you to bless us with your divine grace,
That our lands may be fruitful and teem with life,
And our lives may be blessed with prosperity and growth.

Together, O Enki and Ninhursag,
Your union creates the harmony of creation,
The balance between the waters and the earth.
We offer our prayers and seek your favor,
That we may be blessed with fertile lands and abundant crops,
And that our families may thrive in health and happiness.

In your divine presence, we find solace and guidance,
As we humbly request your blessings upon our lives.
O Enki and Ninhursag, hear our prayer,
And grant us the fertility and abundance we seek.
May your divine influence be forever felt,
As we honor and revere your sacred names. Amen.

Eridu Cleansing Ritual - Ritual purification of individuals and spaces in Eridu

The Eridu Cleansing Ritual is a sacred practice
To purify individuals and spaces in Eridu's embrace.
With reverence and intention, we begin this rite,
To cleanse and purify, to bring forth divine light.

Step 1: Prepare the Sacred Space
Choose a serene area, free from noise and distraction.
Cleanse the space physically and energetically,
Removing any impurities that may hinder the ritual's efficacy.
Arrange sacred items, such as incense and blessed water,
To enhance the purifying energy and create a sanctified atmosphere.

Step 2: Invoke the Divine Presence
As you stand in the sacred space, ready to commence the Eridu Cleansing Ritual, it is time to invoke the divine presence of the deities of Eridu. With reverence and devotion, address Ninhursag, the mother of all creation and fertility, and Enki, the wise and compassionate god of the waters. By invoking their presence, you seek their guidance and blessings for the cleansing ritual, ensuring that it is carried out with pure intentions and effectiveness.

Begin by taking a deep breath, allowing yourself to enter a state of centeredness and receptivity. Focus your attention on the images or symbols representing Ninhursag and Enki, placed on the altar or within your mind's eye. Connect with the essence of these deities, feeling their ancient wisdom and divine energy permeate the space.

With sincerity in your voice, address Ninhursag and Enki, speaking from your heart:

"Ninhursag, mother of all creation and fertility,
Giver of life and sustenance, I invoke your presence.
You who nurture the seeds of abundance,
Guide me in this cleansing ritual, and bless me with fertility and growth."

"Enki, wise and compassionate god of the waters,
Bearer of knowledge and divine wisdom, I call upon you.
You who hold the power to cleanse and purify,
Be with me in this sacred rite, and grant me your guidance and blessings."

Feel the words resonate within you, as you express your genuine reverence and desire for the presence and assistance of Ninhursag and Enki. Envision their divine forms standing before you, radiating their divine energy and wisdom. Open yourself to their presence, inviting their guidance and blessings to infuse the ritual and enhance its potency.

Take a moment of silence, allowing the connection to deepen and the energy to settle within the space. Feel the presence of Ninhursag and Enki surrounding you, enveloping you in their divine embrace.

With a heart filled with gratitude and trust, proceed to the next steps of the Eridu Cleansing Ritual, knowing that the divine energies of Ninhursag and Enki are with you, guiding and blessing your journey towards purification and renewal.

Step 3: Purify the Self
Stand before a basin of blessed water, symbolic of purification.
Take a moment to center yourself and quiet your mind.
Dip your hands into the water and splash it gently on your face,
Allowing the purifying essence to wash away any negativity or impurities.
Recite a personal prayer, expressing your desire for inner purification,
And ask for the divine blessings of Ninhursag and Enki to cleanse your being.

Step 4: Cleanse the Space
With a lit incense stick, move throughout the space,
Wafting the fragrant smoke in every corner and crevice.
As you do so, envision the smoke purifying the energy of the area,
Dispelling any stagnant or negative vibrations that may linger.
Recite sacred words or chants that invoke the divine presence,
Asking for the space to be cleansed and sanctified by the gods.

Step 5: Offerings and Gratitude
Conclude the ritual by offering gratitude to the deities.
Place offerings of food, flowers, or other symbolic items on the altar,
Expressing your appreciation for their presence and blessings.
Offer a heartfelt prayer of gratitude, acknowledging the divine purification,
And expressing your intention to honor the sacredness of Eridu in your life.

May this Eridu Cleansing Ritual bring forth purification and renewal,
Clearing away any obstacles and inviting divine energies to flow.
May Ninhursag and Enki bless you with their grace,
And may the sacredness of Eridu be ever present in your space. Amen.

Prayer to Nusku and Nergal - Prayer to the gods Nusku and Nergal for protection from darkness and evil

Oh, Nusku, radiant god of light,
I beseech you, hear my prayer tonight.
With your fiery torch, banish the dark,
Protect me from evils that seek to embark.

Nergal, mighty lord of the underworld,
Guardian against darkness, evil unfurled,
With your strength and power, I implore,
Shield me from harm, forevermore.

In the depths of night, when shadows loom,
I seek your protection, dispelling gloom.
Nusku, illuminate my path with your flame,
Guide me safely, in your divine name.

Nergal, keeper of justice and divine might,
Wrap me in your protective embrace, tight.
Keep me safe from malevolent spirits' sway,
As I navigate through life's uncertain way.

Together, Nusku and Nergal, I call upon you,
Grant me strength, courage, and wisdom, too.
Protect me from darkness, evil's cruel art,
Shield my soul, body, and every part.

May your divine light dispel all fears,
And banish the darkness that ever nears.
With your guidance, I walk a path so true,
Protected by your power, through and through.

Nusku and Nergal, hear my plea,
Grant me safety, for I trust in thee.
In your names, I find solace and might,
Protect me from darkness, day and night.

With reverence and gratitude, I pray,
To Nusku and Nergal, I humbly say,
Thank you for your watchful care,
For shielding me from darkness' snare.

Amen.

Incantation of Ningishzida - Invocation of the serpent god Ningishzida for healing and protection

O mighty Ningishzida, serpent deity of ancient might,
I invoke your presence on this sacred night.
With healing power and protective embrace,
I seek your aid, your divine grace.

Serpent of the underworld, guardian of life's flow,
Wrap me in your healing energy, bestow
Your wisdom and knowledge upon my being,
Cleanse and heal, my spirit freeing.

Ningishzida, serpent with the divine spark,
Banish illness and pain, light up the dark.
With your transformative essence, I implore,
Restore my body, mind, and spirit's core.

Serpent of the earth, keeper of sacred balance,
Guide me through life's challenges, enhance
My strength and resilience in times of strife,
Shield me from harm, throughout my life.

Ningishzida, serpent coiled, ready to strike,
Grant me protection, like a shield strong and tight.
Defend me from evil, both seen and unseen,
Surround me with your presence, serene.

As I chant your name, let your power surge,
Heal me, protect me, let my spirit emerge.
Through your divine intervention and care,
I find healing and protection, beyond compare.

Ningishzida, I honor your sacred name,
In your presence, I find solace and acclaim.
Thank you for your blessings, so divine,
With gratitude, I offer this prayer of mine.

May your healing touch be felt within,
And your protective energy forever kin.
Serpent god, I place my trust in thee,
Ningishzida, guide and guard me.

Amen.

Prayer to Enlil and Ishtar - Prayer to the gods Enlil and Ishtar for blessings and divine favor

Mighty Enlil, lord of the heavens high,
And Ishtar, radiant goddess of the sky,
I come before you with reverence and praise,
Seeking your blessings in myriad ways.

Enlil, wise ruler, embodiment of strength,
Guide my steps, and grant me success at length.
Bless me with your wisdom, discernment, and might,
Illuminate my path with your divine light.

Ishtar, goddess of love, beauty, and desire,
Fill my heart with passion that never tires.
Shower me with your blessings, gracious and true,
Empower me to radiate love in all I do.

Enlil, master of destinies and fates,
Bestow upon me your divine graces.
Protect me from harm, shield me from strife,
Guard my loved ones and bless our life.

Ishtar, enchantress of joy and fertility,
Infuse my days with blessings of prosperity.
Grant me abundance, in all aspects of life,
And bless my endeavors, amidst joy and strife.

Together, Enlil and Ishtar, I call upon you,
In your presence, may my dreams come true.
With your divine favor, my spirit shall soar,
Embracing blessings that forever endure.

I offer my prayers with a heart sincere,
Knowing that your presence is always near.
Thank you, Enlil and Ishtar, for your divine grace,
Blessings upon blessings, I humbly embrace.

Amen.

Utu's Justice Ritual - Ritual seeking justice and fairness through the god Utu

Step 1: Preparation
Prepare a sacred space, adorned with symbols of justice and balance.
Light candles and incense to create a serene and focused atmosphere.
Clear your mind and open your heart to the presence of Utu, the god of justice.

Step 2: Invocation
Invoke the presence of Utu with reverence and respect.
Call upon his divine guidance and wisdom.
Say:
"Utu, radiant god of justice and truth,
I call upon you with utmost reverence, in my pursuit.
Guide me with your discerning eyes,
Illuminate my path with your righteous skies."

Step 3: Declaration of Intent
Declare your intent for justice and fairness.
State your case, whether personal or on behalf of others.
Express your desire for resolution, balance, and harmony.
Say:
"Utu, I stand before you seeking justice divine,
In this matter, I seek fairness to shine.
Grant clarity to the truth, let it be revealed,
May righteousness prevail, as justice is sealed."

Step 4: Offering
Offer a symbol of gratitude and respect to Utu.
It can be a small token or an item that represents justice.
Place it on the altar as a gesture of devotion and acknowledgment.

Step 5: Prayer for Justice
Offer a heartfelt prayer to Utu, expressing your plea for justice.
Speak with sincerity and conviction, pouring your emotions into your words.
Say:
"Mighty Utu, dispenser of justice and right,
Hear my prayer, as I seek your insight.
May truth prevail, and falsehood be unveiled,
Grant justice and fairness, let it be availed."

Step 6: Meditation and Reflection
Sit in quiet meditation, allowing the energy of Utu to surround you.
Reflect upon the nature of justice and the importance of fairness.
Listen for any guidance or insights that may come during this serene moment.

Step 7: Closure
Thank Utu for his presence and guidance.
Express gratitude for his wisdom and justice.
Conclude the ritual with reverence and respect.
Say:
"Utu, god of justice, I thank you this day,
For your presence and guidance on my way.
May your wisdom and fairness forever abide,
Justice prevails, with you by our side."

Step 8: Closing the Ritual
Extinguish the candles and offer a final moment of reverence.
Leave the sacred space, knowing that your plea for justice has been heard.
Carry the energy of Utu's justice with you, as you navigate the world.

Note: This ritual is intended as a spiritual practice and symbolic representation of seeking justice. Legal matters should be addressed through appropriate legal channels.

Prayer to Nabu and Marduk - Prayer to the gods Nabu and Marduk for wisdom and protection

O Nabu, wise and learned god,
Bearer of knowledge, revealer of secrets,
I come before you with reverence and awe,
Seeking your wisdom and guidance.

Grant me the gift of intellect and understanding,
Open my mind to the depths of knowledge,
May your divine insight illuminate my path,
And lead me towards wisdom's sacred edge.

Marduk, mighty and victorious god,
Protector of the righteous, defender of the just,
I call upon your strength and power,
To shield me from harm and grant me trust.

Wrap me in the mantle of your protection,
Shield me from the perils that surround,
With your divine might and boundless love,
May I walk on solid ground.

Nabu and Marduk, hear my prayer,
Two pillars of wisdom and strength,
Guide me on the path of righteousness,
In your divine presence, I find peace at length.

Grant me the wisdom to discern right from wrong,
The courage to face challenges with a steadfast heart,
With your blessings and protection, I shall thrive,
And embrace the knowledge your grace imparts.

In your names, Nabu and Marduk, I pray,
May your wisdom and protection be my constant stay,
I offer my gratitude and devotion to you,
For in your presence, I find solace and truth.
So mote it be.

Eshnunna Love Divination - Divination ritual for matters of love and relationships in Eshnunna

In the ancient city of Eshnunna, where love and relationships thrive,
We seek the divine guidance that helps our hearts revive.
With reverence and respect, we gather in sacred space,
To perform a divination ritual, seeking love's embrace.

Step 1: Preparation
Create a tranquil and sacred environment,
Adorn the space with symbols of love's enchantment.
Light candles to invite the presence of the divine,
And let the gentle flicker illuminate love's sign.

Step 2: Invocation
Call upon the gods and goddesses of love's domain,
Invoke their presence, so that wisdom they may ordain.
Address Ishtar, the goddess of passion and desire,
And Nergal, the god of love's intense fire.

Step 3: Focus and Intention
Clear your mind and center your heart,
Focus on your intention, let it be your art.
With pure intent, seek answers from above,
To unravel the mysteries of your heart's love.

Step 4: Divination Method
Choose a divination method that resonates within,
Tarot cards, runes, or scrying, let the process begin.
Or consult an oracle, an experienced guide,
To help you uncover the secrets that reside.

Step 5: Pose Your Questions
Frame your questions with clarity and care,
In matters of love, be honest and aware.
Seek guidance on relationships and connections,
Unveil the paths that lead to love's affections.

Step 6: Interpretation
With open eyes and an open heart,
Interpret the divination's message, a divine art.
Trust your intuition, listen to love's whisper,
For in the messages received, love's guidance may shimmer.

Step 7: Gratitude and Closure
Express gratitude to the gods above,
For their guidance, their wisdom, and their love.
Close the ritual with reverence and grace,
Knowing that love's blessings are in place.

May the divination bring clarity and insight,
Guiding your heart towards love's pure light.
In Eshnunna's embrace, may your love flourish and grow,
As the gods of love watch over, may their blessings bestow.

So mote it be.

Prayer to Nanna and Utu - Prayer to the gods Nanna and Utu for guidance and illumination

Oh Nanna, radiant moon god shining in the night,
And Utu, glorious sun god spreading your golden light,
I come before you with a humble heart and open soul,
Seeking your wisdom and guidance to make me whole.

Nanna, with your gentle glow that illuminates the dark,
Guide me through life's challenges, leaving no trace or mark.
Like the moon's phases, may my path wax and wane,
In harmony with your cycles, may I find balance again.

Utu, the radiant sun, source of warmth and clarity,
Illuminate my path, dispelling shadows with your charity.
Through your radiant rays, grant me insight and vision,
That I may make decisions with wisdom and precision.

Oh divine Nanna and Utu, I call upon your sacred names,
Fill my heart with guidance, as I seek to play life's games.
In times of uncertainty, be my guiding light,
And in moments of darkness, banish all blight.

Nanna, lend me your tranquil wisdom from above,
And Utu, bestow upon me your radiant love.
With your divine presence, I find solace and peace,
Grant me clarity and enlightenment, may they never cease.

In this sacred union of moon and sun's celestial dance,
I offer my reverence, my trust, and my humble stance.
Guide me on my journey, in day and in night,
With your blessings and illumination, make my path bright.

Nanna and Utu, I offer my heartfelt prayer,
May your divine guidance always be near.
In your celestial embrace, I find solace and might,
Thank you, oh gods, for your guidance and light.

So mote it be.

Prayer to Enki and Ishtar - Prayer to the gods Enki and Ishtar for fertility and love

Oh Enki, wise and compassionate god of the waters,
And Ishtar, radiant goddess of love and desire,
I come before you with reverence and devotion,
Seeking your blessings for fertility and love's fire.

Enki, from the depths of your sacred domain,
Pour forth your blessings, let life spring forth like rain.
Grant fertility to the earth and to all living beings,
May abundance flourish and new life it brings.

Ishtar, goddess of love, beauty, and passion,
Bless my heart with your divine compassion.
Ignite the flame of love within my soul,
Let it burn bright, making me whole.

Enki, as the water nourishes the seed,
Foster fertility and growth in every need.
Bless my body, mind, and spirit with your grace,
Infuse me with vitality and a fertile embrace.

Ishtar, goddess of desire and enchanting allure,
Guide me in matters of love, pure and secure.
Bring me a love that is true and divine,
A partner whose heart will eternally align.

Oh Enki and Ishtar, I offer my prayers,
Pour your blessings upon me, alleviating life's cares.
Grant me fertility in all aspects of my being,
And love that is boundless, forever freeing.

With gratitude and devotion, I honor your might,
Thank you, gods, for hearing my prayer tonight.
May your divine presence forever be near,
Blessed by Enki and Ishtar, let love and fertility appear.

So mote it be.

Eridu Harvest Ritual - Ritual for a bountiful harvest in the city of Eridu

Step 1: Preparation

Choose a Sacred Space: Select a location that feels sacred and aligned with the energy of fertility and abundance. It can be a garden, a field, or a designated area indoors. Cleanse the space by removing any clutter and creating a welcoming atmosphere.

Symbols of Fertility and Abundance: Decorate the sacred space with symbols that represent fertility and abundance. Use sheaves of wheat, cornucopias, colorful fruits and vegetables, and images of lush landscapes. Incorporate natural elements like stones, shells, or crystals to enhance the connection with the Earth's energy.

Create an Altar: Set up an altar as the focal point of the ritual. Choose a sturdy table or platform and cover it with a beautiful cloth in colors that symbolize harvest and abundance, such as gold, green, or earth tones. Arrange the altar with reverence and intention.

Adorn the Altar: Decorate the altar with harvest fruits, grains, and seasonal flowers. Display baskets of ripe apples, grapes, pomegranates, pumpkins, or any other fruits and vegetables that are abundant during the harvest season. Place bundles of wheat or cornstalks as symbols of fertility and growth. Arrange fresh flowers, such as sunflowers or marigolds, to symbolize the beauty and vibrancy of the harvest.

Offerings of Food and Drink: Prepare offerings of food and drink that represent the bountiful harvest. Choose locally sourced and seasonal items whenever possible. Place a loaf of freshly baked bread, bowls of grains, honey, or jars of preserved fruits on the altar. Pour small cups of wine, cider, or water into sacred vessels. These offerings symbolize gratitude for the abundance of the land and will be presented later in the ritual.

Clearing the Mind and Setting Intentions: Take a few moments to clear your mind and center your intentions on a bountiful harvest. Close your eyes, take deep breaths, and release any distractions or worries. Visualize the land flourishing with abundant crops and envision the joy and satisfaction of a successful harvest. Set your intention to honor and connect with the energy of the Earth and the blessings of the harvest.

Divine Dynamics

Step 2: Invocation of Ninhursag
Call upon Ninhursag, the goddess of fertility and mother of all creation.
Address her with reverence and respect, acknowledging her power and grace.
Speak these words from the depths of your heart:
"Oh Ninhursag, mother of all life,
We invoke your presence in this sacred rite.
Bless our land with fertility and growth,
Grant us a bountiful harvest, overflowing and lush."

Step 3: Invocation of Enki
Invoke Enki, the god of wisdom and the bringer of blessings.
Address him with humility and gratitude, acknowledging his role as provider.
Speak these words with sincerity:
"Enki, generous and wise,
We seek your blessings, hear our cries.
Bestow upon us your abundance and grace,
May our harvest be plentiful, filling every space."

Step 4: Offerings and Gratitude
Place the offerings of food and drink upon the altar, symbolizing gratitude.
Express your thanks to Ninhursag and Enki for their divine blessings.
Speak words of gratitude and appreciation, such as:
"We offer these gifts with gratitude and love,
Thank you, Ninhursag and Enki, above.
For the fertile land and abundant yield,
We give thanks for the harvest, our fields."

Step 5: Harvest Dance and Song
Engage in a joyful harvest dance, celebrating the abundance of the land.
Sing songs of gratitude and praise for the fruitful harvest bestowed upon you.
Let the rhythm of your dance and the melody of your song resonate with the earth's energy, expressing your gratitude for the blessings received.

Step 6: Closing and Blessing
Offer a final prayer of gratitude and blessings for a bountiful harvest.
Speak these words with conviction:
"May our fields be abundant, our crops grow strong,
With Ninhursag and Enki's blessings, all year long.
From seed to harvest, may our efforts bear fruit,
In gratitude and joy, we close this sacred pursuit."

Conclude the ritual with a moment of silence and reflection, allowing the energy of the harvest ritual to permeate the surroundings. Offer thanks once more, and with a heart filled with gratitude, depart from the sacred space, carrying the intention of a bountiful harvest in your heart.

Prayer to Ninurta and Ninhursag - Prayer to the gods Ninurta and Ninhursag for protection and fertility

Divine Ninurta and Ninhursag,
Mighty guardians of the land and its people,
We come before you with humble hearts and reverence.
In your divine presence, we seek your protection and blessings,
For you are the keepers of strength and fertility.

Ninurta, courageous warrior and defender,
Wrap your mighty arms around us, shielding us from harm.
Grant us the courage and resilience to face any challenge,
And bless us with your unwavering protection.

Ninhursag, nurturing mother of all creation,
Bless our land with fertility and abundance.
Let the seeds we sow grow strong and fruitful,
And may our harvests be plentiful and sustaining.

Together, Ninurta and Ninhursag, your union brings balance,
The union of protection and fertility, strength and sustenance.
We offer our gratitude for your watchful eyes and nurturing hands,
For guiding us through life's trials and blessing us with prosperity.

In times of uncertainty, we turn to you for guidance,
To find strength and courage in the face of adversity.
Grant us your divine favor, that we may thrive and flourish,
In body, mind, and spirit, under your loving care.

Divine Ninurta and Ninhursag, we offer this prayer,
With hearts filled with gratitude and devotion.
May your presence be felt in our lives,
And may your protection and fertility grace us always.

Amen.

Incantation of Namtar - Invocation of the god Namtar for protection from disease and death

Namtar, mighty god of fate and plague,
We call upon your power in this solemn hour.
As the guardian against disease and death,
Protect us from harm with your divine breath.

With every word and every chant,
We invoke your name, Namtar, in this sacred rant.
Keep illness and suffering at bay,
Shield us from the grip of decay.

With your divine touch, heal the afflicted,
Banish the darkness that sickness has inflicted.
Grant us strength and vitality anew,
As we offer our prayers to you.

Namtar, we seek your merciful gaze,
To guide us through these uncertain days.
Protect our bodies, minds, and souls,
And keep us safe from all that takes its toll.

In your presence, we find solace and peace,
From the ravages of sickness, please release.
With your grace, we rise above our fears,
And live our lives free from despair and tears.

Namtar, we honor your ancient might,
In this incantation, we call upon your light.
Protect us, O god, with your steadfast care,
And keep us from the clutches of despair.

Amen.

Prayer to Shamash and Nergal - Prayer to the gods Shamash and Nergal for protection and justice

Oh, Shamash, radiant sun of justice and truth,
And Nergal, fierce warrior of righteous wrath,
We humbly offer our prayers to both of you,
Seeking your protection and guidance on our path.

Shamash, with your golden rays so bright,
Illuminate our way with your divine light.
Dispelling darkness, bringing justice forth,
Guide us in the pursuit of fairness and worth.

Nergal, mighty guardian of the oppressed,
With your strength, let injustice be suppressed.
Protect us from harm, shield us from deceit,
And grant us the courage to stand on our feet.

Together, Shamash and Nergal, we implore,
Your blessings and favor we earnestly explore.
In this tumultuous world, uphold what is right,
And let justice prevail, shining ever so bright.

May your watchful eyes be upon us each day,
As we strive for justice in every possible way.
Grant us the wisdom to discern what is just,
And the strength to stand against any unjust.

Shamash and Nergal, we offer our praise,
For your protection and guidance in all our days.
In your divine presence, we find solace and might,
And walk the path of justice, bathed in your light.

Amen.

Prayer to Inanna and Nanna - Prayer to the gods Inanna and Nanna for fertility and divine guidance

Inanna, radiant goddess of love and passion,
Nanna, wise and gentle god of the moon above,
We humbly bow before your sacred presence,
Seeking your blessings, fertility, and divine love.

Inanna, with your enchanting beauty and grace,
You bring forth life's abundance and embrace.
Bless our lives with fertility and fruitful yield,
And let love blossom in every field.

Nanna, with your calming and soothing light,
Guide us through the darkness of the night.
Illuminate our paths with your gentle glow,
And grant us wisdom wherever we may go.

Together, Inanna and Nanna, we implore,
Shower us with blessings forevermore.
Grant us the gift of fertility and creation,
And guide us on the path of divine revelation.

Inanna, we seek your passionate embrace,
To fill our lives with love and grace.
Nanna, we seek your wisdom and insight,
To navigate life's journey with all our might.

May your divine presence be with us always,
Guiding our steps through life's intricate ways.
Bless us with fertility and love's sweet embrace,
And fill our hearts with divine wisdom and grace.

Inanna and Nanna, hear our heartfelt plea,
As we offer this prayer with reverence and glee.
Grant us fertility and divine guidance true,
We place our trust and devotion in both of you.
Amen.

Enuma Elish Ritual - Ritual enactment of the Enuma Elish creation myth

The Enuma Elish, the epic tale of creation,
Shall be enacted in this sacred formation.
Gather in reverence, seekers of divine knowledge,
As we immerse ourselves in this ancient pledge.

Step 1: Preparation
To embark on the sacred journey of the Enuma Elish,
Prepare a space that evokes the essence of cosmic bliss.
Create a sacred sanctuary, a realm of divine connection,
Where gods and mortals meet in sacred introspection.

Find a quiet and dedicated space for the ritual,
Where you can immerse yourself in the cosmic lyrical.
Clear the area of any clutter or distractions,
Creating a sacred space for profound interactions.

Adorn the sacred space with cosmic symbols and signs,
Representing the realms where the gods intertwine.
Hang celestial tapestries and artwork on the walls,
Depicting the cosmic dance and celestial halls.

Place a table or altar at the center of the space,
A sacred focal point, where divine energy will embrace.
Cover the altar with a celestial-colored cloth,
Symbolizing the vastness of the cosmic truth.

Arrange the elements of creation upon the altar,
Representing the birth of worlds and their eternal matter.
Place a bowl of water, symbolizing the primordial sea,
From which life emerged, a sacred decree.

Place a burning incense or candles on the altar,
Their flickering flames invoking divine power.
The fragrant smoke rising, connecting earth to sky,
Creating a sacred ambiance, as the ritual draws nigh.

Scatter celestial objects like crystals or gemstones,

Symbols of the cosmos, each with its unique tones.
Let their energies enhance the sacred space,
Aligning with the gods' presence, embracing grace.

Decorate the space with celestial colors and hues,
Deep blues and purples, shimmering like cosmic clues.
Let the walls and surroundings reflect the vast expanse,
Immersing in the cosmic realm, the gods' grand dance.

As you prepare the sacred space with devotion and care,
Feel the cosmic energy, the divine presence in the air.
Let the symbols and adornments awaken your soul,
Opening the gateway to the gods, making you whole.

In this preparation, the stage is set,
A sacred space where the cosmic forces connect.
May the realm of gods and celestial hymns tremble,
As you prepare for the profound journey of the Enuma Elish ensemble.

Step 2: Invocation
Invoke the presence of the gods with reverence and awe,
Call upon Marduk, the supreme deity, to whom we bow.
Chant the names of the divine beings with devotion,
Summon their energies, their essence, their cosmic motion.

Step 3: Enactment
With symbols and props, recreate the cosmic drama,
The battles, the struggles, the birth of the world's panorama.
Through gestures and movements, embody the divine roles,
As we retell the story that connects our mortal souls.

Step 4: Celebration
Celebrate the triumph of Marduk, the victor of the gods,
With joyous chants, dances, and rhythmic applauds.
Express gratitude for the gift of creation's existence,
Embracing the divine spark within with deep reverence.

Step 5: Reflection and Contemplation
Reflect upon the profound wisdom of the Enuma Elish,
Contemplate the mysteries, the cosmic patterns we cherish.
Seek insights and revelations in this sacred tale,
As we delve into the depths of its meaning without fail.

Divine Dynamics

Step 6: Closing
Offer gratitude to the gods for their presence and guidance,
Bid farewell to their energies with utmost reverence and prudence.
Close the ritual space, knowing that creation's story lives within,
Carrying its profound wisdom as a sacred treasure, akin.

May the Enuma Elish, in its ritual enactment,
Awaken the divine essence within us, a sacred contract.
As we honor the gods and the cosmic dance of creation,
May we find wisdom, connection, and eternal elation.

In the name of Marduk and the celestial realm above,
We honor the Enuma Elish with reverence and love.
Amen.

Prayer to Enlil and Ninurta - Prayer to the gods Enlil and Ninurta for victory and protection

Great Enlil, mighty lord of the heavens,
You who hold the power to shape destinies,
We come before you with reverence and awe,
Seeking your guidance and divine protection.

Ninurta, valiant warrior and protector,
Whose strength and prowess knows no bounds,
We implore you to stand by our side,
Grant us victory and shield us from harm.

Enlil, master of the winds and the storms,
Commander of the celestial forces,
In your wisdom, you discern the path to triumph,
We beseech you to favor us with your blessings.

Ninurta, with your mighty weapons and valor,
Strike down our enemies, scatter their ranks,
Protect us from danger, both seen and unseen,
As we march forward in the pursuit of justice.

Enlil, who holds the key to victory's gate,
Guide our steps, illuminate our way,
Grant us the strength to overcome all obstacles,
And emerge triumphant in the battles we face.

Ninurta, with your unwavering courage and might,
Be our shield, our defender in the darkest hour,
Inspire us with your bravery and unwavering spirit,
As we strive to uphold justice and protect the right.

Enlil and Ninurta, we humbly offer our prayers,
May your divine presence guide us with care,
Grant us victory on the battlefield of life,
And keep us under your benevolent watchful eyes.

Divine Dynamics

In your names, Enlil and Ninurta, we pray,
For victory, protection, and strength every day.
Bestow upon us your blessings and favor,
As we invoke your presence now and forever.

Eridu Marriage Ritual - Ritual for the blessing of marriages in Eridu

Step 1: Preparation

Prepare the sacred space with utmost care,
Adorn it with symbols of love in the air.
Bring forth the colors of passion and devotion,
Setting the stage for a sacred union's emotion.

Create an altar, a centerpiece divine,
Decked with flowers and candles that brightly shine.
Incorporate symbols of fertility and growth,
To bless the couple's journey and strengthen their oath.

Step 2: Invocation of the Divine

Call upon the gods and goddesses of love,
Inanna, radiant and gentle as a dove.
Enki, wise and caring, with boundless grace,
Seek their presence, their blessings to embrace.

Speak their names with reverence and devotion,
Invite them to witness this sacred motion.
Ask Inanna to shower her love from above,
And Enki to bless this union with abundance and love.

Step 3: Exchange of Vows

Let the couple stand face to face, hand in hand,
As they speak their vows, a pledge so grand.
With words crafted from the depths of their hearts,
They promise to walk together, never to part.

Their voices intertwined in love's sweet melody,
Sharing promises of trust, loyalty, and harmony.
May their vows carry the weight of eternity's embrace,
Sealing their bond with love's unbreakable grace.

Divine Dynamics

Step 4: Blessing and Benediction

Let a chosen voice offer a heartfelt prayer,
Invoking the gods' blessings, their love to bear.
May Inanna bless their union with passion's fire,
And Enki grant them abundance, their desires.

May their love flourish like the fields in bloom,
Nurtured by the gods, dispelling any gloom.
May their journey be guided by love's gentle touch,
And may their hearts forever be filled with love so much.

Step 5: Exchange of Rings

In the presence of the gods, the rings are presented,
Circular symbols of love, never to be resented.
Let the couple exchange them, a gesture profound,
As their love story begins, a destiny unbound.

May the rings be a constant reminder each day,
Of the promises made, come what may.
A circle unbroken, representing eternal love,
Sealed in this ritual, witnessed from above.

Step 6: Offering and Celebration

Make offerings of gratitude, sincere and deep,
For the blessings received, forever to keep.
Express thanks to the gods for their divine presence,
And celebrate this union with joyful essence.

Let music fill the air, uplifting and bright,
As loved ones gather to share in the delight.
Dance in celebration of love's sweet embrace,
And rejoice in the union blessed by divine grace.

Step 7: Closing and Wishes

As the ritual comes to an end, hearts aglow,
Offer final prayers, emotions in a gentle flow.
May the gods of love and union forever shine,
Guiding this couple on a path so divine.

May their love be a beacon in the darkest night,
Radiating warmth, filling each day with light.
May their journey be blessed with joy and affection,
United in love, a divine connection.

In this sacred ritual, Eridu's embrace,
A marriage blessed, a bond they shall embrace.
May the gods of love and union forever be near,
Guiding this couple's path, year after year.

With the gods' blessings bestowed from above,
This marriage in Eridu is sealed with love.
May their love story be cherished and adored,
In this sacred union, forevermore.

Prayer to Ishtar and Dumuzid - Prayer to the gods Ishtar and Dumuzid for love and passion

Ishtar and Dumuzid, gods of love and passion,
I beseech you with reverence and utmost admiration.
In your divine presence, I humbly stand,
Seeking your blessings, reaching out my hand.

Ishtar, radiant goddess of beauty and desire,
With your enchanting presence, hearts set afire.
Grant me the bliss of love, deep and true,
Let passion and devotion in my life renew.

Dumuzid, gallant god of fertility and allure,
In your presence, love's essence pure.
Fill my heart with desire, burning bright,
Ignite the flames of passion, day and night.

Together, I invoke your sacred names,
With hopes that love's fire forever flames.
Bless my relationships with harmony and care,
May love's tender embrace always be there.

Ishtar, guide me in matters of the heart,
With your wisdom, let love never depart.
Dumuzid, bless me with passion and zeal,
In love's journey, may I always feel.

Grant me the strength to nurture love's flame,
To cherish and honor, without shame.
May my love be fierce and unyielding,
A bond that is enduring and ever appealing.

Ishtar and Dumuzid, hear my plea,
Embrace me with love's divine decree.
Guide my steps on the path of passion and bliss,
With your blessings, may my love never miss.

In your names, Ishtar and Dumuzid, I pray,
For love and passion to grace my way.

With gratitude, I thank you for your divine embrace,
May love's blessings surround me, in every space.

Amen.

Prayer to Ninhursag and Ninlil - Prayer to the goddesses Ninhursag and Ninlil for protection and fertility

Ninhursag and Ninlil, goddesses of protection and fertility,
I humbly bow before your sacred divinity.
With reverence and gratitude, I offer this prayer,
Seeking your blessings, your loving care.

Ninhursag, nurturing mother of all creation,
Whose fertile embrace brings forth life's manifestation,
Wrap me in your loving arms, keep me safe and secure,
Protect me from harm, of this I implore.

Ninlil, gentle goddess of the fertile land,
Whose abundant blessings are forever at hand,
Grant me the gift of fertility and fruitful bounty,
Let my endeavors bear abundant fruits, plenty.

In your presence, I find solace and strength,
As I walk through life's journey, at any length.
Shield me from troubles, both seen and unseen,
With your divine protection, may I ever glean.

Ninhursag, I call upon your nurturing embrace,
Guide me with your wisdom, shower me with grace.
In times of need, be my comforting shelter,
With your blessings, let my life only prosper.

Ninlil, I seek your bountiful fertility and grace,
Fill my life with abundance, in every space.
Bestow upon me the blessings of growth and renewal,
Let my path be adorned with love and joy, beautiful.

Together, Ninhursag and Ninlil, I pray to thee,
For protection and fertility, bestowed upon me.
May your presence be felt, both near and far,
As I walk this earthly realm, beneath your loving star.

In your names, Ninhursag and Ninlil, I call,
With reverence and devotion, standing tall.
Grant me your blessings, guide me on my way,
In your divine embrace, I forever stay.

Amen.

Incantation of Inanna - Invocation of the goddess Inanna for power and transformation

Inanna, goddess of power and transformation,
I call upon your ancient invocation.
With words of reverence and devotion,
I seek your divine presence and your potent potion.

Inanna, radiant queen of the heavens above,
With your grace and strength, I long to be imbued.
Awaken within me your fierce and fiery might,
Empower me with your transformative light.

From the depths of the underworld to the heights of the sky,
Your journey of self-discovery, I aspire to apply.
Grant me the courage to face my deepest fears,
And the wisdom to learn and grow through the coming years.

Inanna, holder of the sacred me,
Bestow upon me the power to be truly free.
Guide me through the realms of shadow and light,
Ignite within me the spark of divine insight.

By your hand, let me shed the old and embrace the new,
Transforming my limitations into strength and breakthrough.
With your divine presence, let my spirit soar,
Unleashing the power within me, forevermore.

Inanna, I surrender to your divine will,
Knowing that through your grace, I can fulfill.
Grant me the strength to overcome any strife,
And the wisdom to navigate the paths of life.

With deep gratitude and unwavering devotion,
I invoke your name, Inanna, in this sacred incantation.
Empower me, guide me, transform me within,
As I embrace the journey of growth and begin.

So mote it be, in the name of Inanna divine,
May her power and transformation forever intertwine.

With reverence and awe, I honor her name,
Inanna, goddess of power, I forever proclaim.

Amen.

Prayer to Enki and Shamash - Prayer to the gods Enki and Shamash for wisdom and justice

Enki, god of wisdom and knowledge profound,
Shamash, radiant sun god, justice's crown,
I offer this prayer with reverence and respect,
Seeking your guidance and wisdom to connect.

Enki, source of wisdom, the deep and the pure,
In your presence, my understanding shall endure.
Grant me the insight to see beyond the veil,
To navigate life's challenges, never to fail.

Shamash, dispenser of justice and light,
Illuminate my path with your wisdom and might.
Guide me in upholding what's fair and right,
Empower me to seek justice, day and night.

Enki, fountain of knowledge and creativity,
Bless me with wisdom and divine ingenuity.
May your insights flow through my mind and soul,
Inspiring wisdom and solutions to unfold.

Shamash, radiant sun, dispeller of darkness,
Bring forth justice, banishing all unfairness.
Grant me the strength to stand for what is just,
To champion truth, and in integrity to trust.

Enki and Shamash, in your presence I stand,
With open hearts and uplifted hands.
May your wisdom and justice guide my way,
Throughout each and every single day.

I offer my gratitude for your divine presence,
Enki and Shamash, the gods of immense essence.
May your blessings shower upon me from above,
Filling my life with wisdom, justice, and love.
Amen.

Ereshkigal's Lamentation - Ritual lamentation for the goddess Ereshkigal

Oh Ereshkigal, queen of the underworld's domain,
We gather here to honor your sorrow and pain.
In the depths of your realm, where shadows reside,
We lament and mourn, standing by your side.

Ereshkigal, goddess of the land of the dead,
We feel your anguish, the tears that you have shed.
Your domain is one of darkness and despair,
Yet through your lamentation, we show that we care.

Oh Ereshkigal, your anguish is profound,
In your realm, where the lost souls are found.
We join our voices in a sorrowful song,
Expressing our empathy, acknowledging your wrong.

Ereshkigal, we witness your suffering,
As you guard the gates of the underworld, unyielding.
Your tears are a testament to the pain you bear,
We offer our compassion, our love, and our prayer.

Oh Ereshkigal, in your lamentation we find,
The depths of our own sorrows intertwined.
Through your grief, we acknowledge our own strife,
And seek solace and healing in this shared life.

Ereshkigal, goddess of the underworld's might,
We offer this lamentation, embracing the night.
May your sorrow find release, and peace be obtained,
In this sacred lament, your presence is sustained.

As we join our voices in this mournful cry,
We honor you, Ereshkigal, with every sigh.
May your lamentation echo through the realms below,
And bring solace to the hearts that ache and sorrow.

In your sacred presence, we offer this lament,
To honor your sorrow, our voices are sent.

Divine Dynamics

Ereshkigal, goddess of the underworld's domain,
May your pain find solace, and healing remain.

Amen.

Prayer to Nabu and Nusku - Prayer to the gods Nabu and Nusku for knowledge and protection

Oh Nabu, god of wisdom and learning,
We come before you with hearts yearning.
Grant us knowledge, insight, and clarity,
Illuminate our minds with divine clarity.

Nusku, the vigilant and watchful flame,
Protect us from harm and every evil claim.
Surround us with your fiery embrace,
Keep us safe in your radiant grace.

Nabu, the scribe of the gods, we implore,
Guide us to paths of wisdom and lore.
Grant us the gift of knowledge profound,
That our understanding may forever abound.

Nusku, the guardian of sacred spaces,
Shield us from dangers in all its traces.
With your watchful presence, keep us secure,
Defend us from forces that seek to allure.

Nabu, source of inspiration and insight,
Bless us with knowledge that shines so bright.
Expand our minds, open the doors of wisdom,
Lead us to truths that will always be freedom.

Nusku, the protector, strong and resolute,
Guard us day and night, never be mute.
Defend us from darkness, from evil's snare,
Keep us under your watchful, caring stare.

Oh Nabu and Nusku, hear our prayer,
Grant us your blessings, show us you care.
Fill our hearts with knowledge and protection,
Guide us on paths of wisdom's perfection.

Divine Dynamics

We offer our gratitude, reverence, and praise,
To Nabu and Nusku, in sacred ways.
May your presence be felt in every hour,
Enlightening our minds with your divine power.

Amen.

Prayer to Nergal and Ninurta - Prayer to the gods Nergal and Ninurta for strength and victory

Mighty Nergal, fierce god of war,
We call upon you, our spirits soar.
Grant us strength and courage in battle's embrace,
May we stand victorious, in your powerful grace.

Ninurta, valiant god of the storm,
With your might, our foes we'll transform.
Lend us your power, your unwavering might,
Guide our weapons true, in the midst of the fight.

Nergal, the warrior, fearless and bold,
Protect us in the heat, in the cold.
Grant us resilience, in the face of strife,
Lead us to triumph, in every aspect of life.

Ninurta, master of the sacred arts,
In your wisdom, we place our hearts.
Bless us with strategy, cunning, and skill,
May we overcome all challenges, with iron will.

Nergal, lord of the underworld's domain,
Bring us victory, in triumph we shall reign.
Grant us the strength to conquer our fears,
As we march forward, through battle's fierce years.

Ninurta, god of the fertile fields,
With your blessings, abundance shall yield.
Grant us prosperity, in our every endeavor,
May our lives flourish, now and forever.

Nergal and Ninurta, we bow before you,
In your presence, our spirits renew.
Grant us your blessings, your divine might,
As we walk the path, in strength and light.

Divine Dynamics

With hearts filled with reverence, we pray,
Guide us, protect us, both night and day.
To Nergal and Ninurta, our voices raise,
In their names, we offer our hymns of praise.

Amen.

Eridu Blessing of Children Ritual - Ritual for the blessing and protection of children in Eridu

Step 1: Preparation

Gather in a sacred space, adorned with symbols of purity and innocence,
Create an altar, adorned with toys, blankets, and images representing children.
Light candles to create a warm and inviting atmosphere,
Invoke the presence of the gods, inviting their divine blessings to this sacred endeavor.

Step 2: Invocation of the Gods

Call upon the gods of Eridu, with reverence and devotion,
Address Ninhursag, the nurturing mother goddess, and Enki, the wise and compassionate father god.
Invoke their presence, seeking their guidance and blessings,
As you embark on this ritual, dedicated to the well-being and protection of children.

Step 3: Offering and Blessing

Prepare offerings of fresh fruits, sweets, and small toys,
Place them on the altar as a symbol of abundance and joy.
With a sincere heart, offer prayers of gratitude and love,
Requesting the gods' blessings to shower upon the children from below and above.

Step 4: Anointing and Protection

Take a small vial of sacred oil, infused with the essence of protection,
With gentle hands, anoint the foreheads of the children in the room.
Whisper words of love and protection, invoking the gods' divine shield,
May they be guarded against harm, their spirits forever sealed.

Step 5: Songs and Chants

Raise your voices in joyous songs and chants,
Let the melodies fill the space, vibrating with love and enchant.
Sing praises to the gods, expressing gratitude for their divine grace,

May their blessings embrace the children, in every time and place.

Step 6: Closing and Gratitude

Express heartfelt gratitude to the gods for their presence and blessings,
Thank Ninhursag and Enki for their loving protection and guidance.
Offer a final prayer, asking for the continued well-being of the children,
May they grow in health, happiness, and wisdom, in a world that is ever-brightened.

With this Eridu Blessing of Children Ritual complete,
May the gods' blessings shower upon the young and sweet.
May their lives be filled with love, joy, and protection,
Guided by the gods' wisdom and affection.

Amen.

Prayer to Ninshubur and Ishtar - Prayer to the goddesses Ninshubur and Ishtar for assistance and support

Ninshubur, loyal servant and trusted companion,
Ishtar, radiant goddess of strength and passion,
I come before you with reverence and devotion,
Seeking your assistance and support in times of need and action.

Ninshubur, your unwavering loyalty knows no bounds,
You are the faithful ally, the one who surrounds.
I call upon your wisdom and guidance, dear friend,
Stand by my side, from the beginning till the end.

Ishtar, goddess of love and fierce determination,
Your power and beauty inspire admiration.
I beseech you for your strength and divine aid,
In my endeavors, may your blessings never fade.

Ninshubur, your words and actions carry weight,
You are the voice of reason, the one who can relate.
Grant me your wisdom, your insight so keen,
Assist me in navigating the paths unseen.

Ishtar, your presence brings courage and might,
You are the embodiment of passion's light.
Support me in my endeavors, lend me your fire,
Ignite my spirit, as I aim higher and higher.

Ninshubur and Ishtar, I honor your divine grace,
I seek your assistance in every challenging space.
Guide me, protect me, and lend me your aid,
In all my endeavors, may your blessings cascade.

Together, dear goddesses, we shall prevail,
In every hardship, we shall not fail.
With your support and guidance, I shall endure,
In your divine presence, I am forever secure.

Divine Dynamics

Ninshubur and Ishtar, hear my prayer,
Grant me your assistance, show me you care.
I offer my gratitude for your unwavering support,
May your presence be felt, as I move forward.

Amen.

Prayer to Ashur and Enlil - Prayer to the gods Ashur and Enlil for protection and divine favor

Ashur, mighty god of Assyria's realm,
Enlil, great ruler of the celestial helm,
I come before you with reverence and awe,
Seeking your protection and divine favor, I implore.

Ashur, your strength and power know no bounds,
You guard the land, its people and its grounds.
Wrap us in your shield of protection and might,
Keep us safe, day and night.

Enlil, wise and just, ruler of the skies,
Your guidance and wisdom make us rise.
Bestow upon us your blessings and grace,
Illuminate our path, in every time and place.

Ashur, defender of Assyria's might,
Guard us against darkness, keep us in your sight.
Shield us from harm, and lead us through,
With your divine presence, we remain true.

Enlil, master of destinies, we pray,
Guide us through life's intricate array.
Grant us favor, as we navigate each endeavor,
With your divine guidance, we shall never falter.

Ashur and Enlil, hear our plea,
Protect us from all adversity.
In your divine embrace, we find solace and peace,
Bless us with your favor, may it never cease.

Amen.

Incantation of Ea - Invocation of the god Ea for wisdom and magical power

Ea, mighty god of wisdom and the deep,
I invoke your presence, your power I seek.
Grant me your wisdom, deep and profound,
Unveil the mysteries, let knowledge abound.

From the depths of the abyss you rise,
With magical prowess, you mesmerize.
With your command, the elements sway,
Grant me your power, I humbly pray.

Ea, master of incantations and spells,
Inscribe your knowledge in my heart's wells.
Open the doors to realms unseen,
Bestow upon me the gift to intervene.

With your guidance, I navigate the arcane,
Unleash the power that lies in my vein.
Grant me insight into secrets untold,
With your wisdom, let my powers unfold.

Ea, divine sorcerer, I call upon your name,
Inscribe your sigil, ignite the magical flame.
Infuse my being with your ancient might,
Grant me wisdom, and fill me with light.

In your presence, I stand empowered and free,
Ea, god of wisdom, I bow before thee.
Grant me the wisdom, the magical art,
To shape my destiny and play my part.

So mote it be, let the incantation soar,
Ea, god of wisdom, forevermore.
With your blessing, I embrace my fate,
In your divine presence, I elevate.

Amen.

Prayer to Shamash and Utu - Prayer to the gods Shamash and Utu for justice and enlightenment

Shamash and Utu, radiant gods of justice and enlightenment,
I come before you with reverence and sincere intent.
In your divine presence, I seek guidance and clarity,
For justice and enlightenment are the pillars of prosperity.

Shamash, radiant sun god, dispenser of truth,
Illuminate my path and dispel all falsehoods.
Grant me the wisdom to discern right from wrong,
And the courage to stand firm, resilient and strong.

Utu, shining god of justice and divine law,
Guide my actions with fairness, without flaw.
Bring forth the light of righteousness and balance,
And lead me on a path of moral guidance.

Together, Shamash and Utu, your influence reigns,
Your justice and enlightenment heal worldly pains.
Grant me the insight to see through deceit,
And the strength to uphold what is just and meet.

In the pursuit of justice, let my actions align,
With the radiance of your divine design.
Grant me clarity of thought and noble intentions,
As I strive to create a world free from oppression.

Shamash and Utu, I offer my heartfelt plea,
Fill my life with justice and enlightenment, I decree.
May your divine presence forever guide my way,
And may justice prevail in every moment, night and day.

Amen.

Prayer to Enki and Ishtar for Fertility - Prayer to the gods Enki and Ishtar for fertility and abundance

Enki and Ishtar, gods of fertility and abundance,
I come before you with a humble and sincere heart.
In your divine presence, I seek your blessings,
For fertility and abundance in every aspect of life.

Enki, wise and compassionate god of the waters,
You who hold the power to bring forth life,
I beseech you to bless the land with fertile soil,
That it may yield bountiful harvests and sustenance.

Ishtar, radiant goddess of love and beauty,
You who nurture life and inspire desire,
I implore you to shower us with your grace,
That our hearts may be filled with love and joy.

Together, Enki and Ishtar, your union brings forth life,
Your divine essence brings fertility and blessings rife.
I pray for the fertility of the earth and its creatures,
That life may flourish in all its wondrous features.

Enki, with your wisdom and nurturing embrace,
Guide the waters to flow and the seeds to embrace.
Bless the fields, the plants, and the creatures,
That they may thrive and bring forth abundant treasures.

Ishtar, with your charm and allure so grand,
Fill our hearts with love, united hand in hand.
Bless our unions, our families, and relationships,
With the gift of fertility and lasting companionships.

Enki and Ishtar, I offer my devotion and plea,
Grant us fertility and abundance, hear my decree.
May your divine blessings shower upon us all,
And may our lives be filled with fertility's thrall.
Amen.

Eridu New Year Ritual - Ritual to celebrate the New Year in Eridu

The Eridu New Year Ritual, a joyous celebration,
Marks the arrival of a new cycle, a sacred occasion.
In the ancient city of Eridu, we gather as one,
To honor the gods and welcome the year to come.

Step 1: Purification
In preparation for this auspicious event,
We cleanse ourselves, body and spirit, intent.
With water and sacred herbs, we purify,
Releasing the old, embracing the new sky.

Step 2: Invocation
With reverence and gratitude, we invoke,
The presence of the gods, a sacred yoke.
We call upon Enki, the wise and compassionate,
And Ninhursag, the nurturing and bountiful.

Step 3: Offerings
Upon the altar, adorned in vibrant array,
We place offerings of fruits and grains, we say,
To honor the gods and express our devotion,
As we seek their blessings and divine promotion.

Step 4: Ritual Dance and Music
In jubilant celebration, we dance and sing,
To the rhythm of drums and music's sweet ring.
Our bodies and voices harmonize as one,
Ushering in the New Year with joy and fun.

Step 5: Reflection and Resolutions
As the night sky fills with stars so bright,
We take a moment to reflect upon our plight.
We set intentions and make resolutions,
To grow and thrive in the coming revolutions.

Step 6: Feast and Fellowship
With tables abundant in delicious fare,

Divine Dynamics

We share a feast, a communal affair.
In fellowship and merriment, we dine,
Celebrating the blessings of the divine.

Step 7: Blessings and Prayers
Before the night concludes, we gather near,
To offer our blessings and prayers, sincere.
We seek the gods' favor and protection,
For a prosperous and harmonious connection.

Step 8: Closing Ceremony
With gratitude in our hearts, we conclude,
The Eridu New Year Ritual, a joyful interlude.
We carry the blessings of the gods within,
As we embrace the new cycle about to begin.

May the gods of Eridu bless this New Year,
With abundance, joy, and divine cheer.
As we step forward into the unknown,
May their guidance and love be forever shown.

Amen.

Prayer to Nusku and Nergal for Protection - Prayer to the gods Nusku and Nergal for protection from evil forces

O mighty Nusku, radiant flame of protection,
And fearsome Nergal, guardian against affliction,
We bow before you with reverence and devotion,
Seeking your shelter from the depths of commotion.

Nusku, bearer of the sacred fire's glow,
With your flames, repel all malevolent woe.
Wrap us in your warm and vigilant embrace,
Shield us from darkness, keep us safe in every space.

Nergal, fierce warrior, defender of the just,
In your strength, we place our unwavering trust.
Stand by our side, with your mighty sword,
Guard us against evil, protect us, O lord.

Together, Nusku and Nergal, we implore,
Grant us the strength to face challenges and more.
Banish the shadows that seek to harm and deceive,
Grant us the fortitude and resilience to believe.

May your divine presence surround us day and night,
Shield us from harm, guide us toward the light.
With your protection, we fear no evil or ill,
For in your power, we find solace and will.

Nusku and Nergal, gods of protection so strong,
Defend us from harm, may we never go wrong.
In your names, we offer this prayer, sincere,
Grant us your blessings, keep us forever near.

Amen.

Prayer to Ninhursag and Enlil for Healing - Prayer to the gods Ninhursag and Enlil for healing and well-being

O Ninhursag, mother of all life and healing,
And Enlil, mighty ruler and source of our well-being,
We come before you with humble hearts, seeking your divine intervention,
For the restoration of health and the blessings of rejuvenation.

Ninhursag, gentle nurturer of the earth,
In your embrace, all ailments find their worth.
With your healing touch, mend our bodies and minds,
Restore our strength, vitality, and ties that bind.

Enlil, wise and powerful, dispenser of life's breath,
We beseech you to relieve us from pain and distress.
Bring forth your divine energy, heal us with your might,
Renew our spirits, fill us with radiant light.

Together, Ninhursag and Enlil, we implore,
Pour your healing blessings upon us, we adore.
Guide the hands of healers, physicians, and all,
Grant them wisdom and skill, as they answer the call.

May your divine essence flow through our veins,
Rejuvenate our bodies, release us from chains.
Restore our well-being, bring balance and harmony,
With your grace, may we be whole and free.

Ninhursag and Enlil, we offer this prayer,
With gratitude and faith, we lay our burdens bare.
Bless us with healing, restore us with care,
For in your divine presence, we find solace and repair.

Amen.

Incantation of Marduk - Invocation of the god Marduk for protection and victory

Glorious Marduk, mighty warrior and protector,
With reverence and awe, we invoke your name.
In your divine presence, we seek shelter and might,
Grant us protection and lead us to victory's height.

Oh Marduk, the great slayer of chaos and evil,
Your power and strength are unmatched and primeval.
As we face the trials that lay before us,
We call upon you for your guidance and prowess.

With your divine weapon, the sacred bow and arrow,
Strike down our foes and shield us from sorrow.
Unleash your fury upon those who bring harm,
Defend us, O Marduk, with your celestial charm.

Grant us courage to face our battles with might,
And wisdom to discern between wrong and right.
Bestow upon us your victorious spirit,
As we march forward, let our enemies fear it.

Oh Marduk, ruler of gods and champion of the land,
We beseech you to extend your protective hand.
Bring forth triumph and glory to our noble cause,
In your name, we find strength, without pause.

By the power vested in you, O mighty Marduk,
We trust in your guardianship, for we are not stuck.
Victorious we shall be, under your watchful eye,
With gratitude and loyalty, to you, we testify.

Hear our plea, O Marduk, and answer our call,
Wrap us in your divine shield, strong and tall.
Guide us to triumph, in every endeavor we pursue,
For in your name, O Marduk, our victory is true.

Amen.

Prayer to Ninurta and Ninhursag for Agriculture - Prayer to the gods Ninurta and Ninhursag for a successful harvest

Mighty Ninurta, lord of the fields and master of agriculture,
We turn to you with humble hearts, seeking your benevolence.
You who wield the sacred plow and sow the seeds of abundance,
We pray for a bountiful harvest, for your blessings to enhance.

Ninhursag, nurturing mother and giver of life,
With your gentle touch, you make the crops thrive.
You bring forth the fertility of the earth, rich and pure,
We beseech you, grant us a harvest that will endure.

Oh Ninurta, we ask for your strength and protection,
Shield our crops from pests and disease, with your divine intervention.
Grant us favorable weather, with rain and sunlight in perfect measure,
So our fields may flourish, yielding crops of great treasure.

Ninhursag, we honor your role as the guardian of the land,
Bless our soil with fertility, by your loving hand.
Let the seeds we plant grow strong and tall,
May our harvest be abundant, providing for one and all.

Ninurta and Ninhursag, in your union we find harmony,
We offer our gratitude for the blessings you bestow generously.
With each season's cycle, we witness your wondrous grace,
As the fruits of our labor adorn our tables, filling every space.

As the sun rises and sets, as the earth yields its precious yield,
We offer this prayer, with devotion and sincerity, sealed.
Ninurta and Ninhursag, hear our plea this day,
Grant us a plentiful harvest, in your names we pray.

Amen.

Prayer to Nabu and Nanna for Wisdom - Prayer to the gods Nabu and Nanna for wisdom and knowledge

Oh Nabu, god of wisdom and writing,
Grant us your divine guidance, enlightening.
With your sacred words, unlock the gates of knowledge,
Fill our minds with wisdom and understanding in abundance.

Nanna, radiant moon god, source of illumination,
Shine your gentle light upon us, with your divine revelation.
Guide us on the path of wisdom and discernment,
Illuminate our thoughts and actions with your celestial ascent.

Nabu, you who hold the tablets of destiny,
Bestow upon us the gift of intellectual clarity.
Grant us the ability to learn and comprehend,
To seek knowledge and wisdom, without end.

Nanna, you who watch over the nocturnal skies,
Illuminate our minds, make our intellects rise.
In the stillness of the night, in your tranquil embrace,
May we find the answers we seek, the wisdom to embrace.

Oh Nabu and Nanna, we humbly implore,
Open the doors of knowledge, forevermore.
Fill our hearts and minds with your sacred insight,
Bless us with wisdom, that our paths be forever bright.

In your presence, we find solace and truth,
In your guidance, we discover eternal youth.
Oh Nabu and Nanna, we offer our sincere devotion,
Grant us wisdom and knowledge, our souls' eternal motion.

Amen.

Eshnunna Divination by Fire - Divination ritual using fire as a medium in Eshnunna

In the ancient city of Eshnunna, where mysteries unfold,
We gather to seek answers, the future to behold.
Through the flickering flames, a sacred fire burns bright,
We invoke the divine, with reverence and ancient rite.

Step into the sacred space, where the fire dances with glee,
Feel its warmth and energy, as we embark on this decree.
Prepare the offerings, the herbs and sacred wood,
To kindle the flames, as we enter the realm of the good.

With focused intent, let the fire take hold,
Watch the smoke rise, as the divination unfolds.
Inhale the fragrant tendrils, let them guide your mind,
As we seek the wisdom of the gods, one of a kind.

Close your eyes and clear your thoughts,
Let the fire's crackling whispers fill the sought.
Pose your question, let it form in your heart,
As the flames leap and dance, your answers will impart.

Gaze into the fiery depths, where secrets lie,
Allow the flames to speak, with their tongues that fly.
In their flickering dance, symbols may appear,
Whispered messages from the divine, crystal clear.

The crackling embers, the sparks that ignite,
Hold within them the answers, hidden from sight.
Listen to the whispers carried by the fire's breath,
As the divine presence guides you on this sacred path.

When the fire fades and the ritual nears its end,
Offer your gratitude, to the gods we commend.
Thank the fire, the divine, for their wisdom shared,
And carry their guidance, in your heart forever cared.

Eshnunna's divination by fire, a mystical art,
Revealing the secrets, written in the flames' chart.

With reverence and awe, we embrace the fire's lore,
And walk the path of divination, forevermore.

Amen.

Prayer to Nanna and Ishtar - Prayer to the gods Nanna and Ishtar for love and fertility

Nanna, radiant moon god, and Ishtar, goddess of love's embrace,
We come before your divine presence, seeking your grace.
In the twilight hour, under the moon's gentle light,
We offer this prayer, our hearts filled with love and delight.

Nanna, whose soothing beams caress the earth's embrace,
Illuminate our paths, shower us with your gentle grace.
Guide our hearts in matters of love, pure and true,
May our unions be blessed, blossoming like morning dew.

Ishtar, goddess of passion, with a flame that burns bright,
Grant us your favor, ignite our love's eternal light.
Embrace us with your ardor, let our desires be fulfilled,
May our bonds be strong, as destiny's tapestry is woven and skilled.

Nanna, hear our plea as we yearn for fertility's embrace,
Bless us with abundant blessings, the gift of life's grace.
Fill our homes with laughter, with the pitter-patter of tiny feet,
May our families flourish, in love's harmony complete.

Ishtar, hear our cry as we seek love's tender touch,
Unite our souls in a bond that no time can clutch.
Let passion and desire flourish, like a fiery flame,
May our love be enduring, never tarnished or tame.

Nanna and Ishtar, gods of love and lunar light,
We offer our devotion, our hearts shining bright.
In your divine presence, we find solace and bliss,
Grant us the blessings of love, sealed with a sacred kiss.

With gratitude and reverence, we offer this prayer,
To Nanna and Ishtar, gods of love and care.
Guide us on love's journey, in every step we take,
In your embrace, may our hearts forever awake.

Amen.

Prayer to Nergal and Ereshkigal for Justice - Prayer to the gods Nergal and Ereshkigal for justice and retribution

Nergal, fierce god of war and destruction,
Ereshkigal, mighty queen of the underworld's junction,
We beseech you now, with hearts filled with fervor,
To grant us justice, to right every wrong with valor.

Nergal, with your fiery rage and righteous might,
Bring forth justice, dispel the shadows of the night.
Strike down the wicked, those who sow discord and strife,
Let your sword of retribution cleanse the land with righteous life.

Ereshkigal, ruler of the realm beyond mortal sight,
We seek your guidance, your wisdom shining bright.
Bring forth the scales of justice, let truth be unveiled,
Mete out justice, for the righteous have prevailed.

Nergal, with your strength and relentless power,
Protect the innocent in every troubled hour.
Let justice be a shield, a fortress strong and true,
May the guilty face their deeds, their reckoning due.

Ereshkigal, with your deep knowledge of souls and fate,
Guide us on the path of justice, never to deviate.
Unmask the deceitful, reveal their hidden sin,
Let justice prevail, as the righteous hearts within.

Nergal and Ereshkigal, guardians of justice's domain,
We implore you, our plea shall not be in vain.
Bring balance to the world, restore harmony's reign,
Let justice be served, never to be in vain.

As we offer our prayers, let justice be our plea,
Grant us your blessings, in your divine decree.
Nergal and Ereshkigal, champions of what is right,
May justice prevail, dispelling darkness with your might.
Amen.

Incantation of Nuska for Prosperity - Invocation of the god Nuska for wealth and prosperity

Nuska, god of prosperity and abundance divine,
We invoke your presence with reverence and rhyme.
With words of power, we call upon your might,
To bring forth blessings, to make our futures bright.

Nuska, lord of wealth and treasures untold,
Pour your blessings upon us, may they unfold.
From the depths of the earth to the heights of the sky,
Grant us prosperity, as we humbly imply.

By your grace, let the coffers overflow,
Let riches and fortune in our lives grow.
With open hands and hearts, we receive,
Your divine favor, in blessings we believe.

Nuska, master of commerce and trade,
Guide us to success, may our ventures never fade.
Open doors of opportunity, unlock paths unseen,
Lead us towards prosperity, fulfill our every dream.

As we chant your name, the energy ignites,
Envelop us in abundance, like dazzling lights.
Bless our endeavors, our toil and our strife,
With your divine presence, may we thrive in life.

Nuska, we honor you with offerings of devotion,
Grant us your favor, with unwavering emotion.
May our lives be filled with riches and grace,
Prosperity and abundance, in every time and space.

With gratitude and faith, we call upon your name,
Nuska, god of prosperity, our desires we proclaim.
Bring us wealth and blessings, in this sacred rite,
In your benevolent power, may we take delight.
Amen.

Prayer to Enlil and Ninlil for Protection - Prayer to the gods Enlil and Ninlil for protection and guidance

Enlil and Ninlil, mighty gods of protection,
We beseech your aid in times of affliction.
With reverence and respect, we offer this prayer,
Seeking your shelter and guidance, with utmost care.

Enlil, great lord of the heavens above,
With your strength and power, shield us with love.
Wrap us in your divine mantle of defense,
Protect us from harm, both seen and unseen.

Ninlil, gracious goddess of the sacred air,
Wrap us in your nurturing embrace, fair.
Guide us through life's challenges and strife,
Shield us from danger, throughout our life.

Together, Enlil and Ninlil, we implore,
Protect us, our loved ones, forevermore.
Guard our homes, our families, and our lands,
With your divine presence, may we withstand.

Surround us with your divine shield and might,
Illuminate our path with your wisdom's light.
Keep us safe from evil, from every harm,
With your guardianship, we find solace and calm.

In times of danger, we trust in your care,
Enlil and Ninlil, hear our heartfelt prayer.
Guide us on the righteous path each day,
With your protection, we'll never go astray.

We offer our devotion and gratitude to you,
Enlil and Ninlil, gods so steadfast and true.
May your watchful eyes forever be near,
Keeping us safe, dispelling all fear.
Amen.

Prayer to Ishtar and Shamash for Love - Prayer to the gods Ishtar and Shamash for love and harmonious relationships

Ishtar and Shamash, gods of love and light,
We come before you with hearts pure and bright.
With reverence and devotion, we seek your grace,
To bless our lives with love's enchanting embrace.

Ishtar, radiant goddess of passion and desire,
Fill our hearts with love that will never tire.
Guide us in building relationships that are true,
And let our love be steadfast and forever new.

Shamash, radiant god of justice and warmth,
Illuminate our relationships, keeping them strong and calm.
Help us communicate with love and understanding,
And let harmony and compassion be ever expanding.

Together, Ishtar and Shamash, we implore,
Fill our lives with love, now and forevermore.
May your divine energy unite our hearts as one,
And let love's journey be filled with joy and fun.

Bless our relationships with your divine touch,
May they be filled with affection, caring, and such.
Grant us the wisdom to nurture love's flame,
And let our bonds endure, never to wane.

In your presence, Ishtar and Shamash, we find,
The strength to love deeply, with hearts intertwined.
Guide us in creating relationships built on trust,
And may our love shine bright, never to rust.

We offer our gratitude for your loving embrace,
Ishtar and Shamash, gods of love and grace.
With your blessings, our relationships thrive,
Filled with love, joy, and the strength to survive.
Amen.

Eridu Purification Ritual - Ritual purification for individuals and spaces in Eridu

Step 1: Preparation

Before engaging in the Eridu purification ritual, it is important to create a sacred space that is fully prepared for the process of purification. Here are some additional details to enhance this step:

Find a Quiet and Sacred Space: Choose a location where you can have privacy and tranquility, away from distractions and disturbances. It can be a room, a corner of your home, or a designated outdoor area. Ensure that the space resonates with a sense of sacredness.

Cleanse the Space: Before beginning the ritual, ensure that the space is physically clean and organized. Remove any clutter or unnecessary items to create a harmonious environment.

Symbols of Purity and Dedication: Adorn the space with symbols that represent purity and dedication. This can include sacred objects such as crystals, seashells, feathers, or any other items that hold personal significance to you. Arrange them in a meaningful way, creating a visually appealing and spiritually uplifting atmosphere.

Altar Setup: Create an altar as the focal point of the sacred space. Use a small table or any elevated surface where you can arrange your sacred objects. Decorate the altar with white flowers, symbolizing purity, and place candles around them to represent divine light. You can also incorporate other elements such as sacred stones, incense, or images of deities associated with purification.

Sacred Water: Prepare a small vessel of purified water to be placed on the altar. This water will be used during the ritual bath for purification purposes. You may choose to bless the water by saying a prayer or setting an intention for its purifying qualities.

Set the Ambiance: Create a serene ambiance by dimming the lights or lighting soft, ambient candles. You may also play gentle instrumental music or use sound instruments such as chimes or bells to create a sacred atmosphere.

Remember, the preparation phase is crucial for setting the right energy and intention for the Eridu purification ritual. Take your time to arrange the space in a way that resonates with your personal spirituality and creates an inviting environment for the purification process.

Step 2: Invocation
Invoke the presence of the deities, Ninhursag and Enki,
With reverence and respect, we call upon their key.
"Ninhursag, mother of all life, and Enki, the wise,
We seek your blessings for this sacred enterprise.
Purify our beings, cleanse our hearts and souls,
With your divine essence, make us whole."

Step 3: Ritual Bath
Prepare a basin of pure water, blessed and sanctified,
Step into the water, allowing its cleansing tide.
Visualize all impurities washing away,
Leaving you refreshed and pure, ready to convey.

Step 4: Smudging
Take a bundle of sacred herbs, such as sage or cedar,
Light it with a flame, allowing the smoke to spread.
Move the smudge stick around your body and the space,
Let the purifying smoke clear any negative trace.

Step 5: Chanting and Affirmations
Repeat sacred chants or affirmations of purity,
Words that resonate with your intentions surely.
Declare your desire for inner and outer purification,
Affirming your commitment to spiritual elevation.

Step 6: Anointing
Take a small amount of blessed oil in your hands,
Rub them together, activating the energy it commands.
Gently anoint your forehead, heart, and hands,
Symbolizing purification, as the divine plan expands.

Step 7: Closing and Gratitude
Express gratitude to the deities for their presence and aid,
Thank them for guiding you through this sacred crusade.
Release any remaining negativity into the Earth's embrace,
And know that you are purified, in a state of grace.

May this Eridu purification ritual bring you renewed clarity,

Purging all impurities, creating sacred serenity.
May you walk in purity and light, with each step you take,
Blessed by Ninhursag and Enki, your spirit awake.

Amen.

Prayer to Ninurta and Ninhursag for Fertility - Prayer to the gods Ninurta and Ninhursag for fertility and abundance

Mighty Ninurta, courageous warrior and provider,
And nurturing Ninhursag, mother of all creation,
I come before you with a humble heart and sincere devotion,
Seeking your blessings for fertility and abundant provision.

Ninurta, wielder of the sacred plow and guardian of the fields,
You who bring forth bountiful harvests and ensure nature yields,
We beseech you to bless our land with fertile soil and ample crops,
That our fields may flourish, and our harvests never cease to stop.

Ninhursag, divine mother, source of life and nurturing love,
You who shape the earth and guide life's cycle from above,
We implore you to bestow your abundant fertility upon us,
That our bodies may conceive and bring forth new life without fuss.

Together, Ninurta and Ninhursag, your union brings forth abundance,
Your divine energies interwoven, ensuring life's sustenance,
Grant us the gift of fertility, that families may flourish and grow,
And let our lives be filled with joy and prosperity, both high and low.

In your infinite wisdom and benevolence, hear our plea,
As we honor you, Ninurta and Ninhursag, on bended knee,
May your blessings shower upon us, like rain upon the earth,
And may fertility and abundance grace our lives with boundless mirth.

We offer our prayers and gratitude to you, Ninurta and Ninhursag,
For your unwavering protection and blessings without snag,
May our lives be blessed with fertility, abundance, and grace,
In your divine presence, we find solace and embrace.

Amen.

Prayer to Nanna and Utu for Guidance - Prayer to the gods Nanna and Utu for guidance and enlightenment

Radiant Nanna, gentle moon god of wisdom and reflection,
And Utu, radiant sun god of justice and illumination,
I come before you with reverence and sincere intention,
Seeking your divine guidance and profound enlightenment.

Nanna, in your soothing lunar glow, you illuminate the night,
Guiding our paths with your gentle and wise celestial light,
I beseech you to bestow upon me your guidance and clarity,
That I may navigate life's journey with wisdom and prosperity.

Utu, radiant sun, you bring forth the dawn's radiant beams,
Dispelling darkness, illuminating truth, and revealing dreams,
I implore you to shine your light upon my path each day,
That I may walk in righteousness and find my destined way.

Nanna and Utu, in your celestial embrace, I find solace and peace,
Your divine presence fills my heart, providing divine release,
Illuminate my mind, body, and soul with your sacred wisdom,
And grant me the clarity and guidance to overcome any kingdom.

Nanna, grant me the ability to delve deep into introspection,
To understand the depths of my being and seek self-reflection,
Utu, infuse me with the courage to face life's challenges head-on,
To embrace the light of truth and let righteousness be my spawn.

Together, Nanna and Utu, your guidance is an eternal gift,
As I embark upon life's journey, may my spirit uplift,
Fill me with inspiration, knowledge, and profound insight,
That I may walk the path of righteousness, guided by your light.

In your divine presence, Nanna and Utu, I find solace and grace,
Grant me your wisdom and guidance, as I seek my destined place,
May my heart be open to receive your celestial illumination,
And may I walk the path of enlightenment with unwavering dedication.
Amen.

Prayer to Enki and Inanna for Prosperity - Prayer to the gods Enki and Inanna for prosperity and success

Mighty Enki, god of wisdom and abundance,
And Inanna, radiant goddess of love and prosperity,
I come before you with reverence and gratitude,
Seeking your blessings for prosperity and success.

Enki, the bringer of knowledge and divine intelligence,
You hold the key to unlocking the secrets of abundance,
I humbly request your guidance and favor,
That I may prosper in all endeavors I pursue.

Inanna, goddess of love, beauty, and fertile lands,
Your divine energy brings forth prosperity in our hands,
I implore you to shower me with your blessings,
That success may flow into my life without ceasing.

Enki, with your wisdom, bless my endeavors and plans,
Grant me the insight to make wise choices and stands,
Guide me towards opportunities that lead to prosperity,
And protect me from any obstacle or adversity.

Inanna, with your grace, ignite the fire of success,
Bless my efforts with love, joy, and progress,
Infuse my endeavors with your radiant energy,
That I may attract abundance and triumph effortlessly.

Enki and Inanna, together I invoke your divine presence,
May your blessings fill my life with opulence and opulence,
Grant me the strength, resilience, and determination,
To manifest prosperity and success in every situation.

As I walk this path of abundance and achievement,
I offer my gratitude for your benevolent involvement,
With your guidance and blessings, I am assured,
That prosperity and success will be safely secured.

May the blessings of Enki and Inanna be bestowed upon me,
As I embrace the journey of prosperity and victory,
With gratitude in my heart and faith in your divine power,
I know that all my endeavors shall flourish and tower.

Amen.

Eridu Funeral Ritual - Ritual for the proper burial and farewell of the deceased in Eridu

Step 1: Preparation

Gather in a solemn space, honoring the presence of the departed,
A space that holds sacredness, where emotions and memories are charted.
Create an atmosphere of reverence and deep connection,
A space where grief and reflection find their intersection.

Adorn this space with symbols of mourning and respect,
Emblems that signify the loss and the love that we reflect.
Place black cloth, a solemn reminder of the departed's absence,
Symbolizing the void left behind and the sorrowful essence.

Construct a sacred altar as the focal point of the space,
A place where intentions are set and offerings find their place.
Drape the altar in black cloth, representing the shroud of grief,
A reminder of the journey from life to the eternal relief.

Adorn the altar with candles, their flickering flames aglow,
Representing the guiding light that helps the departed's soul to grow.
Each candle holds a sacred purpose and deep significance,
Illuminating the path to peace and providing solace in remembrance.

Place photographs or mementos of the departed upon the altar,
Objects that evoke cherished memories and feelings that won't falter.
These reminders serve as a bridge between the worlds of the living and deceased,
A tangible connection to the one we've loved and now must release.

Surround the altar with flowers, their beauty and fragrance in bloom,
Symbolizing the transient nature of life, its joys, and its gloom.
Select white flowers, pure and serene, as symbols of peace,
Offering a sense of comfort and hope that pain will one day cease.

As the sacred space takes shape, let silence and solemnity prevail,
Creating an ambiance where emotions find expression and unveil.
In this space, honor the presence of the departed with reverence,
Preparing the heart and mind for the funeral ritual's emergence.

In Eridu's ancient traditions, this sacred preparation is embraced,
A space where grief is acknowledged, and the departed's memory is traced.
May it serve as a sanctuary for healing and remembrance,
A place where we honor the journey from life to eternal transcendence.

Step 2: Invocation

Invoke the presence of the gods of the underworld, with solemnity,
Call upon Nergal, the god of death, and Ereshkigal, queen of the eternity.
With words of reverence and respect, address them in prayer,
Seeking their guidance and blessings for the departed's journey there.

"O Nergal, guardian of the realm of the deceased,
And Ereshkigal, ruler of the underworld, our grief is released.
We invoke your presence in this solemn hour,
Guide the departed safely, with your divine power."

Step 3: Farewell and Reflection

Gather the loved ones of the departed, hearts heavy with sorrow,
Share memories and stories, honoring their life's unique and precious borrow.
Reflect on the lessons learned, the love shared, and the bonds formed,
Embrace the grieving process, knowing that healing will be adorned.

Step 4: Ritual Actions

Prepare the body of the departed, with utmost care and reverence,
Cleansing and anointing, ensuring their journey's deliverance.
Wrap them in a white shroud, symbolizing purity and peace,
For their eternal rest in the realm where all sorrows cease.

Step 5: Final Blessing and Farewell

As the time for the burial draws near, gather around the grave,
Offer final prayers and blessings, the soul's peaceful passage to pave.
Lower the body into the earth's embrace, with gentle hands and love,
Bid farewell to the departed, sending them to the heavens above.

Step 6: Commemoration and Mourning

Return to the sacred space, where memories and emotions entwine,
Hold a commemorative ceremony, honoring the departed's life's design.

Divine Dynamics

Light candles, offer prayers, and share words of remembrance,
Support one another through the grieving process, providing solace and acceptance.

Step 7: Closure

With heavy hearts but a sense of peace, the ritual comes to an end,
Knowing that the departed's spirit will forever transcend.
Carry their memory in your hearts, their legacy forever alive,
May they find eternal rest and peace in the afterlife's dive.

In the ancient city of Eridu, this ritual is performed,
Honoring the departed's life, with love and memories affirmed.
May the gods of the underworld guide them on their eternal way,
As we bid farewell, embracing the cycle of life and death's sway.

Prayer to Ishtar and Dumuzid for Passion - Prayer to the gods Ishtar and Dumuzid for passionate love and desire

Oh Ishtar, radiant goddess of love and desire,
And Dumuzid, the beloved shepherd, set my heart afire.
I come before you, seeking your divine embrace,
To ignite the flames of passion, love's fervent grace.

Ishtar, you are the embodiment of beauty and charm,
With your captivating presence, hearts are warmed.
Grant me the allure to captivate and enchant,
To attract a love that's true and passionate.

Dumuzid, the tender shepherd, keeper of desire,
With your gentle touch, set my soul on fire.
Bestow upon me the yearning for passionate love,
A connection so deep, like the heavens above.

Together, Ishtar and Dumuzid, weave your magic,
Infuse my being with desire, both fierce and tragic.
Grant me the courage to surrender to love's embrace,
To experience its intensity and passion, full of grace.

May the fires of desire burn bright within my heart,
Igniting a love that will never falter or depart.
With your blessings, Ishtar and Dumuzid, I implore,
Fill my life with passion, forevermore.

Oh Ishtar, oh Dumuzid, I offer this prayer to you,
In your divine presence, love's flame will renew.
Guide me on a path of passion and devotion,
And let love's ardor be my eternal emotion.

As I call upon you, gods of passion and love,
Grant me the blessings from the realms above.
With your divine favor, may my desires be fulfilled,
In the realm of love and passion, forever thrilled.

Divine Dynamics

Hear my prayer, Ishtar and Dumuzid, I plea,
Fill my life with passion, love's intensity.
I offer my heart and soul, in devotion I stand,
In your hands, I place my love's command.

Oh Ishtar, oh Dumuzid, I humbly adore,
Grant me the passion my heart longs for.
With your divine intercession, let love's flame ignite,
And fill my days and nights with pure delight.

In your names, Ishtar and Dumuzid, I proclaim,
May passion and desire forever be my flame.
Guide me on a path of love's sweet surrender,
With your blessings, may my heart forever remember.

Prayer to Ninshubur and Nusku - Prayer to the goddess Ninshubur and the god Nusku for protection and assistance

Oh Ninshubur, faithful and loyal servant of the divine,
And Nusku, the radiant god of illumination and fire's shine.
I turn to you with reverence and trust in your might,
Seeking your protection, guidance, and heavenly light.

Ninshubur, trusted companion of the great goddess,
You stand by her side, her trusted ally and witness.
Grant me your unwavering strength and steadfast support,
Shield me from harm, as your presence I import.

Nusku, god of sacred fire, burning bright and true,
With your flames, protect me from all that may pursue.
Illuminate my path, banish darkness and fear,
With your guiding light, keep all dangers clear.

Ninshubur, I call upon your unwavering loyalty,
Be my defender, my guardian, with ceaseless fidelity.
In times of trouble, be my ally and advocate,
Shield me from harm, and guide me to the right.

Nusku, bearer of divine light and sacred flame,
Illuminate my way, and keep me safe from shame.
Grant me the courage to face each challenge with resolve,
With your divine protection, my fears will dissolve.

Ninshubur and Nusku, I beseech you this day,
Wrap me in your protective embrace, I pray.
Guard me from ill intentions and malevolent forces,
And assist me in all my endeavors and life's courses.

Ninshubur, your loyalty and devotion I seek,
Strengthen my spirit, make me steadfast and meek.
Be my advocate in times of need and distress,
And guide me to triumph, to victory I profess.

Divine Dynamics

Nusku, your fiery presence I invoke with respect,
Kindle my inner flame, and never let it deflect.
Protect me from harm, with your blazing might,
And lead me to success, shining ever so bright.

Oh Ninshubur and Nusku, hear my plea,
Wrap me in your protective embrace, I decree.
Grant me strength, wisdom, and your divine aid,
In your watchful care, I find solace and serenade.

With gratitude and reverence, I offer this prayer,
To Ninshubur and Nusku, the guardians fair.
Protect me, guide me, with your celestial grace,
In your presence, I find shelter, in your light, I embrace.

Incantation of Nergal for Healing - Invocation of the god Nergal for healing and recovery from illnesses

O mighty Nergal, god of strength and might,
I invoke your presence on this sacred night.
With reverence and trust, I call upon your name,
To bring forth healing, to banish all pain.

Nergal, fierce warrior and bringer of peace,
You hold the power to make all ailments cease.
I beseech you now, with utmost sincerity,
Grant me your healing touch, restore vitality.

From the depths of the underworld, you rise,
With your divine presence, darkness defies.
Bring forth your healing energies, pure and strong,
Cleanse my body, restore it, right any wrong.

O Nergal, master of life and death's domain,
With your mercy and grace, release me from pain.
Heal the wounds within, both seen and unseen,
Revive my spirit, make me whole and serene.

In your wisdom, you hold the secrets of cure,
Pour forth your healing energy, divine and pure.
Banish illness and afflictions that do beset,
With your touch, let my body and soul reset.

Nergal, I trust in your power to heal,
With each breath, let your energy reveal.
Restore balance, strengthen my weakened frame,
Bring health and wellness, in your mighty name.

As I speak this incantation, let it be,
A channel for your healing energy to set me free.
I surrender to your divine authority and might,
Nergal, bring forth healing, restore my inner light.

Divine Dynamics

By the power of Nergal, so mote it be,
May his healing essence flow through me.
With gratitude and reverence, I embrace your cure,
O Nergal, bless me with health, of this I am sure.

Thank you, mighty Nergal, for your healing grace,
May your blessings shower upon me, in this sacred space.
With your presence, I find solace and relief,
Heal me, O Nergal, and grant me lasting peace.

Prayer to Enlil and Ninurta for Strength - Prayer to the gods Enlil and Ninurta for strength and power

O Enlil, mighty god of the heavens high,
And Ninurta, valiant warrior in the sky,
I come before you with reverence and awe,
Seeking your strength, guided by your law.

Enlil, ruler of the cosmos and divine might,
Grant me the strength to face each daunting fight.
Infuse me with your power, make me bold and strong,
To overcome challenges, and right any wrong.

Ninurta, fierce warrior, guardian of the land,
With your courage and valor, by my side I stand.
Lend me your strength, let it course through my veins,
Empower me with might, as I break all chains.

Enlil, from your lofty abode above,
Bestow upon me your strength, unfaltering and tough.
Grant me resilience, both in body and mind,
To face every obstacle, leaving no fear behind.

Ninurta, with your mighty weapon in hand,
Guide me through battles, against all odds I'll stand.
Fill me with your courage, and unwavering might,
To conquer all challenges, with your guiding light.

Together, Enlil and Ninurta, I implore,
Bless me with strength, forevermore.
Grant me endurance and unwavering resolve,
To face life's trials, with courage to evolve.

In your names, I find solace and power untold,
Enlil and Ninurta, mighty gods of old.
With gratitude and reverence, I call upon you now,
Grant me strength and valor, before you I bow.

Divine Dynamics

May your divine presence uplift my spirit within,
Enlil and Ninurta, let your strength begin.
With your blessings, I am fortified and prepared,
To face the challenges ahead, unyielding and unscared.

Thank you, Enlil and Ninurta, for your divine grace,
May your strength empower me in every space.
In your name, I find courage and resilience anew,
Mighty gods, I am grateful for all that you do.

So mote it be, may it be done,
In the embrace of Enlil and Ninurta, I've won.
With their strength, I am boundless and free,
Forever guided by their divine decree.

Prayer to Shamash and Nergal for Protection - Prayer to the gods Shamash and Nergal for protection from enemies and evil spirits

O Shamash, radiant god of justice and light,
And Nergal, fierce warrior of might,
I call upon your power, with humble plea,
Grant me protection, keep me safe and free.

Shamash, with your divine rays that pierce the sky,
Illuminate my path, let darkness pass me by.
Shield me from harm, from foes who seek to harm,
Wrap me in your protective, comforting charm.

Nergal, mighty guardian of the underworld's might,
With your strength, repel all evils that ignite.
Stand by my side, as I face adversity and strife,
Protect me from dangers, throughout my earthly life.

Shamash, in your divine wisdom and sight,
Guide me through shadows, with your radiant light.
Dispel the darkness, reveal truth and the way,
Let your protective gaze keep danger at bay.

Nergal, with your fiery spirit and fierce power,
Banish all evil, let it cower and cower.
Grant me courage and strength to face my foes,
Protect me from harm wherever life goes.

O Shamash and Nergal, gods of protection and might,
I seek your shelter, in the day and the night.
Guard me from enemies and spirits unkind,
Keep me safe and secure, body, soul, and mind.

I offer my reverence and devotion to you,
Shamash and Nergal, gods so true.
Protect me from harm, surround me with your grace,
Let your divine presence shield me in every place.

Divine Dynamics

With gratitude and trust, I place my plea,
Shamash and Nergal, hear my prayer, see.
Keep me safe from harm, enemies at bay,
Guide me through life, each and every day.

In your names, I find solace and peace,
May your protection never cease.
With your divine intervention, I am secure,
Shamash and Nergal, my guardians so pure.

So mote it be, let it be done,
Under the watchful eyes of Shamash and Nergal, I'm one.
Protected and guarded, I walk this earthly ground,
With your divine presence, eternal protection is found.

Thank you, Shamash and Nergal, for your care,
For shielding me from darkness and despair.
I carry your blessings, with strength I stride,
Protected and guided, with you by my side.

Prayer to Inanna and Nanna for Fertility - Prayer to the gods Inanna and Nanna for fertility and the blessing of children

Oh Inanna, radiant goddess of love and desire,
And Nanna, gentle god of the moon's celestial fire,
I come before you with a humble plea,
Grant me the gift of fertility, I beseech thee.

Inanna, embodiment of passion and grace,
Bless me with fertility, in your divine embrace.
Fill my womb with the spark of life's creation,
Let the miracle of conception be my manifestation.

Nanna, with your gentle glow in the night sky,
Bless me with the fertility that money can't buy.
Guide the cycles within me, align them with the moon,
Let fertility blossom and my heart be in tune.

Inanna, goddess of love, fertility, and rebirth,
Bestow upon me the blessings of fruitful earth.
Grant me the joy of conceiving new life,
A precious child, born from love's sacred strife.

Nanna, god of the moon, wise and serene,
Pour forth your blessings, like moonlight so keen.
Favor me with the abundance of fertile lands,
And the touch of your divine, nurturing hands.

Oh Inanna and Nanna, hear my fervent plea,
Bless me with fertility, with the gift to conceive.
Fill my life with the laughter of children's delight,
Guide me through the journey of motherhood's rite.

May my body be a vessel, fertile and strong,
To carry life within, where dreams belong.
Grant me the joy of children's laughter and mirth,
Let fertility flow, a blessing upon this earth.

Divine Dynamics

Inanna and Nanna, I offer my devotion to you,
As I yearn for the miracle of life anew.
Bless me with fertility, grant my deepest desire,
With your divine intervention, let my dreams transpire.

With gratitude and love, I humbly pray,
That you bless me with a child, along life's way.
Inanna and Nanna, hear my heartfelt plea,
Grant me the gift of fertility, so mote it be.

So be it, let it be done,
Under the watchful eyes of Inanna and Nanna, the One.
May their blessings of fertility and love,
Descend upon me like a gentle dove.

Thank you, Inanna and Nanna, for your divine grace,
For showering me with fertility's embrace.
With trust in your power, I surrender my plea,
Bless me with fertility and the gift of a child, I decree.

Eridu Harvest Offering - Offering to the gods for a bountiful harvest in Eridu

In the fertile lands of Eridu, where abundance thrives,
We gather to offer gratitude for nature's bountiful lives.
With humble hearts and grateful souls, we come to pay tribute,
To the gods who bless our harvest, their blessings we salute.

Oh gods of Eridu, guardians of the land,
We offer our reverence with open hands.
For the fruits of the earth, so generously bestowed,
We gather to honor you, our gratitude bestowed.

To Enlil, mighty lord of the harvest's yield,
With reverence, we offer the first fruits of the field.
May your blessings grace our lands with fertility and rain,
So that our crops may flourish, abundant and without strain.

To Ninhursag, mother of all creation's glory,
We present the golden sheaves, a testament to your story.
May you bless our fields with fertile soil and gentle breeze,
Nourishing our crops with your divine expertise.

To Utu, radiant god of the sun's warm embrace,
We offer the ripened grains, a symbol of life's race.
Illuminate our harvest with your golden rays,
Granting us abundance and prosperous days.

To Ninurta, valiant protector of the crops and fields,
We bring the harvest's bounty, abundant and revealed.
Guard our crops from pests and blight's destructive might,
So that we may reap the rewards of a fruitful sight.

To Nanshe, goddess of abundance and flowing waters,
We pour libations, celebrating life's offerings she proffers.
May our rivers and streams overflow with nourishing flow,
Sustaining our harvest, as the tides of abundance grow.

To Enki, wise and benevolent god of the waters,
We offer prayers for rain, a gift that truly matters.

Divine Dynamics

Bless our fields with showers, gentle and pure,
Saturating the earth, ensuring a harvest secure.

Oh gods of Eridu, hear our humble plea,
Accept our offerings, given with reverence and glee.
In gratitude, we honor your divine grace,
For the blessings of abundance, we forever embrace.

As we partake in the bountiful harvest's feast,
We offer thanks to the gods, our gratitude increased.
May the blessings of Eridu forever abound,
With fertile lands and abundance all around.

With hearts full of gratitude, we offer this prayer,
May our harvest be plentiful, beyond compare.
Bless us, oh gods of Eridu, with your divine might,
As we celebrate the harvest, with joy and delight.

Prayer to Ninurta and Ninhursag for Healing - Prayer to the gods Ninurta and Ninhursag for healing and well-being

Oh mighty Ninurta, courageous and strong,
Master of battles and vanquisher of wrong.
We come before you with hearts heavy and frail,
Seeking your healing touch that will never fail.

In your hands, Ninurta, lies the power to mend,
To restore our bodies, our spirits to transcend.
With your divine strength, banish illness and pain,
Bring forth healing and wellness like gentle rain.

Ninhursag, mother of all, source of life's creation,
With your nurturing touch, grant us restoration.
We beseech you, goddess of fertility and growth,
To heal our ailments and bestow blessings of both.

Gentle Ninhursag, with your wisdom and grace,
Guide us through illness, restore us to a healthy pace.
By your divine touch, let our bodies rejuvenate,
And let our souls find solace, free from any weight.

Together, Ninurta and Ninhursag, we implore,
Pour your healing energies upon us, we adore.
Release us from afflictions that burden our days,
And fill us with vitality in myriad ways.

In this sacred space, we offer our prayer,
To Ninurta and Ninhursag, gods beyond compare.
We trust in your power to heal and restore,
With gratitude and reverence, we forever adore.

As we emerge from the darkness of pain and strife,
May your healing light guide us to a vibrant life.
Ninurta, Ninhursag, we seek your divine embrace,
Grant us healing and well-being, by your grace.

Divine Dynamics

With hearts uplifted and spirits made whole,
We thank you, oh gods, for the blessings you bestow.
May your healing touch forever remain,
And in our lives, your love and guidance sustain.

Hail Ninurta, hail Ninhursag, we sing,
With gratitude and reverence, our praises we bring.
Heal us, protect us, and keep us ever strong,
With your blessings, may we thrive, our lives prolong.

Prayer to Nabu and Nusku for Knowledge - Prayer to the gods Nabu and Nusku for knowledge and wisdom

Oh wise Nabu, god of wisdom and words,
In your presence, our knowledge unfurls.
Grant us insight and understanding profound,
Illuminate our minds, let wisdom resound.

Nusku, bearer of light and sacred flame,
With your guidance, we shall never be tame.
Ignite within us the fire of knowledge and truth,
Illuminate our path, renew our youth.

Nabu, dispenser of wisdom's divine gift,
Inscribe upon our minds knowledge to uplift.
Unveil the secrets of the universe's expanse,
Enlighten our hearts with your cosmic dance.

Nusku, guardian of the sacred flame's glow,
We seek your guidance, your wisdom to know.
Illuminate the darkness, banish ignorance's haze,
Lead us towards wisdom's bright and righteous ways.

Together, Nabu and Nusku, we invoke your might,
Grant us clarity of thought, insight shining bright.
Open the doors of knowledge wide and clear,
Let wisdom flow through us, dispelling all fear.

In this sacred space, we offer our plea,
To Nabu and Nusku, gods of wisdom, hear our plea.
Bless us with knowledge, understanding, and light,
Illuminate our minds, guide us through the night.

Nabu, Nusku, we beseech your divine grace,
Fill us with wisdom and knowledge's embrace.
Empower our thoughts, expand our horizons vast,
Grant us discernment, let ignorance be surpassed.

Divine Dynamics

With hearts open and minds prepared to receive,
We honor you, Nabu and Nusku, and believe.
In your presence, wisdom's treasures we find,
Enlighten our spirits, let knowledge unwind.

Hail Nabu, hail Nusku, we offer our praise,
For the wisdom and knowledge that in us you raise.
Guide us on the path of enlightenment's bliss,
With your blessings, may our minds never miss.

Grant us knowledge's key and wisdom's guiding light,
Nabu, Nusku, in your presence, all is bright.
We thank you for your wisdom's sacred bestowal,
May it illuminate our lives and spirits eternal.

Incantation of Ea for Protection - Invocation of the god Ea for protection from malevolent forces

Ea, mighty god of wisdom and magic,
With your power, we seek protection from the tragic.
In your name, we invoke your divine might,
Shield us from darkness, keep us safe day and night.

Ea, master of the great waters deep,
Guard us from harm, let no evil seep.
Surround us with your divine shield,
Protect us from malevolent forces that wield.

By the power of your sacred name,
We call upon you, Ea, to claim
Our sanctuary, our hearts, and our souls,
Keep us safe, make us whole.

With your wisdom and ancient knowledge,
Deflect all negativity and bondage.
Banish darkness with your guiding light,
Grant us strength to stand and fight.

Ea, protector of mortals and gods,
Embrace us within your protective odds.
Let no harm come near, no danger befall,
As we answer your divine call.

By the strength of your enchantments and charms,
We invoke your presence, free from all harms.
Shield us from curses, hexes, and foes,
Let your divine protection enclose.

Ea, we place our trust in your sacred care,
In your shelter, we find solace and repair.
Protect us from all malevolence and strife,
And guide us towards a harmonious life.

Divine Dynamics

With reverence and devotion, we pray,
Ea, keep us safe each step of the way.
May your divine presence be our shield,
And may your protection never yield.

In your name, Ea, we find respite,
With your power, we overcome any plight.
Protect us, defend us, and keep us secure,
Ea, we surrender to your safeguard pure.

As we invoke you in this sacred rite,
Grant us protection both day and night.
Ea, divine guardian, we call upon you,
Keep us safe, strong, and true.

Hail Ea, protector of life's sacred dance,
We seek your shelter, we entrust our chance.
Protect us from all harm, evil, and despair,
With your divine presence, let us be aware.

Ea, we thank you for your watchful eye,
For your protection that's ever nigh.
With your mighty power, we are fortified,
Under your guidance, we safely reside.

Ea, great protector, we offer our plea,
Protect us always, keep us forever free.
With your divine power, we are defended,
Ea, our guardian, our fears are transcended.

Prayer to Shamash and Utu for Guidance - Prayer to the gods Shamash and Utu for guidance and clarity of vision

Shamash, radiant god of justice and light,
Utu, the shining sun, whose presence is bright,
We beseech you for guidance, wisdom, and sight,
Illuminate our path, make our decisions right.

Shamash, dispenser of truth and divine law,
Utu, whose rays bring clarity and awe,
We turn to you, seeking guidance and insight,
Guide us through darkness, make our choices bright.

Shamash, beacon of justice, shining so strong,
Utu, whose light exposes all that is wrong,
Grant us discernment, clarity, and precision,
Illuminate our minds, grant us decision.

Shamash, who sees all with your watchful eye,
Utu, whose radiance never does shy,
We invoke your presence, oh gods so wise,
Guide us with your light, make our way rise.

Shamash, judge of all, we seek your advice,
Utu, whose rays pierce through the darkest skies,
Illuminate our path, help us see the way,
Lead us with your wisdom, day by day.

Shamash, bringer of truth and cosmic order,
Utu, whose rays touch every border,
We call upon you for guidance and vision,
Show us the path with divine precision.

Shamash, the just, and Utu, the divine,
We look to you, our hearts and minds align,
Grant us clarity and wisdom in our quest,
Illuminate our way, and let us be blessed.

Divine Dynamics

Shamash, source of justice and righteous power,
Utu, whose light shines in every hour,
Guide us with your wisdom, grant us your grace,
Lead us on a path of truth and embrace.

Shamash, god of truth, we seek your embrace,
Utu, whose brilliance lights up every space,
Fill our hearts with wisdom, our minds with clarity,
Guide us on a journey of purpose and prosperity.

Shamash, dispenser of justice and law,
Utu, whose light brings truth into raw,
We invoke your presence, our minds open wide,
Illuminate our path, let our vision be clarified.

Shamash, god of the heavens and the earth,
Utu, whose radiance brings rebirth,
Guide us with your wisdom, grant us clear sight,
Lead us on a path of truth and infinite light.

Shamash, dispenser of fairness and grace,
Utu, whose rays illuminate every place,
We call upon your guidance, oh gods divine,
Show us the way, let your light shine.

Shamash, god of the day, Utu, god of the sun,
We seek your guidance, our spirits you have won,
Bless us with clarity, grant us your illumination,
Guide us on a path of righteous revelation.

Shamash, the just, and Utu, the bright,
We beseech you for guidance, with all our might,
Illuminate our hearts and minds with your divine rays,
Lead us on a path of wisdom and righteous ways.

Hail Shamash, the illuminator of truth,
Hail Utu, whose radiance provides clear proof,
We offer our prayers, seeking your guidance and sight,
Grant us your wisdom, lead us towards the light.

Shamash, the all-seeing, Utu, the brilliant,
We implore your guidance, our path to be resilient,

Illuminate our way, grant us discerning eyes,
Lead us towards wisdom, let your presence arise.

In your names, Shamash and Utu, we pray,
Guide us through life's challenges, day by day,
Grant us clarity, wisdom, and a vision clear,
May your divine guidance forever be near.

Prayer to Enki and Ishtar for Love - Prayer to the gods Enki and Ishtar for love and harmonious relationships

Enki, wise and compassionate god of waters,
Ishtar, goddess of love and passion,
We come before you with hearts full of longing,
Seeking your blessings for love's divine fashion.

Enki, you who understands the depths of emotion,
Ishtar, you who ignites the flames of desire,
We invoke your presence, oh gods of devotion,
Fill our lives with love that will never tire.

Enki, source of wisdom and nurturing care,
Ishtar, embodiment of love so fair,
We beseech you to bless our hearts and souls,
Grant us love that unites and makes us whole.

Enki, guide us to waters of love's deep well,
Ishtar, inspire us with desires that swell,
May our hearts find solace in your embrace,
And may love's enchantment forever grace.

Enki, bestow upon us the gift of understanding,
Ishtar, ignite within us a passion so commanding,
May our love be a beacon of light and bliss,
Radiating warmth and tenderness with every kiss.

Enki, bring forth the waters of love's healing tide,
Ishtar, let our hearts and souls forever abide,
Grant us love that knows no bounds or strife,
And bless us with a harmonious and joyous life.

Enki, master of creation and flowing streams,
Ishtar, goddess of love's ethereal dreams,
We humbly pray for love's blessings divine,
May our hearts entwine, forever in love's shrine.

Enki, the wise counselor and giver of life,
Ishtar, the passionate goddess, banisher of strife,
We call upon your divine presence and grace,
Bless us with love's embrace in every place.

Enki, the bringer of harmony and sweet delight,
Ishtar, the enchantress, filling hearts with light,
We seek your blessings for love's sacred dance,
May our union be blessed with romance.

Enki, the architect of love's sacred design,
Ishtar, the muse of desires intertwine,
Grant us love that is deep, true, and pure,
A love that will forever endure.

Enki, the provider of nurturing and care,
Ishtar, the embodiment of love so rare,
We seek your favor in matters of the heart,
May our love never waver or depart.

Enki, the bringer of love's gentle flow,
Ishtar, the goddess of passion's fiery glow,
We pray for love's blessings to fill our days,
May our hearts be united in love's eternal maze.

Enki and Ishtar, we beseech your divine grace,
Shower us with love, make our hearts embrace,
Bless our relationships with harmony and trust,
And may our love be forever just.

In the names of Enki and Ishtar, we pray,
Grant us love that grows stronger each day,
Guide us on a path of love's pure delight,
And fill our lives with passion's eternal light.

Eridu Festival of Music and Dance - Ritual celebration of music and dance in Eridu

Step 1: Preparation

Gather in the festive square of Eridu,
A bustling hub of joy and merriment true.
Transform the square with vibrant hues,
Adorned with colorful banners and ribbons anew.

Bring forth the essence of celebration and delight,
As the atmosphere becomes a captivating sight.
Hang streamers in every shade and tone,
Creating an ambiance that truly sets the tone.

Create a grand stage in the center of it all,
A focal point that beckons and enthralls.
Adorn the stage with a tapestry of flowers and lights,
A visual feast that ignites the senses and excites.

Let the fragrance of blossoms fill the air,
As petals cascade and dance without a care.
Illuminate the stage with twinkling lights,
Creating a magical backdrop that ignites.

Position the instruments with utmost care,
Awaiting skilled hands that will soon be there.
Arrange the drums, the flutes, and the lyres,
Ready to create melodies that the soul inspires.

On the edges of the square, set up seating,
For spectators to enjoy the performances fleeting.
Line the benches with cushions and soft fabrics,
Providing comfort to all who revel in the antics.

Ensure there is ample space for movement and dance,
For bodies to sway and twirl in joyful trance.
Clear pathways for performers to make their way,
With ease and grace, they'll enchant the display.

As the stage is set and the square adorned,
The spirit of celebration is brightly adorned.
In Eridu's festive square, the excitement is ripe,
A vibrant space where music and dance take flight.

Step 2: Invocation of the Muses
Call upon the Muses, guardians of artistic inspiration,
Their presence brings forth divine celebration.
Invoke their names with reverence and praise,
As they bless the festivities in magnificent ways.

Step 3: Offerings to the Gods
Present offerings to the gods of music and dance,
A melody of fragrant incense and fruits in abundance.
Express gratitude for the gift of rhythm and melody,
And seek their blessings for a joyous ceremony.

Step 4: Musical Performances
Let the melodies of lyres and harps resound,
As skilled musicians fill the air with beautiful sounds.
Dancers adorned in vibrant attire and graceful moves,
Bring forth the essence of joy and rhythmic grooves.

Step 5: Communal Dancing
Join hands and hearts in a circle of unity,
As the community dances with joy and glee.
Let the rhythm guide your steps and movements,
As the spirit of music and dance truly enthralls.

Step 6: Celebration of Cultural Heritage
Showcase the diverse traditions of Eridu's people,
Through dances that tell stories, ancient and regal.
Embrace the rich tapestry of cultural expressions,
And honor the ancestors through rhythmic sessions.

Step 7: Expressions of Individual Creativity
Open the floor to individual talents and artistry,
Allowing performers to shine with their unique ability.
Let singers, instrumentalists, and dancers take their turn,
As the festival becomes a platform for personal yearn.

Step 8: Culmination and Reflection
In the final moments, pause and reflect,
On the power of music and dance to connect.
Express gratitude to the gods and the community,
For the shared experience of this spirited jubilee.

Step 9: Closing Invocation and Blessings
Offer a closing prayer, expressing gratitude and admiration,
To the gods who bestowed this musical inspiration.
Seek their continued blessings for creativity and expression,
As the echoes of the festival linger with joyous impression.

In Eridu, the city of music and dance divine,
Let the festival fill every heart and mind.
May the rhythms and melodies forever resonate,
And the spirit of celebration eternally elevate.

Prayer to Nusku and Nergal for Banishing Evil - Prayer to the gods Nusku and Nergal for banishing evil influences and negativity

Great gods Nusku and Nergal, hear my plea,
I come before you seeking your divine decree.
As the flames of Nusku flicker and dance,
And the strength of Nergal stands in a steadfast stance.

In this sacred moment, I beseech your might,
To banish evil from my presence, shining bright.
Grant me protection from negativity's grasp,
And shield me from all that seeks to harm and clasp.

Nusku, god of the sacred fire's glow,
With your flames, purify and bestow.
Consume the darkness that lingers within,
Let your radiant light wash away the sin.

Nergal, fierce warrior of righteous might,
In your name, I call upon your divine light.
Stand beside me, with your power and force,
Defend me against the evils that try to course.

Together, Nusku and Nergal, I implore,
Banish the shadows that darken my door.
With your divine presence and strength,
I seek refuge from all that is malevolent.

Cleanse my spirit, my mind, and my soul,
Let negativity and darkness lose control.
Protect me from harm, both seen and unseen,
And guide me to a place where I'm serene.

Nusku, Nergal, guardians of the flame,
With gratitude, I invoke your holy name.
Banish evil, negativity, and strife,
And fill my life with love, peace, and life.

Divine Dynamics

May your power and grace surround me here,
Dispelling darkness, bringing light so clear.
I offer my devotion and faith, pure and strong,
To Nusku and Nergal, to whom I belong.

With heartfelt gratitude, my prayers ascend,
To the gods who protect and eternally defend.
Nusku and Nergal, I trust in your care,
Banish evil from my life, let goodness be my share.

Prayer to Ninhursag and Enlil for Protection - Prayer to the gods Ninhursag and Enlil for protection and security

Mighty Ninhursag, mother of all creation,
And Enlil, protector of realms with dedication,
I come before you, seeking your divine might,
To shield me from dangers, both day and night.

Ninhursag, nurturing goddess of the earth,
Whose embrace gives life and grants rebirth,
Wrap me in your loving and protective embrace,
Guard me from harm, in your sheltered space.

Enlil, great lord of the celestial skies,
Whose presence brings order and strength that lies,
Stand by my side with your formidable power,
Defend me from threats that may come to devour.

In your names, Ninhursag and Enlil, I pray,
Grant me protection each and every day.
Surround me with your divine energy and might,
Keep me safe and secure, both day and night.

Ninhursag, bless me with your nurturing grace,
Shield me from harm, in your embrace.
Enlil, fortify my boundaries and keep me strong,
Guard me against all that may cause me wrong.

Together, Ninhursag and Enlil, I implore,
Protect me from dangers that may explore.
Create a shield of divine energy around me,
Keeping me safe and secure, forever free.

In times of adversity and moments of fear,
Let your presence be my refuge and my gear.
Guide my steps and lead me on the right path,
Shield me from harm and spare me from wrath.

Divine Dynamics

Ninhursag and Enlil, I offer my devotion,
With reverence and gratitude, a sacred notion.
Protect me, watch over me, day and night,
With your divine presence, keep me in your sight.

May your blessings encompass me from above,
Filling my life with security and love.
Ninhursag and Enlil, my eternal protectors,
I trust in your guardianship, my divine selectors.

With utmost faith, I offer this prayer to you,
Ninhursag and Enlil, to whom I am true.
Thank you for your protection, unwavering and sure,
I am forever grateful, now and evermore.

Incantation of Marduk for Victory - Invocation of the god Marduk for victory in battles and conflicts

Mighty Marduk, the great god of victory,
Whose strength and valor shine through history,
I call upon you in this hour of need,
To grant me triumph, as I proceed.

Marduk, wielder of the fearsome weapons,
Master of battles and noble aggressions,
Infuse me with your fierce and relentless might,
Guide me through the darkest of fights.

By the power vested in your divine name,
I invoke your aid, your glory I proclaim.
Grant me victory in this battle I face,
Bestow upon me your unwavering grace.

Marduk, with your mighty bow and arrow,
Strike down my foes with a righteous blow.
Fill me with courage and unwavering strength,
As I fight for justice, regardless of length.

I beseech you, Marduk, in this solemn plea,
Grant me success and triumph, set me free.
May your divine presence shield me from harm,
And lead me to victory with your mighty arm.

Grant me the wisdom to strategize and plan,
To overcome all obstacles, as only a champion can.
Guide my hand, steady my aim, and clear my mind,
So that I may emerge victorious, leaving my enemies behind.

Marduk, I honor you with devotion and respect,
As I seek victory, may your blessings intersect.
Grant me the courage to face any foe,
And the strength to triumph and conquer, I bestow.

Divine Dynamics

With your divine intervention and unwavering support,
I shall prevail in this battle, of any sort.
Marduk, I call upon you with unwavering faith,
Grant me victory, triumph, and an honorable wraith.

In your name, Marduk, I offer this invocation,
With utmost reverence and complete dedication.
Grant me victory and let my foes be undone,
By your divine power, let me be the chosen one.

Hail Marduk, the god of triumph and might,
In your name, I claim victory with all my might.
With gratitude and praise, I sing your praise,
For in your presence, I find strength and raise.

Marduk, I thank you for your divine intervention,
For granting me victory and eternal ascension.
I carry your name with honor and pride,
With your blessing, I conquer all sides.

May your victory be my victory, oh Marduk divine,
In battles fought, may your glory forever shine.
I am forever grateful for your guiding light,
Grant me victory, oh god of celestial might.

With this incantation, I seal my plea,
Marduk, the bringer of victory, I summon thee.
In your name, I claim triumph and success,
By your power, my enemies I suppress.

Hail Marduk, the mighty god of war and might,
Grant me victory, in your name, I fight.
So mote it be, may it be done,
In Marduk's name, my victory is won.

Prayer to Ninurta and Ninhursag for Agriculture - Prayer to the gods Ninurta and Ninhursag for a prosperous agricultural season

Mighty Ninurta, god of fertility and abundance,
Whose strength nurtures the fields and makes them grow,
I beseech you on this sacred day,
To bless our land and ensure a bountiful harvest flow.

Ninhursag, mother goddess of the earth,
Whose nurturing hands bring forth life's sustenance,
We turn to you with humble hearts,
Seeking your blessings for agricultural brilliance.

Ninurta, with your powerful bow and divine spear,
Protect our crops from pestilence and fear.
Let your fertile energy embrace the land,
As we sow the seeds with care, hand in hand.

Ninhursag, creator of all living things,
Your gentle touch makes the earth to sing.
We pray for your blessings upon our toil,
That our fields may yield abundant soil.

Together, Ninurta and Ninhursag, we implore,
Grant us a prosperous agricultural lore.
With your guidance and abundant grace,
May our crops flourish in every place.

Ninurta, mighty warrior of the heavens,
Command the rains to nourish our fertile plains.
Bring forth the sunshine, warm and bright,
To nurture the growth of plants day and night.

Ninhursag, mother of all that is green,
Bless our seeds with life, unseen.
Let the earth embrace their tender roots,
As they sprout and grow in joyful pursuits.

Divine Dynamics

We honor you, Ninurta and Ninhursag,
For the gifts you bestow upon the land.
With gratitude, we tend the fields with care,
Knowing that in your hands, success is grand.

As we till the soil and sow the seeds,
May you bless our efforts and fulfill our needs.
May the crops flourish and abundance flow,
Under the watchful eyes of Ninurta and Ninhursag, we shall grow.

With hearts filled with gratitude and devotion,
We offer our prayers, an earnest notion.
Bless our fields, bless our hands,
Grant us a prosperous harvest across the lands.

Ninurta and Ninhursag, we seek your favor,
In this sacred bond, may our efforts never waver.
Guide us through the seasons, gentle and kind,
And may the fruits of our labor be divinely aligned.

In your names, Ninurta and Ninhursag, we pray,
For a prosperous agricultural season, day by day.
With gratitude in our hearts, we honor your might,
And trust in your blessings to bring forth abundance and light.

Hail Ninurta! Hail Ninhursag!
We invoke your presence, we raise our voice.
Bless our fields, bless our crops,
With your divine power, may abundance rejoice.

May our harvest be plentiful and our spirits soar,
Under the watchful eyes of Ninurta and Ninhursag, forevermore.
We offer our thanks and prayers to you,
For the blessings of agriculture, strong and true.

With gratitude and reverence, we stand,
Ninurta and Ninhursag, take our humble hand.
Bless our fields, bless our crops,
With your divine essence, never-ending, never stops.

Hail Ninurta! Hail Ninhursag!

May our agricultural endeavors never lag.
With your blessings, our harvest will be grand,
As we walk together, hand in hand.

Prayer to Nabu and Nanna for Wisdom - Prayer to the gods Nabu and Nanna for wisdom and intellectual prowess

Mighty Nabu, god of wisdom and knowledge,
Whose sacred words unveil the mysteries of the ages,
I beseech you on this solemn day,
To bestow upon me your wisdom and intellectual sage.

Nanna, celestial deity of the moon,
Whose gentle light guides us in the darkest of nights,
I humbly come before you,
Seeking your guidance and profound insights.

Nabu, with your mighty quill and scholarly might,
Illuminate my path with your intellectual light.
Grant me the gift of wisdom and understanding,
So I may unravel life's complexities, demanding.

Nanna, with your serene glow and tranquil grace,
Bless my mind with wisdom, in every space.
Open the doors of perception and intuition,
So I may seek truth with fervent resolution.

Nabu, master of the written word,
Inspire me to learn, explore, and be heard.
Infuse my thoughts with clarity and insight,
As I delve into knowledge, day and night.

Nanna, keeper of hidden secrets and dreams,
Awaken my intellect to the cosmic streams.
Grant me the ability to perceive beyond the mundane,
And connect with the realms of wisdom's domain.

Together, Nabu and Nanna, I implore,
Fill my mind with wisdom, forevermore.
Guide me on a path of intellectual growth,
And help me discern what is of true worth.

Nabu, god of scholarship and the arts,
Ignite my intellect, let wisdom impart.
May my words be eloquent and profound,
As I seek knowledge and truths to expound.

Nanna, goddess of lunar inspiration,
Illuminate my mind with divine revelation.
Grant me the wisdom to discern right from wrong,
And let my actions be guided by knowledge strong.

I honor you, Nabu and Nanna, with deep respect,
For the wisdom you offer and the intellect you protect.
Grant me the ability to learn and to teach,
And let wisdom's flame within me ever reach.

As I seek knowledge and understanding each day,
May your blessings guide me along the way.
Nabu, Nanna, I offer my heartfelt plea,
Grant me wisdom's essence, forever to be free.

In your names, Nabu and Nanna, I pray,
For wisdom's blessings to illuminate my way.
May your divine insights fill my mind,
And may intellectual prowess be forever enshrined.

Hail Nabu! Hail Nanna!
Grant me wisdom, bright as a star.
With your guidance, may I grow,
In knowledge and understanding, may I flow.

May my mind be sharp and my insights keen,
Under the watchful eyes of Nabu and Nanna, serene.
I seek your wisdom, I yearn to learn,
And with your blessings, may my intellect discern.

Hail Nabu! Hail Nanna!
In your wisdom, I find solace and grace.
With your guidance, may I navigate,
The vast realms of knowledge, without a trace.

In your names, Nabu and Nanna, I invoke,
The power of wisdom, a celestial yoke.

Divine Dynamics

Grant me insight, grant me clarity,
So I may unlock the treasures of intellectual prosperity.

Hail Nabu! Hail Nanna!
Bless me with wisdom, profound and deep.
May your divine teachings forever keep,
My mind enlightened, my spirit steeped.

With gratitude and reverence, I stand,
Nabu and Nanna, take my humble hand.
Guide me on the path of wisdom's embrace,
And let knowledge and understanding interlace.

Hail Nabu! Hail Nanna!
In your wisdom, I find solace and might.
Grant me intellect, grant me insight,
As I seek wisdom's treasures, day and night.

Prayer to Ishtar and Shamash for Justice - Prayer to the gods Ishtar and Shamash for justice and fairness

Glorious Ishtar, radiant goddess of justice,
Whose scales weigh the deeds of all humankind,
I come before you, humbled and sincere,
Seeking your guidance and righteous mind.

Shamash, mighty god of the sun,
Whose light illuminates the path of truth,
I beseech you on this solemn day,
To bring justice and fairness to all, from youth.

Ishtar, with your sword of righteousness,
Strike down the oppressors and unjust.
Protect the weak and the downtrodden,
In your name, may justice be thrust.

Shamash, with your divine gaze,
Pierce through deceit and false claims.
Illuminate the courts and the hearts of the just,
With your radiance, reveal the true aims.

Ishtar, champion of the wronged,
Defender of the innocent and pure,
Unleash your wrath upon the wicked,
And let justice prevail, swift and sure.

Shamash, dispenser of divine laws,
In your hands lies the balance of equity.
Guide the judges and the lawmakers,
To uphold justice and create harmony.

Ishtar, goddess of righteous retribution,
Instill in us a passion for fairness and right.
May our actions align with your principles,
And in the pursuit of justice, we find delight.

Divine Dynamics

Shamash, source of wisdom and order,
Grant us clarity and discernment of the law.
May justice be dispensed without bias or favor,
And let fairness prevail, without a flaw.

Ishtar, in your name, we seek redress,
For the oppressed, the silenced, and the weak.
Let your divine presence be our strength,
As we fight for justice, bold and meek.

Shamash, your radiance reveals all truth,
Shine upon the courts, the systems, and the land.
May every decision be rooted in fairness,
And let the rule of law firmly stand.

Ishtar and Shamash, together we pray,
For justice and fairness to guide our way.
Grant us the courage to fight for what's right,
And let justice prevail, in the brightest light.

In your names, Ishtar and Shamash, we implore,
Bring justice to the oppressed and the poor.
May your divine presence be our guide,
As we strive for justice, side by side.

Hail Ishtar, goddess of righteousness!
May your scales of justice never sway.
Hail Shamash, god of truth and order!
May your light guide us, night and day.

In your wisdom and might, we trust,
To uphold justice, to be fair and just.
Ishtar and Shamash, hear our plea,
Grant us a world where justice is free.

Hail Ishtar! Hail Shamash!
In your names, we seek justice's flame.
May fairness and equity be our aim,
As we honor your divine, righteous name.

With gratitude and devotion, we pray,
To Ishtar and Shamash, each and every day.

Guide us in the pursuit of justice and right,
And let fairness prevail, in every sight.

Hail Ishtar! Hail Shamash!
May justice reign, in every land.
With your blessings, may we firmly stand,
For justice and fairness, hand in hand.

In your names, Ishtar and Shamash, we call,
For justice's triumph, one and all.
May righteousness prevail in every nation,
And bring forth a world of harmony and elation.

Hail Ishtar! Hail Shamash!
May justice's flame forever burn bright.
In your guidance, we find strength and might,
To uphold justice, and fight for what's right.

Eshnunna Divination by Water - Divination ritual using water as a medium in Eshnunna

In the ancient city of Eshnunna, where wisdom and divine knowledge abound,
We gather now to seek guidance through the sacred medium of water, profound.
As the flowing rivers and shimmering lakes hold secrets untold,
We turn to the gods for insight, their wisdom to unfold.

Step 1: Preparation

In a tranquil and consecrated space, we assemble with reverence and care,
Adorning the area with symbols of divination, creating an atmosphere rare.
A vessel of pure water is placed upon a sacred pedestal, shimmering and clear,
Reflecting the heavens above, a mirror of truth we hold dear.

Step 2: Invocation

We invoke the presence of the gods, the divine entities supreme,
With humble hearts and solemn words, we call upon their esteemed.
"O mighty gods and goddesses, guardians of fate and destiny,
Bless us with your divine guidance, as we seek answers through this ceremony."

Step 3: Purification

Before the divination begins, we purify ourselves, body and soul,
Cleansing away all impurities, allowing our spirits to become whole.
With reverence, we wash our hands and face, preparing to receive,
The messages and insights that the water's divination will conceive.

Step 4: Offering

In gratitude and respect, we present offerings to the gods so wise,
Fruits, flowers, and precious herbs, a tribute to their celestial ties.
With each offering placed near the vessel, we express our devotion,
Seeking their favor and blessings in this sacred communion.

Step 5: Focus and Intent

With minds clear and hearts open, we focus our thoughts and desires,
Formulating questions and seeking guidance from the divine sires.

We express our intentions to the gods, laying them bare,
Asking for their wisdom and insight, to navigate life's intricate affair.

Step 6: Divination

The water, calm and still, becomes our conduit to the other realm,
We peer into its depths, searching for answers at the helm.
With unwavering concentration, we observe the subtle signs and shifts,
Interpreting the ripples and patterns, where destiny's veil uplifts.

Step 7: Interpretation

The gods speak to us through the language of the water's dance,
Symbolic messages and visions, imbued with divine chance.
With deep intuition and ancient knowledge, we decipher their voice,
Translating the meaning behind the fluid patterns, the guidance of choice.

Step 8: Gratitude and Closure

As the divination comes to an end, we express our gratitude and awe,
Thanking the gods for their presence and wisdom, as we withdraw.
We honor their divine counsel and guidance, forever in our hearts,
Knowing that through the sacred water, their wisdom forever imparts.

In Eshnunna, the ancient city steeped in mystic tradition and lore,
We honor the gods through divination by water, seeking knowledge galore.
May their wisdom guide us in every step we take,
And may their blessings surround us, for the gods' sake.

Prayer to Nanna and Ishtar for Fertility - Prayer to the gods Nanna and Ishtar for fertility and abundance

O gracious gods, Nanna and Ishtar, radiant and divine,
We come before you with hearts full of reverence and entwine.
In the realm of fertility and abundance, we seek your blessed presence,
To bestow upon us the gift of life, and grant our hearts' deepest essence.

Nanna, gentle moon god, with your luminous glow,
You watch over the earth and its creatures below.
As the cycles of the moon wax and wane,
We beseech you to bless us with fertility's reign.

Ishtar, mighty goddess of love and desire,
Your radiance sets hearts aflame with the eternal fire.
We call upon your sacred essence, oh goddess fair,
To shower us with your blessings, and answer our prayer.

Together, Nanna and Ishtar, in unity divine,
We implore you to bless us with children, a precious sign.
May our bodies be fertile, our spirits pure and bright,
Grant us the gift of conception, with your celestial might.

In the name of Nanna, we ask for the moon's gentle embrace,
May it bring forth abundance and prosperity, filling every space.
In the name of Ishtar, we seek love's passionate embrace,
May it fill our lives with joy and blessings, leaving no trace.

Oh gods of fertility, hear our heartfelt plea,
Fill our lives with the miracle of new life to be.
Bless our unions with love, fertility, and grace,
And shower us with abundance in every time and place.

Nanna and Ishtar, we offer our devotion and praise,
As we walk this sacred path, seeking your divine ways.
Guide us, protect us, and bless us with your divine might,
As we honor your names, in this prayer for fertility's light.

In your holy names, we humbly pray,
Nanna and Ishtar, hear us today.
Grant us the blessing of fertility and abundance,
And fill our lives with joy, love, and radiance.

Prayer to Nergal and Ereshkigal for Retribution - Prayer to the gods Nergal and Ereshkigal for retribution against enemies

Mighty gods Nergal and Ereshkigal, lords of the underworld,
We come before you seeking your wrath, fierce and unfurled.
As gods of retribution, we invoke your fearsome might,
To punish those who've wronged us and restore justice's light.

Nergal, powerful warrior, fierce and unyielding,
With your burning gaze, the enemy's fate you are sealing.
Grant us your strength, as we stand against our foes,
Unleash your fury, and let retribution impose.

Ereshkigal, queen of the underworld, dark and sublime,
In your realm of shadows, the wicked pay for their crime.
We call upon your divine judgment, just and severe,
To bring swift retribution and make our enemies fear.

Nergal and Ereshkigal, hear our plea,
Inflict upon our enemies the punishment they decree.
Let your vengeance be swift and righteous,
As we seek retribution for the wrongs they've done to us.

Strike down our foes with your relentless might,
Bring forth justice, and set all wrongs to right.
May their transgressions be met with your fierce ire,
As we invoke your names, fueling our righteous fire.

In your name, Nergal, we seek triumph and victory,
Grant us the strength to face our enemies with audacity.
In your name, Ereshkigal, we invoke the power of the abyss,
May their deeds be repaid, their treachery dismissed.

Oh gods of retribution, we beseech you today,
To avenge our grievances, and show them the way.
Let your divine presence guide our righteous cause,
And let our enemies tremble, in awe of your laws.

Nergal and Ereshkigal, we pledge our loyalty,
As we seek retribution and regain our dignity.
With your wrath, we shall triumph and emerge,
From the ashes of vengeance, our enemies will surge.

Grant us the strength to face our adversaries,
And bring about justice with your divine mercies.
In your names, we offer our devotion and plea,
Nergal and Ereshkigal, hear us and set us free.

By your power, let retribution befall,
And restore balance and justice for all.
Nergal and Ereshkigal, we bow before your might,
Bring forth retribution and set everything right.

In your names, we pray with hearts full of zeal,
Nergal and Ereshkigal, our prayers you shall seal.
Grant us the retribution we seek so dire,
And let justice prevail, fueling our righteous fire.

Incantation of Nuska for Success - Invocation of the god Nuska for success in endeavors and endeavors

Hear me, mighty god Nuska, bearer of success,
With reverence and devotion, I call upon your blessedness.
By your divine presence, I seek to excel and achieve,
Grant me your favor, that my efforts may prosper and receive.

Nuska, the bringer of fortune and favorable fate,
I beseech you now, may success be my destined state.
Infuse my endeavors with your divine energy and might,
Guide me on the path of triumph, shining ever bright.

With each step I take, may your blessings surround,
Empower my actions, let success be unbound.
Through obstacles and challenges, may I prevail,
As I invoke your name, may fortune never fail.

Nuska, the god of prosperity and favorable outcomes,
I invoke your essence, as I embark on new realms.
In business, in creativity, and every endeavor I pursue,
May your divine presence lead me to success anew.

Grant me the vision to see opportunities arise,
The wisdom to seize them and claim the ultimate prize.
With your guidance, may my path be paved with triumph,
And may success be woven into every fiber and stratum.

Nuska, I call upon your sacred powers so immense,
Fill my life with abundance, and make success my recompense.
By your hand, may my ventures flourish and thrive,
As I walk in the light of your blessings, I shall strive.

With gratitude in my heart, I honor your divine grace,
And trust that with your aid, success I shall embrace.
Nuska, hear my plea, as I offer this incantation,
Bestow upon me success and unwavering determination.

In your name, Nuska, I invoke this sacred rite,
Grant me success, may it shine ever bright.
Guide my steps, bless my efforts, and make them prevail,
As I offer my devotion, may success never fail.

So mote it be!

Prayer to Enlil and Ninlil for Guidance - Prayer to the gods Enlil and Ninlil for guidance and wisdom

Oh Enlil, mighty god of wisdom and power,
And Ninlil, gentle goddess of guidance in every hour.
I bow before you with reverence and awe,
Seeking your divine wisdom, abiding by your law.

Enlil, the great lord of the heavens above,
You hold the keys to knowledge, justice, and love.
Guide me on the path of righteousness and truth,
Illuminate my mind with your wisdom's soothing sooth.

Ninlil, compassionate goddess, mother and queen,
Your nurturing presence is serene and serene.
Wrap me in your guidance, like a comforting shroud,
Teach me the ways of the world, both silent and loud.

Together, Enlil and Ninlil, your wisdom I implore,
Grant me discernment and knowledge to explore.
In times of doubt and confusion, be my guiding light,
Show me the way, and make my choices right.

Enlil, with your profound wisdom and might,
Help me discern between wrong and right.
Guide my actions and decisions, I pray,
That I may walk a righteous and virtuous way.

Ninlil, with your gentle and nurturing hand,
Lead me through life's intricate and complex strand.
Instill in me the compassion and understanding,
To navigate the challenges that life is demanding.

Enlil and Ninlil, I call upon your divine grace,
Shower me with wisdom, in every time and space.
Illuminate my path, as I journey through life,
With your guidance, may I conquer every strife.

I offer my prayers and reverence to both of you,
Enlil and Ninlil, gods of wisdom and virtue.
Guide me with your infinite wisdom and care,
In your divine presence, I find solace and dare.

Oh Enlil and Ninlil, hear my plea,
Grant me the wisdom I seek, so I may be free.
With your guidance and blessings, I shall abide,
Walking the path of wisdom, with you by my side.

In your names, Enlil and Ninlil, I pray,
Grant me guidance and wisdom each and every day.
May your divine influence forever be near,
As I navigate this journey, with reverence and sincere.

So mote it be.

Prayer to Ishtar and Shamash for Protection - Prayer to the gods Ishtar and Shamash for protection from harm and danger

Mighty Ishtar, radiant goddess of love and war,
And Shamash, the sun god, whose light travels far,
I come before you with humility and reverence,
Seeking your divine protection and defense.

Ishtar, fierce protector, with your fiery sword,
Shield me from dangers, both known and untoward.
Wrap me in your loving embrace, powerful and bold,
Guard me from harm, as your divine strength unfolds.

Shamash, radiant god, whose light banishes the dark,
Protect me with your rays, both fierce and spark.
Illuminate my path with your celestial glow,
Guide me away from perils, wherever I may go.

Ishtar and Shamash, I call upon your might,
Defend me against all evil, day and night.
Surround me with your divine energy and power,
Keep me safe in every moment and every hour.

Ishtar, shield me from malice and ill intent,
Let your presence be a barrier, strong and unbent.
May your love and protection embrace my being,
Keeping me safe from harm, forever decreeing.

Shamash, shine your light upon my way,
Dispel the shadows that seek to lead me astray.
Illuminate the truth, expose deceit and lies,
Guide me towards safety, under your watchful eyes.

Together, Ishtar and Shamash, I seek your grace,
Wrap me in your protective embrace.
Keep me shielded from harm, both seen and unseen,
Let no danger or fear disturb my serene.

I offer my prayers, my heart, and my trust,
To Ishtar and Shamash, gods so just.
With gratitude, I seek your watchful gaze,
Protect me always, in all my days.

Oh Ishtar and Shamash, hear my plea,
Keep me safe and secure, wherever I may be.
With your divine protection, I am free,
Under your care, I find solace and glee.

In your names, Ishtar and Shamash, I pray,
Protect me from harm, each and every day.
May your divine presence be my shield and guide,
With your protection, I fear no tide.

So mote it be.

Prayer to Ninurta and Ninhursag for Fertility - Prayer to the gods Ninurta and Ninhursag for fertility and abundant harvests

Mighty Ninurta, god of war and agriculture,
And Ninhursag, goddess of fertility and creation,
I offer my prayers to you, seeking your divine favor,
For bountiful harvests and abundant fertility.

Ninurta, mighty warrior, whose strength knows no bounds,
Bless our fields with fertility, enriching the grounds.
Grant us strength and skill to cultivate the land,
That our harvests may be plentiful, by your guiding hand.

Ninhursag, nurturing mother of all living things,
Goddess of fertility, with blessings that life brings,
Pour forth your abundant blessings upon the earth,
Let the seeds we sow bring forth abundant birth.

Ninurta, protector of the fields and crops,
Defend us from pests and blights, until harvest tops.
Let your divine energy infuse every plant and tree,
That they may thrive and yield, abundantly and free.

Ninhursag, source of life and abundance divine,
Bless us with fertility, like the fruitful vine.
Nurture the seeds we sow, with your loving care,
Bring forth a bountiful harvest, beyond compare.

Together, Ninurta and Ninhursag, I beseech you now,
In your divine presence, I humbly bow.
Grant us fertility, abundance, and prosperous days,
That our crops may flourish, in myriad ways.

Ninurta, god of the plow and the battle's might,
Guide our hands as we toil, from morning till night.
Protect our fields from drought, storms, and blight,
That our harvest may be abundant, shining bright.

Ninhursag, mother of all, bringer of life,
Nurture the soil, relieve it from strife.
Bless us with fertile lands and fertile hearts,
That we may partake in nature's abundant arts.

I offer my gratitude, my prayers, and my devotion,
To Ninurta and Ninhursag, in this sacred notion.
May you bless our lands, our crops, and our kin,
With fertility and abundance, let the harvest begin.

In your names, Ninurta and Ninhursag, I pray,
Grant us fertility and blessings, day by day.
May our fields yield plentifully, with love and mirth,
And may we be blessed with abundant harvests on Earth.

So mote it be.

Prayer to Nanna and Utu for Illumination - Prayer to the gods Nanna and Utu for enlightenment and understanding

Oh, Nanna, radiant moon god, and Utu, shining sun god,
I turn to you in reverence, seeking your divine illumination.
Grant me the gift of enlightenment and understanding,
That I may walk the path of wisdom and knowledge.

Nanna, gentle and serene, your silver light guides the night,
Illuminate my mind and soul with your celestial sight.
In your gentle glow, reveal the mysteries hidden deep,
Grant me clarity and insight, as I journey and seek.

Utu, radiant and mighty, your golden rays pierce the day,
Illuminate my path with your brilliant, guiding ray.
In your radiant warmth, bestow upon me divine clarity,
Fill my heart with wisdom and discernment, for all to see.

Nanna, moon god of wisdom and dreams,
Fill my mind with knowledge, like a flowing stream.
Open my eyes to the secrets of the universe,
So I may understand its wonders and traverse.

Utu, sun god of justice and truth,
Illuminate my path with your radiant, eternal youth.
Grant me the wisdom to discern right from wrong,
And the courage to stand firm, resolute and strong.

Together, Nanna and Utu, I beseech you now,
In your celestial presence, I humbly bow.
Grant me the gift of enlightenment and understanding,
That I may walk the path of wisdom, expanding.

Nanna, Utu, I seek your divine light,
To guide me through the darkness, day and night.
Illuminate my mind, my spirit, and my way,
So I may walk in wisdom and enlightenment each day.

In your names, Nanna and Utu, I offer my plea,
Grant me illumination, so I may truly see.
Fill my being with knowledge, insight, and grace,
And lead me on the path of wisdom, in every place.

I express my gratitude for your benevolent grace,
Nanna and Utu, gods of enlightenment and embrace.
May your radiant light forever shine upon my soul,
Guiding me with wisdom, making me whole.

So mote it be.

Prayer to Enki and Inanna for Success - Prayer to the gods Enki and Inanna for success in endeavors and ventures

Oh, Enki, wise and cunning, and Inanna, radiant and bold,
I come before you seeking your divine guidance and support.
Grant me the blessings of success in all my endeavors,
And empower me to achieve greatness and fulfillment.

Enki, the master of wisdom and knowledge,
With your boundless intellect, guide me through each challenge.
Grant me the insight to make wise decisions,
And the creativity to find innovative solutions.

Inanna, goddess of love, beauty, and strength,
Wrap me in your divine embrace, and inspire me to go to any length.
Infuse my actions with passion and determination,
And bless my ventures with success and elevation.

Enki, the shaper of destinies and the bringer of prosperity,
Pour your blessings upon me and open doors to opportunity.
Grant me the skills and resources to excel in my pursuits,
And may success follow me wherever I choose.

Inanna, the embodiment of courage and ambition,
Empower me to face obstacles with unwavering conviction.
Ignite the fire within me, fueling my aspirations,
And let triumph be the culmination of my dedications.

Enki and Inanna, I offer my heartfelt plea,
With reverence and gratitude, I bend my knee.
Guide me on the path to triumph and victory,
And let success be my everlasting story.

I thank you, Enki and Inanna, for your divine grace,
For your guidance and blessings that I embrace.
May my endeavors be crowned with success and achievement,
As I walk the path of fulfillment, with your divine agreement.
So mote it be.

Eridu Purification Bath - Ritual bath for purification of the body and spirit in Eridu

Step 1: Preparation
Create a serene and sacred space for your purification bath by gathering the necessary items:

Basin or Tub:
Choose a basin or tub that is large enough to comfortably immerse yourself in. Ensure it is clean and free from any debris. Fill it with clean, lukewarm water to a level that allows you to fully submerge your body.

Purifying Herbs:
Select purifying herbs that resonate with you and your intentions for the bath. Common choices include rosemary, lavender, sage, or any other herbs known for their cleansing properties. These herbs can be used in the form of loose dried leaves or tied together in a bundle.

Clean Towel or Robe:
Prepare a clean towel or robe to use after the bath. It should be soft, absorbent, and solely dedicated to this ritual. Choose a fabric that feels comforting against your skin and enhances the sense of purity and renewal.

Soft Candlelight or Dim Lighting:
Create a soothing ambiance by using soft candlelight or dim lighting in the bathing area. The gentle flickering of candles or the warm glow of dimmed lights can help create a tranquil atmosphere, promoting relaxation and introspection.

Arrange the items thoughtfully, ensuring they are easily accessible within your bathing space. Place the basin or tub in a comfortable and quiet area where you can fully immerse yourself in the experience. Set the herbs, towel, and candles nearby, ready to be incorporated into the ritual.

Before proceeding to the next steps, take a few moments to center yourself and set your intention for the purification bath. Reflect on the cleansing and renewing qualities of water, herbs, and light, envisioning how they will support your purification journey.

By mindfully preparing the necessary items and creating a sacred space, you set the stage for a profound and transformative purification experience. This step lays the foundation for the subsequent stages of the ritual, enhancing your connection to the elements and promoting a sense of tranquility and purification.

Step 2: Setting the Intention

Clear your mind and focus on your intention for the purification bath. This could be cleansing your body and spirit, releasing negative energies, or seeking inner peace and renewal. Take a few moments to center yourself and connect with your inner self.

Step 3: Cleansing the Space

Before entering the bath, cleanse the space around you. Light purifying incense or smudge sticks, such as sage or palo santo, and let the smoke waft through the room. This helps purify the energy and create a sacred atmosphere.

Step 4: Herbal Infusion

To enhance the purification bath, you will create an herbal infusion by incorporating the purifying herbs into the basin or tub of water. Follow these steps to prepare the infusion:

Place the Herbs:

Take the purifying herbs, such as rosemary, lavender, sage, or any other herbs of your choice, and gently scatter them into the water-filled basin or tub. Allow the herbs to float freely or gently submerge them in the water.

Steep the Herbs:

Let the herbs steep in the water for a few minutes, allowing their essence to infuse into the liquid. As the herbs steep, they release their aromatic properties and energetic vibrations, amplifying the purifying qualities of the water.

Optional: Add Essential Oils:

If desired, you can further enhance the herbal infusion by adding a few drops of essential oils associated with purification. Eucalyptus, peppermint, or tea tree oil are popular choices known for their cleansing properties. Remember to use high-quality essential oils and dilute them properly according to the instructions.

Stir or Swirl:

Gently stir or swirl the water in the basin to distribute the herbal essence and essential oils evenly. This helps to ensure that the purifying qualities are infused throughout the bath.

As you prepare the herbal infusion, take a moment to connect with the healing and cleansing energy of the herbs. Visualize their properties blending with the water, creating a potent elixir of purification. You may even silently or verbally express your intention for the bath, inviting the herbs to assist in your purification process.

Once the herbs have steeped, and the water is infused with their essence, you are ready to proceed with the purification bath. The herbal infusion acts as a catalyst, working synergistically with the other elements of the ritual to cleanse and purify your body, mind, and spirit.

Step 5: Enter the Bath
Undress and slowly immerse yourself in the bath, allowing the water to envelop your body. As you do so, visualize the water washing away any impurities, both physical and spiritual. Feel the purifying energy of the herbs and water embracing you, cleansing and renewing your entire being.

Step 6: Intentional Reflection
While in the bath, take time for self-reflection and introspection. Connect with your inner thoughts, emotions, and desires. Focus on releasing any negativity or stagnant energy within you, allowing the purifying properties of the bath to work their magic.

Step 7: Affirmations and Prayers
In this step, you will recite affirmations or prayers that align with your intention for purification. It is an opportunity to connect with higher powers or deities of your choice, expressing your gratitude and seeking their blessings for the cleansing of your body and spirit. Here's how you can approach this step:

Set the Tone:
Create a serene and peaceful atmosphere around you. Find a comfortable position either inside or near the bath. Light candles or use soft lighting to create a soothing ambiance. Take a few deep breaths, allowing yourself to relax and center your mind.

Express Gratitude:
Begin by expressing gratitude for the opportunity to purify your body and spirit. Acknowledge the presence of higher powers or deities, recognizing their guidance and support. You can say something like, "I am grateful for the presence of divine energy in this moment. I thank the [higher powers or deities] for their blessings and guidance as I embark on this purification journey."

State Your Intention:
Clearly state your intention for the purification bath. This could be specific to cleansing negative energy, releasing emotional burdens, or purifying your physical body. For example, you may say, "I affirm my intention to cleanse and purify my body, mind, and spirit. I release all negativity and invite in divine light and healing."

Call Upon Higher Powers:

If you have specific deities or higher powers you resonate with, address them directly in your prayers. Call upon their presence, wisdom, and blessings to assist you in the purification process. You can use the following format as a guide: "I call upon [deity or higher power's name], the embodiment of [their qualities], to bless and cleanse me. I seek your guidance and support as I purify my body and spirit."

Recite Affirmations:

Recite affirmations that resonate with your intention. These affirmations should affirm the purification process, uplift your energy, and align you with the desired outcome. Choose affirmations that resonate with you personally, or you can use examples such as:

"I am cleansed and purified from within. I release all that no longer serves me."
"I am open to receiving divine healing and transformation. I embrace the purity of my being."
"I am surrounded by divine light and love. I am restored and renewed."

Speak from the Heart:

Feel free to speak from your heart during this step. Share your personal thoughts, emotions, or requests with the higher powers or deities. This is an intimate moment to connect with the divine and express your deepest desires for purification and healing.

Take your time with the affirmations and prayers, allowing their words to resonate within you. Feel the presence and energy of the higher powers or deities as you speak. Remember that sincerity and intention are key in this process. When you feel complete, take a few moments to bask in the energy of your affirmations and prayers before proceeding to the next step.

By incorporating affirmations and prayers into your purification bath, you invite divine blessings, guidance, and transformative energy into your experience, amplifying the effects of the ritual.

Step 8: Soak and Relax

Spend a significant amount of time soaking in the bath, allowing the purifying energy to permeate your entire being. Close your eyes, breathe deeply, and let go of any tension or stress. Feel yourself being refreshed, renewed, and purified from within.

Step 9: Final Rinse

When you feel ready, stand up and rinse your body with the water from the bath, allowing it to wash away any remaining impurities. Visualize all negative energies being washed down the drain, leaving you cleansed and revitalized.

Step 10: Closing the Ritual

Step out of the bath and wrap yourself in a clean towel or robe. Take a moment to ground yourself and express gratitude for the purification process. You may choose to light a candle or perform a closing prayer to seal the energy of the ritual.

Remember, the Eridu purification bath is not only a physical act but also a spiritual one. Allow yourself to be fully present in the moment, embracing the transformative power of the water and herbs. With each bath, you can experience a deeper sense of purification and rejuvenation for your body, mind, and spirit.

Prayer to Ninurta and Ninhursag for Protection - Prayer to the gods Ninurta and Ninhursag for protection from harm and evil

Mighty Ninurta, brave warrior of the heavens,
You who wield the divine weapon and protect the realms,
I call upon you in this sacred hour,
To guard and shield me from all harm and evil.

Ninhursag, nurturing mother of all creation,
You who give life and sustain the world with your love,
I seek your presence and benevolence,
To wrap me in your protective embrace.

Together, Ninurta and Ninhursag, I beseech you,
Watch over me with your vigilant eyes,
Defend me from the forces that seek to harm,
And keep me safe in your divine sanctuary.

Ninurta, with your unwavering strength,
Strike down the malevolent forces that threaten my being,
Grant me courage and resilience to face adversity,
And may your divine shield be my armor.

Ninhursag, with your gentle and nurturing touch,
Surround me with your loving energy and wisdom,
Guide my steps on the path of righteousness,
And shield me from the darkness that lurks.

In your sacred union, Ninurta and Ninhursag,
I find solace and protection from all directions,
May your divine presence be my fortress,
And may your power shield me from every harm.

I offer my gratitude for your unwavering protection,
And I vow to honor your divine grace and guardianship.
Ninurta and Ninhursag, I trust in your mighty presence,
For in your embrace, I find true safety and peace.
So mote it be.

Prayer to Nabu and Nusku for Inspiration - Prayer to the gods Nabu and Nusku for creative inspiration and ideas

Oh Nabu, god of wisdom and knowledge,
Bearer of the divine tablet and the scribe of the gods,
I call upon you in this sacred moment,
To grant me your divine inspiration and guidance.

Nusku, radiant god of illumination and fire,
Keeper of the sacred flame that ignites creativity,
I seek your presence and your blessed spark,
To awaken the depths of my creative potential.

Nabu, with your ancient wisdom and profound insight,
Open the gates of inspiration within my soul,
Unleash the rivers of creativity that flow within,
And guide my hand as I put thoughts into words.

Nusku, with your flickering flame of inspiration,
Illuminate the pathways of my imagination,
Ignite the fire that fuels my creative spirit,
And illuminate the world with my unique expression.

Together, Nabu and Nusku, I beseech you,
Infuse my mind and heart with divine inspiration,
Unlock the depths of my creativity and imagination,
And guide me in bringing forth ideas of beauty and significance.

Nabu, grant me the gift of clarity and eloquence,
That my words may flow with grace and purpose,
May my writings inspire and uplift others,
And bring forth wisdom and enlightenment.

Nusku, bestow upon me the creative fire that burns,
That I may express myself with passion and authenticity,
May my artistic endeavors shine with brilliance,
And touch the hearts and souls of those who witness.

Divine Dynamics

In your sacred union, Nabu and Nusku,
I find the wellspring of inspiration and creativity,
I surrender myself to your divine guidance,
And trust in the gifts you bestow upon me.

I offer my gratitude for your divine inspiration,
And vow to honor and nurture my creative gifts.
Nabu and Nusku, I embrace the creative journey,
With your blessings, I shall bring forth beauty and meaning.

So mote it be.

Incantation of Ea for Healing - Invocation of the god Ea for healing and restoration of health

Ea, great and compassionate god of wisdom,
Master of the sacred waters and healer of afflictions,
I beseech your divine presence in this moment,
To bring forth your healing power and restore my health.

Ea, with your deep knowledge and understanding,
I call upon you to banish illness and suffering,
Let your divine essence flow through my body,
Cleansing and rejuvenating every cell and fiber.

By the sacred waters that embody your essence,
I invoke your healing energy to permeate my being,
Wash away all ailments, pains, and discomforts,
And replace them with vitality, strength, and well-being.

Ea, ancient and wise, I seek your intervention,
To mend the wounds and restore balance within,
Guide the hands of physicians and healers,
That their treatments may be effective and swift.

With each breath, I draw in your healing essence,
Infusing every part of me with your rejuvenating power,
Let your divine light illuminate the darkest corners,
And dispel all illness, leaving only radiant health.

Ea, I trust in your benevolence and healing gifts,
I surrender myself to your divine wisdom and care,
Grant me the strength and resilience to overcome,
And bless me with a speedy and complete recovery.

May your healing energy flow through me,
Restoring me to a state of perfect health and vitality,
I am grateful for your divine intervention, Ea,
And I honor you as the great healer and bringer of restoration.
So mote it be.

Prayer to Shamash and Nergal for Strength - Prayer to the gods Shamash and Nergal for strength and courage

Mighty Shamash, radiant god of justice and light,
And powerful Nergal, fierce warrior of the underworld,
I humbly come before you, seeking your divine strength.

Shamash, source of cosmic order and divine justice,
Grant me the courage to face the challenges before me,
Illuminate my path with your guiding light,
And bestow upon me the strength to overcome all obstacles.

Nergal, formidable and relentless in battle,
Infuse me with your unwavering determination,
Ignite the fire of bravery within my heart,
And grant me the strength to face adversity head-on.

Together, Shamash and Nergal, I implore your aid,
Empower me with the resilience and fortitude I seek,
Fill me with unwavering confidence and conviction,
That I may overcome all trials with unwavering strength.

May I draw upon your divine essence, Shamash,
To guide my actions with fairness and integrity,
And may I channel the ferocity of Nergal,
To stand strong in the face of adversity and emerge victorious.

In your combined might and wisdom, I find solace,
Knowing that your divine protection surrounds me,
With your strength, I am unyielding, unshakable,
And I walk the path of courage and triumph.

Shamash and Nergal, I offer my deepest gratitude,
For your unwavering support and empowering presence,
May your strength flow through me in times of need,
And may I embody your valor and resilience in all I do.

Blessed be.

Prayer to Inanna and Nanna for Protection - Prayer to the gods Inanna and Nanna for protection from misfortune and harm

Mighty Inanna, radiant queen of heaven and earth,
And wise Nanna, guardian of the night sky,
I humbly call upon your divine presence for protection.

Inanna, fierce and powerful goddess,
Wrap me in your loving embrace,
Shield me from misfortune and harm,
And guard me against all evil that may seek to harm me.

Nanna, gentle and vigilant protector,
Guide me through the darkness of the unknown,
Illuminate my path with your celestial light,
And keep me safe from dangers seen and unseen.

Together, Inanna and Nanna, I seek your shelter,
As I navigate the challenges of life's journey,
Surround me with your divine grace and strength,
And protect me from all negative influences.

Inanna, with your sacred powers,
Defend me against those who wish me ill,
Bestow upon me the courage to face adversity,
And fill me with your unwavering confidence.

Nanna, with your watchful eyes,
Keep me safe in the embrace of the night,
Guide me with your wisdom and foresight,
And shield me from the perils that lie in wait.

In your divine union, Inanna and Nanna,
I find solace and sanctuary,
Wrap your protective energies around me,
And keep me secure from all harm.

With gratitude in my heart, I thank you,

Divine Dynamics

For your constant vigilance and loving care,
May your divine protection be my shield,
And may I walk in the world with confidence and peace.

Blessed be.

Eridu Ancestral Ritual - Ritual honoring and connecting with ancestors in Eridu

The Eridu Ancestral Ritual is a sacred practice that honors and connects us with our ancestors, those who came before us and shaped our lineage. It allows us to acknowledge their wisdom, seek their guidance, and express our gratitude for the gifts they have bestowed upon us. Here is a general outline of the ritual:

Step 1: Preparation
Create a dedicated space, adorned with ancestral symbols and items of significance. Arrange photographs or mementos of your ancestors on an altar or table. Light candles and incense to create a sacred atmosphere. You may also want to have a journal or paper and pen nearby for reflection.

Step 2: Invocation and Opening
Stand before the altar and take a few deep breaths to center yourself. Call upon the energies of Eridu and the divine forces that guide and protect ancestral connections. You can use a simple invocation such as:
"O mighty spirits of Eridu, I call upon you. Hear my voice and presence as I honor my ancestors and seek their guidance. May their wisdom guide me in this sacred space and throughout my life's journey."

Step 3: Ancestral Recognition and Appreciation
Take a moment to acknowledge and recognize your ancestors individually or collectively. Gaze upon their photographs or mementos, feeling their presence and the connections that bind you together. Express your gratitude for their love, sacrifices, and the blessings they have bestowed upon you. Speak from your heart, sharing your appreciation and love for each ancestor.

Step 4: Ancestral Communication
Begin a dialogue with your ancestors, speaking aloud or in your mind. Share your thoughts, questions, or any challenges you may be facing. Seek their guidance and wisdom, asking for their insights and support. Be open to receiving their messages and signs, trusting in their love and desire to assist you.

Step 5: Ancestral Offering
Prepare an offering for your ancestors as a symbol of gratitude and respect. This can be food, drink, flowers, or any other item that holds significance for them or your lineage. Place the offering on the altar with reverence, expressing your intention for it to be a symbolic gesture of your appreciation and connection.

Step 6: Meditation and Reflection
Sit in stillness and silence, allowing yourself to be receptive to the presence of your ancestors. Engage in meditation or reflection, opening yourself to their wisdom and guidance. Listen to any thoughts, feelings, or insights that arise during this time. You may also choose to write down any messages or reflections in your journal.

Step 7: Closing and Gratitude
Express your gratitude to your ancestors and the divine forces that have facilitated this sacred connection. Offer thanks for their presence, guidance, and blessings. Close the ritual with a simple statement of gratitude, such as:
"Thank you, beloved ancestors, for your love, guidance, and protection. May our bond remain strong, and may your wisdom continue to guide me. I honor and cherish you. Blessed be."

Step 8: Grounding and Integration
Take a few moments to ground yourself, feeling your connection to the earth beneath you. Breathe deeply, allowing the energy of the ritual to settle within you. When you are ready, extinguish the candles and release any remaining energies, knowing that you can carry the connection with your ancestors in your heart.

Remember, this is a general outline, and you can adapt and personalize the ritual to align with your beliefs and practices. It is a sacred time to honor and connect with your ancestors, fostering a deep sense of belonging and gratitude within your lineage.

Prayer to Ninurta and Ninhursag for Healing - Prayer to the gods Ninurta and Ninhursag for healing and well-being

Mighty Ninurta and compassionate Ninhursag,
I come before you with a humble heart,
Seeking your divine presence and healing touch.
In your wisdom and power, I place my trust.

Ninurta, valiant god of strength and vitality,
With your mighty weapon, you vanquish all adversity.
I beseech you, grant me the strength to overcome,
To heal and rise above the challenges that come.

Ninhursag, nurturing goddess of life and fertility,
You who bestow health and nourishment abundantly.
I implore you, bless me with your healing embrace,
Restore my body, mind, and spirit with grace.

Together, Ninurta and Ninhursag, I call upon you,
Unite your energies and blessings in all that you do.
Heal my wounds, physical and emotional alike,
Bring balance and well-being, like a soothing hike.

May Ninurta's strength fortify my weakened parts,
His healing energies mending my broken hearts.
May Ninhursag's gentle touch nurture and restore,
Her healing power flowing through me evermore.

With gratitude, I thank you, noble deities divine,
For your presence, love, and blessings so fine.
In your healing embrace, I find solace and peace,
May your divine intervention bring my healing release.

Ninurta and Ninhursag, I offer my prayers sincere,
Grant me the healing I seek, drawing you near.
With reverence, I embrace your divine intervention,
And I trust in your healing for my complete restoration.

Divine Dynamics

Blessed Ninurta and nurturing Ninhursag,
I thank you for hearing my plea,
May your healing powers flow abundantly,
And may I be restored to health and vitality.

So mote it be.

Prayer to Nabu and Nusku for Learning - Prayer to the gods Nabu and Nusku for academic success and knowledge acquisition

Mighty Nabu, god of wisdom and knowledge,
With your sacred pen, you inscribe the truth,
I come before you seeking your guidance,
In my pursuit of learning, I seek your eternal youth.

Nusku, radiant god of illumination,
You who kindle the flame of intellect and inspiration,
I beseech you, shine your divine light upon me,
Ignite my mind with wisdom, grant me revelation.

Nabu, master of scribes and keeper of records,
Inscribe your teachings upon the tablet of my soul,
Guide me through the realms of knowledge and wisdom,
Grant me clarity of thought, make my mind whole.

Nusku, bearer of the torch, illuminator of paths,
Illuminate my way as I tread upon the learning's road,
Grant me understanding, clear away the shadows,
Reveal the hidden truths that lie untold.

Together, Nabu and Nusku, I invoke your presence,
Bless my endeavors with your divine essence,
Grant me a thirst for knowledge that never wanes,
And the ability to absorb and retain what my mind contains.

Nabu, instill in me a love for learning,
May my studies be fruitful, my mind discerning,
Guide my thoughts and words, sharpen my intellect,
So I may excel in my academic pursuits, unrestricted.

Nusku, ignite the flame of passion within,
May it burn bright and lead me to wisdom's kin,
Illuminate my mind, empower my understanding,
So I may unravel the mysteries that life is demanding.

Divine Dynamics

With reverence, I offer my prayers to you,
Nabu and Nusku, gods of knowledge true,
Grant me the gifts of learning and insight,
Bless my studies, guide me in the pursuit of what is right.

May my mind be a vessel for wisdom's elixir,
May my journey through knowledge be richer,
In your names, I seek knowledge's balm,
Grant me success, let my learning be calm.

Honor and gratitude I extend to you,
Nabu and Nusku, gods so wise and true,
May your blessings flow abundantly,
And may I find enlightenment through your decree.

So mote it be.

Prayer to Enlil and Ninlil for Prosperity - Prayer to the gods Enlil and Ninlil for prosperity and abundance

Mighty Enlil, lord of the heavens and earth,
You who hold the power of creation and birth,
I humbly come before you with reverence and awe,
Seeking your blessings, for prosperity I implore.

Ninlil, radiant goddess of grain and fertility,
You who nurture life with abundant divinity,
I beseech you, gracious mother of all,
Bestow upon me your blessings, answer my call.

Enlil, mighty ruler and provider of wealth,
In your hands lie the keys to abundance and health,
I ask for your favor, for blessings to flow,
Grant me prosperity, let my fortune grow.

Ninlil, gentle nurturer of life's golden seeds,
With your fertile touch, fulfill my needs,
Bless my endeavors, from the smallest to the grand,
Guide my steps, let prosperity be at hand.

Enlil, master of fortunes, bringer of prosperity,
Open the gates of abundance for me,
Pour forth your blessings, shower me with grace,
Lead me on the path to a prosperous embrace.

Ninlil, goddess of harvest and fruitful lands,
With your divine touch, prosperity expands,
Fill my life with abundance, in all forms it takes,
Let success and prosperity be the path my life makes.

Enlil and Ninlil, I offer my sincere devotion,
In your divine presence, I find profound emotion,
Bless me with prosperity, let abundance reign,
Guide my steps, remove all obstacles and pain.

Divine Dynamics

May my efforts bear fruit, may my ventures thrive,
Under your watchful gaze, may prosperity arrive,
With gratitude and reverence, I honor your might,
Enlil and Ninlil, bring prosperity's radiant light.

So mote it be.

Incantation of Marduk for Protection - Invocation of the god Marduk for protection from malevolent forces

In the presence of Marduk, the great protector,
I invoke your name, O mighty deity of power.
With reverence and respect, I call upon your might,
To shield me from darkness, to guide me with light.

Marduk, the conqueror of chaos and strife,
With your divine presence, dispel all that is rife.
Wrap me in your protective embrace,
Guard me from harm, keep me in safe space.

From the depths of Tiamat, you emerged,
A champion of justice, your power surged.
I beseech you, Marduk, hear my plea,
Grant me your protection, set my spirit free.

By the force of your sacred words and spells,
Banish all evil, where darkness dwells.
With your divine sword, cleave through the night,
Defend me, O Marduk, with your celestial might.

Shield me from malice, shield me from harm,
Wrap me in your divine armor, strong and warm.
Let no malevolent force penetrate my soul,
Under your watchful eye, I am made whole.

O Marduk, protector of the righteous and just,
In your presence, all malevolence is crushed.
I offer my devotion, my trust and belief,
Protect me, O Marduk, in times of grief.

By the power of your name, I invoke your aid,
Shield me from danger, come to my aid.
With gratitude and reverence, I honor your might,
Marduk, protector, guide me through the night.
So mote it be.

Prayer to Ishtar and Shamash for Harmony - Prayer to the gods Ishtar and Shamash for harmonious relationships and balance.

In the presence of Ishtar and Shamash, radiant and divine,
I offer my prayer, seeking harmony and love to intertwine.
Goddess Ishtar, embodiment of beauty and desire,
And Shamash, the sun god, whose light never tires.

Ishtar, the queen of love and passion so pure,
I beseech you, grant me love that will endure.
Bless my relationships, bring them into accord,
Fill them with compassion, let love be their reward.

Shamash, the bringer of justice and radiant light,
Illuminate the path of harmony, make all things right.
Guide us in finding balance, both day and night,
Let our interactions be harmonious and bright.

Together, Ishtar and Shamash, your powers combined,
Bring forth harmony, where love and peace are enshrined.
In our hearts and souls, let kindness prevail,
May our connections flourish, never to fail.

Grant us understanding, empathy, and grace,
In every encounter, let love find its rightful place.
Heal the wounds of discord, mend the bonds torn,
Let our relationships blossom, like flowers newly born.

Ishtar, Shamash, I offer my gratitude and trust,
In your divine presence, I know love is a must.
With your blessings, let harmony be our guide,
In all our relationships, may love forever reside.

So mote it be.

Milton Keynes UK
Ingram Content Group UK Ltd.
UKHW030053040823
426310UK00010B/199